All You Need Is Food

A scrapbook of food & music
for the mind, body & soul

by
Mary Joseph

Cover design by Aaron Burtch
Illustrations by Jason Turner

"And Juan Makes Three" reprinted from *Monkey Puzzle Volume 6*, published by
Monkey Puzzle Press (2009) and copyright (2009) Kona Morris.

ISBN - 978-1-61623-085-2

This book is dedicated
to Sito & Busia who, through
the passing down of their
recipes, rooted my soul firmly
in the kitchen.

And to my musician friends
here, there & everywhere.
You have overflowed my
heart & life with your
beautiful music.
My life has been forever
changed because of
each & every one of you.

An Expression of Appreciation!

This book is everything I wanted it to be and then some. This wouldn't be so without the following people who have contributed and helped me along the way.

First of all, thanks to everyone who contributed their stories, quotes, poems, art, doodles and recipes: Bethany Taylor, Willy Tea, Octavio Hernandez, John Elmasian, Josh Schmidt, Tom Vanden Avond, Soda, Matt "The Professor" Smith, Wayne Joseph, Jeshua Marshall, Chris Doud, "Auntie" Marci Halabis, Mary Silvers, John Garner, Dave Hanley, Mattee Daniel, Scott McDougall, Randy Duax, "Uncle Bob" Meisenbach, Micah Garbarino, Gabriel Garbarino, Pat "My Mom" Joseph, Emily Ihrke, George Joseph, Andrew Carew, Jason Turner, Dan "My Dad" Joseph, Joey Eisinger, Alexander Ayers, Dallin Bulkley, John Dodds, Dave Maclure, Shelly Cimoli, Marissa Garbarino, Travis Mamone, Ian Cook, T.J. Birman, Anastüblychin, Dean Haakenson, Wesley Haakenson, Jamin Marshall, Anna Cecil, Wendolyn Garbarino-Cooper, Punam Shaida, Wiley Bull Taylor, Ray Vazira, Eddie Nader, Matt "The Gambler's Prayer" Cordano, Amber Cross, Sean Ford, Heaven Lindsey-Burtch, Aaron Burtch, Kona Morris, Maria Safi, David Burtch, Travis Gruber, Casey Weber, Sebastian "Seabass" St. John, Grace Taylor, Kim Brown, Dustin "Walter Mitty" Hayes, Tawny Dunn and Mikey Dunn.

Aaron Burtch: For designing the most rad cookbook cover *ever*. You, my friend, are truly a talent and I'm honored to be able to combine my art with yours.

Jason: Your illustrations are exactly what I didn't even realize I needed, they add such a fun touch to the book. The same can be said for your presence in my life.

Larry & His Flask: Meeting you guys changed my life. You inspired me to be free and got me out of the city and back home where I belong. You are everything that is right with music. Keep on keepin' that world alive, my brothers.

A special thank you to Emily Webster for helping me with a million different things, far too many to list here. You have been a godsend!

Thanks to my testers and editors: Jason Turner, Timothy Burgess, Lily Nichols, Ipek Tuncer, Kathi Pethoud, Ellen McManis, Taylor Webster, Deanna Tate, Christina Weber, Leslie Richardson, Linda Stewart, Stacy Wimmer, Meril Smit, Elizabeth Milsark, Heidi Roseler, Stephanie Franklin, Monica van Adrichem, Hillary Gruber, Marti Sichel, Kim Brown, Miriam Doner, Christina Randall, Becca Weitzel, Lisa Mistiuk, Heaven Lindsey-Burtch, Angie Aveiro and Mary Ratliff.

Mom & Dad: Thanks for letting me spend hours using your kitchen as my office and eating your food while I frantically worked to get this thing wrapped up.

A special thanks to everyone who continued to believe in this project as the months dragged into years. Your enthusiasm would breath new life into me. Especially: Wendy, Bethany, Will, Mom, Dad, Cristina and Auntie Marci.

Last but not least, thanks to my daughter Sydney for coming right on time.

Table of Contents

To view pictures of my recipes visit
www.AllYouNeedIsFood.com

Note from the Author

This book started as a collection of recipes to give to my mom and sisters for Christmas. Five years later, it is a proper 200+ page cookbook. Cooking has been my passion since I was a young girl and feeding musicians has become my favorite past-time. I will cook for music, they will sing for food - it's a match made in heaven.

What some people may not realize is that cooking is one thing, while writing a recipe is another. Most cooks and chefs don't even follow recipes. They cook using instinct and view cooking as an art form. Ask your grandmother how to make her famous Bolognese, stuffed grape leaves or tortillas and she'll most likely say things like: "A handful of dried basil", "A few pinches of salt", "Fill a bowl half way with flour, add butter until it feels right."

My cooking is fueled so much by instinct that sometimes, when I've translated it onto paper, it has proven difficult. I'd make something spontaneously one day, write down what I did, make it again according to my notes, only to have it turn out different. I've made many of the recipes in this book over and over only to have different results each time. It all came to a head when I made some meatballs two nights in a row. I was frustrated that they were different each night and I began to doubt whether or not my recipes were ready to be published. But then I remembered that there are always different variables that affect the outcome of any recipe: altitude, freshness of the ingredients and humidity, to name a few. This is why a recipe made the same way many times can come out slightly different.

Recipes should never make one lazy. Recipes are the guide and cooking the journey. That said, I want to encourage you to listen to the voice inside, find your cooking instinct and get creative. For instance, if you'd like to add a fresh herb that isn't mentioned or would prefer less cheese (which may happen since I love cheese) go with your gut! Stray from the recipe and get personal, make *my* recipes *your* recipes.

These pages are filled with so much love. This book is my dream come true and, because of everyone involved, it has become a dream more beautiful than I ever imagined. With contributions from over 50 musicians, music lovers, artists and poets, every page contains something straight from the heart. *All You Need Is Food* is my love letter to food and music. This is me gathering these people in one place, group-hugging them all and showing them off.

With this book I hope to show that there is talent beyond what we see on television or hear on the radio. There are real people - unknown people - making music, writing great songs, creating masterpieces and cooking amazing meals. We may not be cooking in 4-star restaurants or playing to crowds of thousands, but we cook, we make music and, in more than a small way, it enriches our lives and the lives of the people around us.

- Always read the recipe from start to finish before you start cooking.

- If a recipe calls for chopping, shredding, dicing etc., do this before you begin.

COOKING DEFINITIONS:

Finely Chop/Dice:	Cut into very small pieces, about ⅛" to ¼" in size
Chop:	Cut into small ¼" to ½" pieces
Rough Chop:	A few chops of the knife making large, non-uniform pieces

- Remember that cooking times may vary depending on altitude, humidity or the type of stove/oven you have. So try to become familiar with how things smell, taste and look when they are done.

- Meat should always be cooked at room temperature - so remove it from the fridge about 10 minutes before cooking.

- It's important to cook meat properly to avoid getting sick. When cooking meat that's already chopped, cut the largest piece to see if it's done. When cooking meat whole (like a chicken breast or a steak), use a meat thermometer to see if it's done.

TEMPERATURE CHART:

Ground beef/lamb	160°F	71°C
Whole beef/lamb - medium rare	145°F	63°C
Whole beef/lamb - medium	160°F	71°C
Whole beef/lamb - well done	170°F	77°C
Ground chicken/turkey	165°F	74°C
Chicken/turkey breasts/whole	165°F	74°C

CONVERSION CHART:

1 ½ teaspoons = ½ tablespoon	½ cup = 4 fluid ounces
3 teaspoons = 1 tablespoon	1 cup = 8 fluid ounces
4 tablespoons = ¼ cup	2 cups = 16 fluid ounces
⅓ cup = ¼ cup + 2 teaspoons	16 fluid ounces = 1 pint

Introduction

by Wendolyn Garbarino-Cooper
Chef/Musician/Soul-sister

Music and Food: At a glance, perhaps they seem like an odd coupling. But, I promise you, they are a blessed union: two beautiful art forms linked together by qualities and characteristics that, while different in nature, are similar in essence when it comes to the affect they have on us as human beings. Music primarily nourishes our souls, while food nourishes our bodies. One satisfies our spirit, while the other satisfies our palates and appetites. Delicious meals are created from an infinite spectrum of ingredients and flavor combinations, while the songs we hear, from an endless range of chord progressions, various scales, and key changes. And the two of them, as they have for generations and generations, will live on and evolve with us through time and culture.

In all these years of human existence, we, from master chef to homemaker, famous composer to unknown folk artist, have never run out of new things to create, to taste and to hear - a splendid myriad of compositions. Washing, dicing, mixing, steaming, cooking, smelling, tasting; strumming, playing, dancing, singing, writing, feeling, sharing. New recipes and songs are being written every day all over the world, and in this unique and daring cookbook we get to see these two glorious worlds collide in a way that will bring insight into the vital role that music and food have in our lives.

Music and food connect us at a very core level that, perhaps, many of us fail to truly realize. We eat for survival and we would starve without food. But, we also eat to enjoy and to savor, to have fellowship and experience the very human and intimate act of hunger being satisfied as we share a meal together. True, music does not feed us in the same way that food does, but it is most definitely food for our souls and is just as vital for a healthy human life. Whether we are listening or composing to be comforted, uplifted, understood or to vent frustration, music connects us to something on a deeper level - something higher. I am sure you have experienced it: that potent combination of lyrics and poetry paired with just the right chord progression that grips your heart and soul to move you beyond reason or understanding. That perfect song, in the perfect moment, resounding in your soul. It is not far from the same euphoria one savors when tasting that perfect bite: where flavor, textures, and aroma are married in perfect harmony.

For any of you who are skeptical of our claim that music is *just* as vital for survival as food, I welcome you to first, please, take a few moments and close your eyes. Now, as John Lennon would ask, "imagine all the people" in a world that has never experienced music: weddings without love songs, movies without soundtracks, children without "twinkle, twinkle little star" to sing, nothing to dance to, no symphonies to revel in! The picture I see is dreary and deafeningly quiet. I see hearts and minds starved for the divine connection that music provides, as our bodies would be starved for food in a famine.

We eat, enjoy, and create food because we are human. We listen to, create, and need music because we are humans with *souls*.

Contributor's Manifesto

by Mikey Dunn

Friend

They say we can't live without food. They say music might just be a luxury. They say in times of trouble, necessity should not be mixed with frivolity.

We rebuke.

We say, especially in tough times, that food shall be dressed, that music shall flow, that a healthy and vibrant culture is imperative to our survival and well being. And we will say it with passion, and we will live it with fervor. And Love.

We say that the colors and smells and sounds and tastes that make our every day are what make us as well. The flowers we decide to plant that bloom fire orange with purple tips; the eucalyptus tree that draws our noses to its bark and leaves; the gentle guitar or fired up banjo echoing from the barn; the pungent, spicy crisp of a radish pulled right from the ground and put in my mouth as a fire lights up the faces and instruments of those around me . . . We say these are connected – in us and out of us, by ourselves and as a community.

And we say we will make our senses sing and dance with every occasion. We will put them together and create not just a meal, not just a song, but an experience, a design of unity, a symbol of our own potential when we come together and enrich, enliven, and live.

Finally we will be done saying, and we will create. We will create songs, bands, poetry. We will create gardens, fields, and recipes. We will create festivals, music programs, and books. We will create for the kindergartner, for the cowboy, for the soccer mom. We will create for our futures, for our children's futures, and for their children.

Mary Joseph says that food can be music, and music can be food. I agree. A recipe, like a song, has instructions, but can be "played" differently every time. And a song, like a good meal, fills us with life, reminds us even breathing – an involuntary action necessary to our survival – can still be a sweet breath, can still be done next to a flowering jasmine. This perspective seems so in line with how we all choose to live so many other ways. If we must travel, might we do it in comfort? If we must stand, might we be in comfortable shoes? And of course, we all know that if we must eat, might it taste good (or, in Mary's case, heavenly)?

So if we must cook, might it be seasoned with a good song? And if we're drawn to sing, to play, might it be to truly enhance someone's life? As with food and music, we are all connected; and we, in this book, choose to embrace that connection and be filled with joy and energy from it.

So we say, that the music tastes great and the food sounds delicious.

Starters & Dips

Tzatziki - 4

Auntie Marci's Veggie Dip - 4

Messy Tomato-Feta Dip - 5

Chunky Tomato Guacamole - 6

Tomato Salsa! - 6

Black Bean Dip - 8

Creamy BLT Bruschetta - 9

Chicken Bean Dip - 12

Fancy Garlic Bread - 13

Baked Brie with Bacon
& Red Onions - 13

Mozzarella Stuffed
Meatballs - 14

Feta Stuffed
Kalamata Olives - 17

Mini Ham & Cheddar
Quiche - 19

Garlic Parmesan Twists - 19

Jalapeno Poppers with
Cilantro Ranch - 21

Chicken Basil Stuffed
Tomatoes - 23

Cold Veggie Pizza - 24

Pesto Feta Crostinis - 25

Serrano Ham &
Manchego Crostinis - 26

1

Feta Stuffed Kalamata Olives - Page 17

Garlic Parmesan Twists - Page 19

Jalapeno Poppers - Page 21

Mini Ham & Cheddar Quiche - Page 19

Mozzarella Stuffed Meatballs - Page 14

Chicken Basil Stuffed Tomatoes - Page 23

Tzatziki

(serves 4-6)

1 ½ cups Lebne (a.k.a. Kiefer cheese or Greek yogurt*)
¼ cup chopped fresh dill
½ cup finely chopped English cucumber**
2 tablespoons lemon juice
2 tablespoons olive oil
½ teaspoon salt

*You can use plain yogurt if you can't find either of these.

Add all ingredients to a medium sized bowl and mix with a fork until completely combined.

This traditional Greek dip is generally served with hot pita bread. You can also use it as a vegetable dip or as a salad dressing.

**You don't need to peel an English cucumber - their skins aren't as tough as a regular cucumber.

Auntie Marci's Veggie Dip

(serves 4-6)

1 cup mayonnaise
1 cup sour cream
2 cups shredded Swiss cheese
1 bunch green onions, chopped
½ teaspoon salt
1 teaspoon secret ingredient*

Add all ingredients to a bowl and mix well. This is best if made the day before serving. Serve with baby carrots, celery, broccoli, button mushrooms or any kind of veggie you want.

You'll feel like you're being healthy because you're dipping veggies in this, but don't let the carrots fool you... mayo + sour cream + cheese does not = diet food.

*see Auntie Marci for details

Messy Tomato-Feta Dip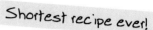

(serves 4-6)

6 vine-ripe tomatoes
8 ounces Feta cheese

Shortest recipe ever!

Slice the tomatoes in half lengthwise. Scoop the seeds and juices - what I call the "tomato guts" - into a bowl. Slice the tomatoes into quarters (lengthwise) and set on a plate. Add the Feta to the tomato guts and mash with a fork until combined.

Use the tomato shells to scoop and eat the dip. You can also use pita, toasted pita, sourdough bread, etc.

Does music have to be in a language you understand? If you're a lyrics lover, maybe it does. Good music, though, is all about transporting us to other places. And people speak other languages in other places. I fell in love with a Brazilian many years ago and married her. And, I've been falling in love with the music of her country ever since.

Caetano Veloso. The name may not mean anything to you. But, to Brazilians he is Elvis, Tony Bennett and Bob Dylan rolled into one - except he's aged better than all of those men and his music is still credible and popular. In fact, it's not fair to compare him to the greats of American popular music. Caetano is Caetano - a Brazilian vocal legend who penned and then personally sang the soundtrack to Brazil's modern history. Exiled for his protest music in the 1960's, welcomed as a hero on his return in the 1970's, he has continually provided a commentary, an explanation, an interpretation for and about his country. And all this with a knowing smile which masks a rigorous work ethic directed toward constant innovation. Now, in his mid-60's he is an elder statesman of World Music.

I saw Caetano perform live in 2006. Aptly, it was in Rio – Caetano's spiritual home. And even more aptly, it was with my wife to celebrate our wedding anniversary. I have never seen a performer who so effortlessly transfixed his audience. He did not mock us, he did not frighten us, he did not overwhelm us. Instead, he gently took us by the hand and led us on a dazzling journey. We floated to other places.

Does music have to be in a language you understand? Of course it doesn't. Senhor Veloso has made over 30 studio albums all in Portuguese and you don't need to understand his every word to have your soul moved. But, if your music has to be in English then you'll be pleased to know he recorded, once, a record entirely in English. *A Foreign Sound*, released in 2004, featuring covers of well-known American tunes old and new, could be your portal into the wonderful world of Caetano.

- Dave Maclure - Natal, Brazil

Chunky Tomato Guacamole

(serves 4-6)

2 avocados
2 de-seeded and chopped vine-ripe tomatoes
2 green onions, chopped small
1 clove garlic, minced

2 tablespoons chopped fresh cilantro
¼ cup sour cream
2 tablespoons lemon juice
½ teaspoon salt

Cut each avocado in half and take the pit out. Use a spoon to scoop the flesh into a bowl. Mash with a fork and mix until mostly creamy with some chunks.

Add tomatoes, green onion, garlic, cilantro, sour cream, lemon juice and salt. Stir until combined.

Allow guacamole to sit for at least an hour in the fridge before serving.

I hated avocados for most of my life. One day, I ate some guacamole at a restaurant in Sacramento. It was similar to this recipe and now I love 'em!

Tomato Salsa!

(serves 4-6)

2 cups (about 3-4) chopped vine-ripe tomatoes
1 cup diced white onion
1 jalapeno, de-seeded and finely diced
1 (4 ounce) can diced mild green chilies
2 large cloves garlic, minced

1 cup roughly chopped (gently
   packed) cilantro
1 teaspoon salt
½ cup lime juice

Cut 2 of the tomatoes in half. Scoop out and discard all of the seeds and juice. Dice these along with the other 2 tomatoes and put into a bowl. (You only want the juice/seeds from 2 of the tomatoes.)

Add the rest of the ingredients to the bowl with the tomatoes and mix well. You can serve this as is (chunky), or puree in a blender or food processor until smooth.

Allow salsa to sit for at least 2 hours before serving.

Starters & Dips

"Food Song"

by Andrew Carew - Larry & His Flask - Bend, OR

When I wake up, when I get outta bed,
Can you guess who it is already
Running through my head?
Baby, it's you.
I've never known a love that's lasted so long,
21 years and I know it'll be that strong
On the day that I die.

You're almost always on my mind.
More than girls and beer and songs
For years it's been that way,
Oh that's how it's gonna stay with you…
My delicious food.

I love you almost every different way you come.
Spicy or sweet you're always #1...in my book.
I know it's a silly topic for a song like this,
But what better way to rejoice the one at the top of my list?

Words can't explain the euphoria I feel
After a wholesome double-helping of a
Finely prepared, awesome homemade meal.
Oh it's simply unreal,
That's why I'm thankful every day for you…
My delicious food!

Andrew on banjo

Black Bean Dip

(serves 4)

1 (15 ounce) can black beans, drained but not rinsed
¼ cup lime juice
¼ cup sour cream
½ cup roughly chopped cilantro
1 teaspoon salt
½ cup crumbled Queso Fresco cheese

or lemon juice!

Add all ingredients to the bowl of your food processor and process until smooth. Serve cold or hot. If you want to serve this hot, just spread the dip into an 8x8 baking dish and bake in a 350 degree oven for 10-15 minutes. Serve with chips or veggies.

If I take a trip down memory lane, I recall the moment I truly discovered music. As a kid, growing up with a skateboarding brother and 1970's Punk Rock uncle, one could say that I was fortunate enough to experience the non-pop music of the 70's and 80's. I loved to listen to it. It fueled my rage when I skated. It peppered my dreams as I slept. It wasn't until a warm evening in 1990 that the music finally wormed its way into my heart and inspired me to make my own.

Under the ruse of sleeping over at a friend's house, my buddies and I made the 45-minute trip to Sacramento so we could see some bands play at the Cattle Club (an old Sacto favorite). In between bands, the DJ played random songs from Punk's past. That's when I heard it. Blaring over the PA system was "Amoeba" by the Adolescents. The simplicity of the guitar rhythm and power packed between each snare snap had my heart thumping. I dissected every sound. The guitar separated from the bass. My mind envisioned the faces the singer made as he strained over the symbols. Each player was unique to his art. Each one melted into the other to form this song. I wanted to make people feel the way they made me feel.

I heard a lot of music that night, but nothing gave me the high or left me with the feeling that the Adolescents did. It was the first time that I stopped picturing strangers on a stage playing for everyone's amusement. For once, I saw me.

- Mattee Daniel - Sacramento, CA

Creamy BLT Bruschetta

(serves 4-6)

This recipe was given to me for this book by
my dear, scary friend, Travis Gruber.
This recipe is one of the best things I've ever eaten.
I didn't let him come over unless he brought it with him.
True story.

Ingredients For Recipe
1 pound bacon
1 medium sized tomato
⅓ cup chopped chives - or so
2 tablespoons chopped fresh parsley
½ cup mayonnaise
¾ cup sour cream
1 ½ teaspoons minced garlic - it ain't gotta be fresh - that stuff in a jar is fine
Grated parmesan cheese - to taste...look this isn't science, it's food
1 large loaf of sourdough bread - cut into large chunks for dipping

Ingredients for chef
One Dirty Vodka or Gin Martini

Instructions:
Take drink of martini to get loose.

Cut bacon into small squares and cook it. Set it aside on a plate with a paper towel to drain. Get yourself a good sharp knife and dice the shit out of that tomato. Next chop them chives. Chop 'em so good.

Take a drink of your martini - you deserve a reward.

Mince the parsley. Make it so tiny that even midgets would be all like, "Damn, that's some tiny parsley."

Eat olive from martini - chefs deserve snacks.

Mix all ingredients, except the bread, into a large mixing bowl. Mix with spoon to retain large chunks of ingredients. Don't use an electric mixer - that's abuse.

Cover and place in fridge so them flavors get to "know" each other.

Finish martini then make another.

Place chunks of bread on cookie sheets. Place in oven (about 350 degrees) until slightly crispy and warm. Obviously you'll want to turn the oven on, but there are no specifics for that. Look, you're just making cubes of toast in the oven. If that's too complicated, I don't know how you've made it this far.

Down martini in one drink 'cause it's getting close to party time.

Once bread is toasted, serve everything up all fancy style and try not to drop it as you drunkenly stumble from the kitchen, you lush.

Not that there's anything wrong with that...

...the lush thing I mean...you drop food and you make angels cry.

And now, a word from Travis...

I am a lover of both music and cooking. A master of neither art – but a dabbler in both – I have had one great influence in my life in each regard.

In my more musically inclined days I was a drummer, and in the pantheon of my craft one man stood head and shoulders above the rest: Jimmy Chamberlain. Jimmy played drums for the Smashing Pumpkins and when behind the drum kit seemed less like a man and more a god - a man possessed of abilities that no mere mortal should have. The first time I heard the opening drum salvo of "Quiet", a mere three second drum-fill off the Pumpkins sophomore release *Siamese Dream*, it became apparent to me that this man was not sitting behind a drum set but rather in possession of a machine gun that he had somehow managed to coerce music out of. In each subsequent track on said same record he oscillated between heavy metal machine-gunner and artful poet. Quiet and reserved when needed - as on the song "Soma" - and blowing the doors off of the recording studio when given the chance - as on the aforementioned "Quiet" - Jimmy Chamberlain was a musical anachronism. And a mind boggling one at that.

Hearing him play was awe inspiring, but to watch Jimmy play was akin to watching Michelangelo paint the Sistine Chapel. On each song he was a flurry of motion and emotion, but never a wasted movement. He was meticulous in his playing. An economy of motion where nary a muscle flexed was wasted, but always bordering on a becoming a whirling dervish comprised of nothing but arms and drum sticks. When I picked up my first set of drumsticks at fifteen years old there was ONLY one goal: to play like Jimmy.

In the epicurean realm there was only one person I ever looked up to: my Nana. My maternal grandmother was a California raised southern woman who could coax four-star flavor out of shoe leather if need be. Growing up poor we never had a lot of "options" at the dinner table. But when Nana was in front of the stove it didn't matter.

With the bounty of my Grandfather's garden in the back yard, and a lifetime of experience behind her, my Nana would could make droll and boring ingredients into a sublime miasma.

As a child I spent a lifetime sitting on the counter next to her as she hand made each meal of the day. Breakfast was biscuits and gravy, made from scratch with the occasional interruption by yours truly snatching bits of uncooked biscuit dough from under her rolling pin. Lunch was almost always a family dish called 'Ronis and Juice', a simple concoction of shell macaroni boiled and then drowned in home-canned tomato juice. And dinner spread the gamut of the traditional southern delicacies: fried green tomatoes, okra, breaded catfish (caught by myself and my Grandfather) cornbread and mustard greens - dishes that held a legacy, food that told a story.

But, the penultimate was always birthday dinner. My Nana's standing order was that on your birthday you got to have whatever you wanted. And I always wanted pizza. So my ever patient Grandmother would hand roll the dough and lovingly add any topping I wanted, no matter how ridiculous the request. It was my birthday and the greatest gift she could give me was to make sure my taste buds were placated with any order of flavor that would please my palate.

Sadly both of my heroes no longer practice their chosen craft. Jimmy is apparently retired from music and my Nana, god rest her soul, prepares meals for a more divine audience. But from each I learned a great many lessons.

From Jimmy I learned to be passionate in your pursuits. To be sparing with your energy and precise in your movements - waste energy now and there won't be enough left for the big finish. To be satisfied with being in the background when necessary, but when given a chance to be the center of attention, blow 'em away!

From Nana I learned to make something from nothing. To always be satisfied with what you have because even the most meager ingredients can a great feast make. That home-made always beat store-bought, because you can't mass market care and affection. You will learn more about your family around the dinner table than anywhere else. And on his birthday, the boy gets whatever he wants to eat.

But from them both I learned the most important lesson: food and music are transcendental. Almost 17 years after the release of *Siamese Dream*, that opening drum beat of "Quiet" still gives me goose bumps. And almost ten years after her death my Nana's recipes - the entire library of which I am in possession of - still make me feel like a cared for and loved little boy in a world where nothing can go wrong. And I'm sure these things will make me feel the same way until it's time for me to shuffle off my mortal coil.

And if my son so desires, I'll make him homemade pizza. Like Nana always said, "On his birthday, the boy gets whatever he wants."

- Travis Gruber - Stand-up comedian & former member of The Hour Lilies & Absent Me - Roseville, CA

Chicken Bean Dip

(serves 4-6)

1 tablespoon olive oil
1 pound boneless, skinless chicken breasts,
   chopped small
½ teaspoon salt
½ teaspoon pepper
½ cup sour cream

½ cup mayonnaise
1 cup tomato salsa
½ cup shredded Cheddar cheese
½ cup shredded Monterey Jack cheese,
3 green onions, diced
1 (2.5 ounce) can sliced black olives

Preheat oven to 350 degrees.

Heat oil in a large skillet over medium heat. Add chicken, salt and pepper. Cook and stir until done, about 10 minutes.

Meanwhile, in a large bowl, mix sour cream, mayonnaise, salsa, cheese, green onions and olives. When chicken is done add to the bowl and combine. Spread evenly in an 8x8 baking dish. Bake for 20-30 minutes or until brown and bubbly. Serve hot with corn chips.

From 52 Week "Mooner" by Ray Vazira

A grain of sand is all I am,
I watch it all go by here as I stand.
Kingdoms they come and kingdoms they go,
Left, right, center: It's all a show.
This life we live is a one way road,
I'm not too sure but that's what I was told.
My mind is weary I can't go to sleep,
I'd rather stay up and watch the deep blue sea.
The rich get richer and the poor they stay poor.
The sick and the tired are all left at the door.
All I can do is just speak my mind.
Life is too short and I'm running out of time.
That's why all I wanna do is stare at the moonlight.

To read more about the 52-Week Club see pages 87-88

Starters & Dips

Fancy Garlic Bread

(serves 4-6)

3 cloves roasted garlic, minced
1 (4 ounce) package Feta cheese
4 ounces softened cream cheese
2 green onions, finely chopped
2 tablespoons olive oil

⅛ teaspoon salt
⅛ teaspoon pepper
1 loaf sourdough bread, sliced into ½ inch
   thick slices

First, roast the garlic. For directions, see page 17.

Preheat broiler.

(This is as fancy as I get folks)

Add Feta, cream cheese, roasted garlic and green onions to the bowl of your standing mixer (or use an electric hand mixer) and mix until smooth. If you don't have either of these just mix well with a wooden spoon or similar utensil.

In a separate bowl whisk together olive oil, salt and pepper. Brush sliced sourdough with oil mixture and broil for about 1 minute, until lightly toasted. Remove from oven. Spread cheese mixture on the bread and return to the broiler until brown and bubbly on top.

Baked Brie with Bacon & Red Onions

(serves 4-6)

½ pound bacon, cooked and crumbled
½ medium red onion, chopped
1 (8 ounce) wedge Brie cheese

Recipe courtesy of Wendolyn Garbarino-Cooper - Yuba City, CA

Preheat oven to 350 degrees.

Heat a large skillet over medium heat. Add bacon and cook until crispy. Remove bacon and drain on a paper towel. Pour about half of the grease out then heat up the rest of the grease over medium heat. Your skillet and the grease should still be hot, so this won't take very long. Add the chopped red onion, cook and stir until soft, about 3-5 minutes.

Meanwhile, crumble the bacon. Place the Brie in an 8x8 baking dish or on a cookie sheet. When the onion is done, spread it on top of the Brie and top with crumbled bacon.

Heaven on a plate

Bake for 10-15 minutes. Serve hot with sliced bread or crackers.

Mozzarella Stuffed Meatballs

(makes 20-something meatballs)

1 tablespoon olive oil
½ small onion (about ½ cup), finely
  chopped
3-4 cloves garlic, minced
½ pound lean ground beef
½ pound Hot Italian sausage
1 egg, beaten
1 ½ tablespoons Worcestershire sauce

½ cup chopped flat-leaf (Italian) parsley
½ cup chopped fresh basil
1 teaspoon salt
½ teaspoon pepper
½ cup breadcrumbs
½ cup grated Parmesan cheese
3-4 sticks of Mozzarella sticks

Preheat oven to 350 degrees. **a.k.a. String cheese**

Heat oil in a large skillet over medium heat. Add onions, cook and stir for about 2 minutes. Add garlic and cook for another minute. Put into a large bowl. To the same bowl add beef, sausage, egg, Worcestershire, parsley, basil, salt, pepper, breadcrumbs and Parmesan cheese. Use your hands to mix until completely combined. Form into 1 ½ inch balls.

Cut each string cheese stick into 8 pieces. Press a piece of cheese into the middle of each meatball and re-shape neatly. Place the meatballs on a foil-lined cookie sheet.

Bake for 15-20 minutes. Check the middle of the largest meatball. The inside should have an internal temperature of 160-165 degrees and not be pink inside.

Serve with 'Red Pizza Sauce' on page 147.

14

Traveling. Eating. Music. I'm not really sure which one my body requires more for sustenance. I'll put my money on traveling and music. But due to that, I have been afforded some amazing meals. And by amazing I don't always necessarily mean the flavor. The all around sensation of food in travel is breathtaking, even if the vittles are not. It started out for me as traveling every year from California to Oklahoma and Arkansas, eating highway rations on the way, only to gorge myself on home cooked Okie grub upon arrival at the doorsteps of my long missed relatives. Now there is something to be said for that country cookin'. And to me, it is as good as any French cuisine I've tasted. But let us not forget the relativity of the matter. When you are on the highway and your only means of nutriment are what's in the ice chest or what's at the next truck stop, well if you're the traveling kind, you tend to get creative and also learn to enjoy the food you have.

Any hobo can tell you the importance of a wide palette of mini-mart condiments in the making of a traveler's feast. The creativity in food I regrettably feel is something missing in most of America. Oh, sure, we have a flood of T.V. shows dedicated to cooking and beating the next chef and such, but when it comes down to the actual exercise of creating something new, enjoying something unique and hopefully tasty, we are a sad lot indeed. Fortunately for me, I have had the opportunity to travel to many places where that is not the case. From America to Europe to Asia and abroad there are really some truly amazing dishes out there. Not all tasty, but each its own. When you add that creative cooking with the scenery around you that you might be seeing for the first time, and then combine those two with the sounds of your friends playing music on tour or the local musicians performing their regional music it, to me, is complete bliss.

For me, nothing will ever top my Momma's biscuits and gravy while listening to Hank Williams over a Budweiser in Lone Oak, Texas during a thunderstorm. And no one will ever come close to her mashed potatoes.

The regional Czech fare I experienced was dreadful in a way that it was comical. So, I learned to cope with sticking my fork into a chicken breast only to have it deflate before my eyes with a smile. Listening to beautiful piano concertos in a city as beautiful as Prague makes one more apt to forgive the grub. Germany. Can't stand the country. But the fact that I was eating amazing Bratwurst and enjoying great beer while finding the first Suicidal Tendencies album for two American dollars in a thrift store made up for it. What can I say about Italy that hasn't already been said? The food is amazing. I could listen to a tarantella while drinking the village wine and walking up cobblestone alleyways in Imperia for the rest of my life and be fine with that. England. Not my bag. But hanging out with S.F.A and talking to the locals in Wales while eating beer battered fish and chips is. In Thailand, don't even bother going to a restaurant. Just hit up the street carts and enjoy the best Pad Thai you will ever get while listening to the shouts and engines of the tuk tuk drivers. I will never forget the spicy squid on a stick at a giant flea market in Bangkok while I sat and listened to two Thai gentleman play bluegrass music on their banjo and mandolin with the same precision as anyone I've seen in the States.

There was the time that I hired a Cambodian mobster to drive me to Phnom Penh in the middle of the night. Crazy beautiful Cambodian music was coming from some cracked out ghetto blaster.

They handed me a bowl. It was so dark I could not see any trace of what I was eating. Which, of course, meant who knew what was going into the food in the first place. As soon as I had swallowed the first spoonful I knew it was every piece of the inside of a cow, water buffalo or something that they could scrape up so as not to waste. It was cold and the texture was what I would imagine the inside of a lung feeling like. It was so completely strange and unappetizing to me that I asked for a second helping just to experience it again.

Ever had Hot Vit Lon? In Vietnam it is fetal duck egg. Sounds gross, I know. I was enjoying the fireworks and parades of a small delta village celebrating the Tet Offensive when I first enjoyed one of these. I love them. Borneo with their longhouse dances and Otak (chunks of fish wrapped in Banana leaves and cooked over charcoal). Bali and its monkey god ceremonies and funeral march music while I eat nasi goreng (fried rice with a fried egg on top). The best food I ever made for myself was while fishing in the Bering Sea. I would save up a bag of fresh halibut cheeks until I had enough for a burrito and then cook it up in the galley while blasting Motorhead so I wouldn't have to listen to the tow wench.

And speaking of burritos-nothing beats the ones at the taco trucks in Modesto, Ca on 9th St., when I finally take that Central Modesto exit coming in from my latest travel destination. And the best pizza I have ever had wasn't from New York or Italy. It was from Oakdale, Ca. From the creator of this book. From someone who puts as much love and enjoyment into her cooking as any other person or place on this earth that I've been to. So, if you are ever around Oakdale and hear about some good homemade music, with good homemade food at a good ol' barn, you should think about that before heading to someplace as ordinary as the next and as boring as the most. You might experience a food, a music and a place you will never forget. Food, travel and music make my world go round. And as far as I will ever go, I know it can all be found right here at home as well.

- John Garner - Fort Smith, AR

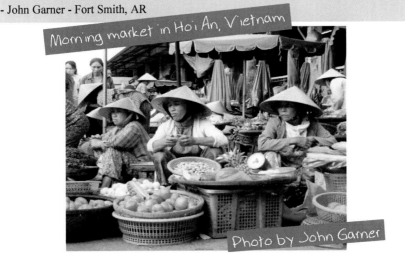

Morning market in Hoi An, Vietnam

Photo by John Garner

Feta Stuffed Kalamata Olives

(makes about 100 olives)

3 cloves roasted garlic, minced
2 tablespoons extra-virgin olive oil
7 ounces Feta cheese

1 (9.5 ounce) jar Kalamata olives
6 ounces thinly sliced prosciutto

(Time consuming, but worth it)

To roast garlic:
Heat oven to 400 degrees. Place unpeeled cloves of garlic in the middle of a large square of tin foil. Drizzle liberally with olive oil - about 2 tablespoons. Fold up the ends of the foil tightly, completely sealing the opening so that no air can escape. Place on a cookie sheet and roast in oven for 15 minutes. Remove and allow to cool enough to handle. Cut an end off of each clove, squeeze from the shell and mince.

In a food processor blend roasted garlic, olive oil and Feta. Spoon cheese mixture into a thick zip top bag and smoosh the mixture down into one corner. Seal bag and use sharp scissors to snip a small bit off of the corner of the bag. Pipe the cheese into each olive and set aside. This will probably be messy, it certainly was for me, but that just means you get to taste the filling as you go.

Cut the prosciutto into approximately 2 ½ x ¾ inch strips and wrap around each olive. Secure with toothpick and serve.

From 52 Week "Bus Fare" by Mary Joseph

When life gets like this,
Sweet music, music saves my soul.
And it reminds me I'd have no songs
If I had no words to sing.
So I tip my hat to all the moments
That made me turn it inside out,
To lonely nights and broken hearts
And being left out of the club.
To cold winters and quiet days,
To keeping it all inside until it comes pouring,
Pouring out in song

To read more about the 52-Week Club see pages 87-88

How To Chop Basil

Step #1
Stack leaves on
top of each other

Step #2
Roll leaves
(tube-like)

Step #3
Chop!

Now they're in fun strips. You can keep them like
this or keep chopping until they're really small.

Mini Ham & Cheddar Quiche

(makes 48 mini quiches)

4 eggs, beaten
2 cups finely diced cooked ham
2 cups shredded Cheddar cheese
¾ cup sour cream

½ teaspoon pepper
2 pie crusts
 (the kind you unroll)
mini-muffin tins

Preheat oven to 350 degrees. In a medium bowl mix beaten eggs, ham, cheese, sour cream and pepper. Set quiche mixture aside while you prepare the crust.

Use a shot glass to cut 24 circles into each crust. Place one circle into the bottom of each mini-muffin mold. Spoon 1 tablespoon of the quiche mixture into each mold.

Place quiche in oven. Check at 15, then every 5 minutes. These shouldn't take more than 25 minutes to cook. Stick a toothpick in the middle to check if they're done. The toothpicks should come out with very little moisture on them, the tops of the quiche should be lightly browned.

Remove from oven. Let sit for about 5 minutes, then remove each mini-quiche onto a cooling rack. You can serve these cold or hot.

xoxoxoxoxox

Garlic Parmesan Twists

(serves 4)

½ recipe 'Pizza Dough' (page 146)
6 cloves roasted garlic, minced (page 17)
¼ cup 'White Pizza Sauce' (page 147)
¼ cup shredded Parmesan cheese

2 tablespoons finely chopped flat-leaf
 (Italian) parsley
2 tablespoons shredded Parmesan cheese

Preheat oven to 400 degrees. *(check out page 2 for a visual)*

On a floured surface roll pizza dough into a circle ¼ inch thick. Spread the roasted garlic over half of the dough. Spread sauce on top of the garlic, cover with ¼ cup of cheese and sprinkle parsley over the cheese. Fold the side *without* toppings over the topping side. Use a pizza cutter to cut the dough into 1 inch strips, starting at the folded end, working out to the open edge.

Grab the strips at each end and twist a few times. Place on an un-greased cookie sheet. Use a pastry brush to brush the twists with a little more of the white sauce. Sprinkle with 2 tablespoons of cheese and bake for 7-10 minutes or until golden brown.

The sauce may leak out and cause smoke - be prepared if your smoke detectors are sensitive.

Most musicians I know can cook at least one good dish, and sometimes even a great meal or two. Most cooks I know can scratch out a tune or two on guitar or piano and maybe even sing a little. Historically, both kitchens and tour vans have appealed to the same boozed-up-tattooed-ex-con-anti-authority-piratey-crazed-druggie types. Only in these hot, cramped and stinky underworlds can this person breathe and survive.

When you go to a restaurant, you only see 10% of what it takes for your order to magically appear before you. You don't witness the hours of prep work cutting, slicing, stock making and snaking of the wash tank that backed up with gray grease sludge (again) in the middle of a Friday night dinner rush. You don't hear the swearing, see the blood or feel the tension.

When you go to a show, you only see 10% of what it takes for the band to magically appear before you. You don't witness the years of individual practice, hours of band rehearsals, late-night scrutinizing of lyrics, the $1,200 clogged fuel filter that stranded the van in the middle of nowhere Montana for two days in negative five-degree weather. You don't hear the swearing, see the blood or feel the tension.

What most normal people don't understand is that this person doesn't really have a choice. They know that they do what they do better than anyone else. Hell, no one else CAN do it. Can you see your accountant repeatedly scarring their hands on the grill and chopping off bits of extremities, or waking up in a different place every morning with their sleeping bag being the only familiar thing in sight?

This sado-masochistic breed thrives on all of the inconsistencies, uncertainties, last-minute emergencies, long days, dedication, late hours, end-of-night exhaustion, sweat-soaked uniforms and the pride that comes with knowing they did their job really well, and that tomorrow it will all happen again...and they'll enjoy it.

Maybe that musician doesn't know the secret to light and fluffy mashed potatoes is to simmer the potatoes - not boil; boiling extracts too much starch - and too much starch makes them heavy and pasty once mashed. And maybe that cook doesn't know how to properly hold a pick. But, if you're ever fortunate enough to find yourself sitting down with a bowl of the musician's mash and listening to the cook slowly demolish "Stairway to Heaven" with a sledgehammer, take the time to really appreciate how lucky you are at that moment.

- Sebastian "Seabass" St. John - Fiddle Player For Hire - On The Road

Authors Note: Seabass is a very gifted fiddle player and has played with the likes of Flogging Molly, Beck, Jack White and Reverend Peyton's Big Damn Band. Once, while visiting the Tea Farm, he was playing his fiddle in the barn. Almost in a trance I had to stop what I was doing to listen. It was a very surreal moment, like something out of a beautiful dream.

Starters & Dips

Jalapeno Poppers with Cilantro Ranch

(makes about 40 poppers)

20 jalapenos, sliced in half, seeds and veins removed*
1 (8 ounce) package cream cheese brought to room temperature
1 ½ cups shredded Mexican 4-Cheese mix
¼ cup mayonnaise
1 teaspoon onion powder
1 teaspoon garlic salt
1 cup crushed corn chips
2 tablespoons butter, melted

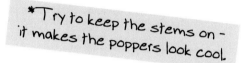

*Try to keep the stems on – it makes the poppers look cool.

Preheat oven to 350 degrees.

Place halved jalapenos (seeds and veins removed!) cut side up on a cookie sheet. Drizzle lightly with olive oil and sprinkle with salt and pepper. Roast for 7 minutes. Remove and set aside to cool. Don't turn the oven off.

In the bowl of your food processor or standing mixer add cheeses, mayonnaise, onion powder and garlic salt. Mix until well blended. Using all of the cheese mixture, spoon evenly into the jalapenos.

In a small bowl mix crushed corn chips and melted butter. (The chips should be crushed into fine crumbs, so use a food processor or a zip top bag and rolling pin.) Divide evenly over the cheese stuffed jalapenos to form a crust.

Bake for 7-10 minutes. (Don't let them boil over!) Allow to cool a little before serving.

To make these the day before serving: Roast the jalapenos and keep them in the fridge in a zip top bag. Make the cheese mix and keep it in a covered bowl in the fridge. Take the cheese mix out of the fridge about 20 minutes before you stuff the jalapenos so it softens a bit.

Serve with Cilantro Ranch.

Cilantro Ranch:
½ cup mayonnaise
¼ cup sour cream
¼ cup buttermilk
1 teaspoon apple cider vinegar
2 tablespoons chopped fresh cilantro
¼ teaspoon salt
½ teaspoon garlic powder
½ teaspoon onion powder
2½ teaspoons hot sauce (optional)

Add all ingredients to a small bowl and whisk until creamy.

Only add the hot sauce if you like it really spicy – the poppers can be spicy enough on their own.

Being from a blue collar town, my parents both put in a lot of hours. When I grew up - from when I was born until I was twelve or so - my "babysitter" was a professional guitar player from Muscle Shoals, Alabama. He toured with a lot of acts, and within certain circles, he's one of those "Greatest Unknown Guitarist" types whose bootlegs are traded back and forth on tour buses via "only copy" cassette tapes.

I picked up a guitar in an effort to relate to him; he was a great man, but a very shy one. I knew him, and consider him a family member, but playing guitar, learning from him, introduced me to one of the deepest forms of communication I've ever had with another human being. And past that, to this day I'm still utterly amazed that, at times, it was the only way this man could communicate. With the greats, with musical geniuses, you don't need fancy rigs, either---it could have been a thousand dollar Stratocaster or a $10 beater he'd picked up at a garage sale, three or four notes, a bend here, some vibrato there, and you knew it was him on guitar.

I'd play him song after song; albums, CDs and cassettes I brought in. "How do I play this?" I'd ask him over and over. Within seconds of hearing something, often for the first time, he'd show me how to rip into Zeppelin, the Stones, old Robert Johnson licks. Every single song I ever loved, I've a memory of him teaching me how to play it and giving me histories and back stories of each of the musicians involved.

When he died suddenly, I wasn't just unable to pick up a guitar---I couldn't listen to music for years. I blocked it all out, because it was too painful. I'm unable to express what it's like to have something so wonderful and beautiful in your life be altered in such a tragic fashion, other than to say those years were dull and numb. Everything feels gray without music---it charges and energizes so many other aspects of your life that to live without it is simply to exist. Rocks exist. People are meant to live.

One day, while going through some old boxes, I came across a cassette he'd made of himself playing. I hadn't forgotten I'd had it, but I was so nervous to play it I kept it on the periphery of my consciousness---it was that same feeling when you haven't been to church in awhile and have to go to confession, or when you're finally going to tell a girl you love her.

There he was. On the stereo. Like he'd never left. In every note I heard his voice, and every strum I felt him with me.

I play guitar a lot more these days.

- Randy Duax - New York City, NY

Chicken Basil Stuffed Tomatoes

(makes 100 tomato bites)

I know 100 is a lot, but these are tiny bite-sized appetizers - people will most likely eat at least 4 or more of them. It's the perfect amount for a baby/bridal shower or some other such party.

2 (12.5 ounce) cans chicken
½ cup mayonnaise
½ tablespoon lemon juice
¼ teaspoon salt
¼ teaspoon pepper

½ teaspoon onion powder
2-3 cloves garlic, minced
¾-1 cup chopped fresh basil
50 cherry tomatoes
½ cup tomato guts (explained below)

In a medium bowl mix chicken, mayonnaise, lemon juice, salt, pepper, onion powder, minced garlic and basil.

Slice each tomato in half. Use a spoon or a knife (whatever works best for you) to scoop out the insides (the guts) of each tomato. Put the "tomato guts" into a small bowl. When you're done, add ¼ cup of the guts into the chicken mixture and discard the rest.

Divide chicken mixture evenly between the tomatoes, stuffing each one with some filling. Serve immediately.

You can make this mixture the night before, but don't prepare the tomatoes until you're almost ready to serve.

From 52 Week "Turtle" by Chris Doud

Well he never did have no roller skates,
And he never had use of a flying cape.
He never put on no runnin' shoes,
Well he never did run, so what's the use.
He never did drive no sports car,
He never had a reason to go that far.
He never hopped on the lightnin' train,
Well he was plenty fast on his own four legs.
Sugar Envelopes Bread the Turtle,
Big ol' grin on his green ol' face.
Livin' the life of ease and leisure,
Yeah, slow and steady, wins the race.

To read more about the 52-Week Club see pages 87-88

Cold Veggie Pizza

(serves 8-10)

1 (10 ounce) tube croissants
1 (8 ounce) container softened cream cheese
½ (1 ounce) packet ranch dressing mix
1 to 2 cups finely diced veggies of any combination*
 (carrots, celery, red bell peppers, green peppers, etc.)
1 cup finely shredded Cheddar cheese

Recipe courtesy of Emily Ihrke - Las Vegas, NV

Preheat oven to 350 degrees.

*Add more or less veggies as you'd like. You can't really go wrong here.

Open the croissants and gently unroll the dough on a lightly floured surface. Using your fingers, pinch along the perforated edges to seal the triangular pieces together. You want all of the pieces to become one big, rectangular piece of dough. Carefully flip the dough over and do the same on the other side. You need to be pretty thorough about this because, when it bakes, it will come apart at the perforated edges if it's not sealed well.

Place onto a cookie sheet. Bake for 8-10 minutes or until cooked through and it's a nice, crispy brown. Let it sit on the cookie sheet for about 5 minutes. Carefully remove and place on a cutting board to cool.

In a small bowl mix cream cheese and ranch dressing until thoroughly combined. Let the mixture sit out so it softens - this makes it easier to spread.

Allow dough to cool completely. When cool, spread the cream cheese mixture over the dough. Top with veggies and cheese. Cut into squares and serve.

Music is love in every sense of the word. It captures all different emotions possible, but the essence is love and will always be beneath every thing else. Music is a universal language created to translate love to all people. I am a very, very blessed young man, to be a part of such a great power. If only all people could know and understand this love that is available to every one. I often think about the devastating things people do to each other, to their own family and children and to the earth. This violence plagues my mind. It's the fear of being silenced that imprisons me. Being jailed for 3 days was hell for me; there is nothing to be proud about being a prisoner. So many people are locked away just to be silenced and I pray each and every day that I will be able to keep my voice and not lose it to the muffling walls and bars. Beautiful things do come from anger, but it is hard to know when to quiet that anger. I used to use music to express my anger. Over the years of growing up in a traveling band I have realized the power and the strength of music. The many people I meet and the many songs I hear teach me I can use music to convert anger into love and pain into hope. Sadness and anger are inevitable, but without them love and strength could not be conceived.

- Jeshua Marshall - Larry & His Flask - Redmond, OR

Pesto Feta Crostinis

(makes about 28 crostinis)

¼ - ½ cup 'Spinach Pesto' (recipe below)
1 cup (about 1-2) finely diced vine-ripe tomatoes
½ cup crumbled Feta cheese (about 4 ounces)
1 baguette (about 28 slices, ½ inch thick)

Preheat oven to 350 degrees.

Spread a teaspoon or so of pesto on each slice of bread and place on a large cookie sheet. Top with a sprinkling of the diced tomatoes and crumbled Feta.

Crostinis are little slices of toasted bread served with different toppings or drizzled with olive oil.

Bake for 5 minutes or until warmed through.

If you prefer crunchy bread: Before you spread the pesto and add the toppings, place the bread on a cookie sheet. Bake for about 5-7 minutes, depending on how crispy you want your bread. Top with the pesto and toppings and bake for another 5 minutes.

Spinach Pesto
(makes about ¾ cup)

2 tablespoons pine nuts
¼ cup chopped fresh basil
2 cups chopped baby spinach
¼ cup shredded Romano cheese
2 cloves garlic, minced

2 tablespoons lemon juice
¼ cup + 1 tablespoon extra-virgin olive oil
½ teaspoon salt
¼ teaspoon pepper

Add pine nuts, basil, spinach, cheese, garlic, lemon juice, olive oil, salt and pepper to the bowl of your food processor (or blender). Process (or blend) for about 10 seconds. Use your spatula to scrape the sides of the bowl. Process again until smooth, about 1 minute or so.

Music can bring me to tears, take me back in time, bring me inspiration, keep me grounded or take me above the clouds. It has power, it has influence, it can bring people together, it can inspire love, it can inspire hate and it can inspire change. It's something we all have in common regardless of race or creed - we all have our music. We may prefer different tunes, we may be affected by different words, but music, in its purest form, reaches into places deep inside of us that nothing else can touch, except maybe food.

-Mary

Serrano Ham & Manchego Crostinis

(makes about 28 crostinis)

¼ to ½ cup 'Parsley Pesto' (recipe below)
¼ pound chopped Serrano ham
½ cup finely shredded Manchego cheese
1 baguette (about 28 slices, ½ inch thick)

Preheat oven to 350 degrees.

Serrano ham and Manchego cheese are Spanish in origin and can usually be found at specialty food shops.

Heat a large skillet over medium heat. When hot, add chopped Serrano ham to the skillet. Cook, tossing frequently, until just a little crispy, about 2-3 minutes. Set aside on a paper towel to cool.

A good substitution for Serrano ham and Manchego cheese is prosciutto and Parmesan.

Spread about a teaspoon or so of pesto on each slice of bread and place on a large cookie sheet. Top with ham and Manchego cheese.

Bake for 5 minutes or until warmed through and cheese is a melted.

If you prefer crunchy bread: Before you spread the pesto and add the toppings, place the slices on a cookie sheet. Bake for about 5-7 minutes, depending on how crispy you want the bread. Top with the pesto, ham and cheese and bake for another 5 minutes.

Parsley Pesto
(makes about ¾ cup)
3 cups roughly chopped flat-leaf (Italian) parsley
1 clove garlic, minced
2 ½ tablespoons lemon juice
¼ cup + 1 tablespoon extra-virgin olive oil
½ teaspoon salt
¼ teaspoon pepper

about 1 large bunch

Add parsley, garlic, lemon juice, oil, salt and pepper to the bowl of your food processor (or blender). Process (or blend) for about 10 seconds. Use your spatula to scrape the sides of the bowl. Process again until smooth, about 1 minute or so.

The Beatles... if history proves nothing, it's that four kings are better than one. Down with tyranny!

- Micah Garbarino - Oklahoma City, OK - When asked "Elvis or The Beatles?"

Hummus!

Roasted Garlic - 29

Feta - 31

Tabbouleh - 31

Sicilian - 31

Spicy Tomatillos - 32

Tomato & Goat Cheese - 32

Creamy Lebne - 32

Spinach - 34

Cilantro Lime - 34

Chunky Tomato - 34

Roasted Red Pepper - 35

Black Bean - 36

Kalamata Olive - 36

Sour Cream & Onion - 36

Artichoke - 36

Sun-Dried Tomato - 37

Curry - 37

Pesto - 37

Guacahummus - 37

Spicy Spanish - 37

ما شين حمص

Roasted Garlic Hummus - Page 29

Sicilian Hummus - Page 31

Cilantro Lime Hummus - Page 34

Roasted Garlic Hummus

4-6 cloves roasted garlic, minced (directions below)
½ cup tahini
1 (15 ounce) can garbanzo beans*
⅓ cup lemon juice
1 tablespoon olive oil
1 teaspoon salt
1 teaspoon cumin

A food processor works best for hummus. It blends everything perfectly without any fuss. If you don't have one you can use your blender. If it's not a good blender - and even sometimes if it is - it'll be a little frustrating, but not impossible. You'll just need to be patient. I'll give directions for both a food processor and a blender.

First, roast the garlic (see directions below).

To roast garlic:
Heat oven to 400 degrees. Place unpeeled cloves of garlic in the middle of a large square of tin foil. Drizzle liberally with olive oil - about 2 tablespoons. Fold up the ends of the foil tightly, completely sealing the opening so that no air can escape. Place on a cookie sheet and roast in oven for 15 minutes. Remove and allow to cool enough to handle. Cut an end off of each clove, squeeze from the shell and mince.

Blender Directions:
Add roasted garlic, tahini, ¼ of the beans, lemon juice, olive oil, salt and cumin to the blender. Blend until smooth. Stop often to scrape the sides and the cover of the blender. If you don't, my mother will scold you.

Add more beans, blending little by little, until completely smooth. If it seems too thick to blend, alternate (small!) splashes of olive oil and lemon juice. By the time I'm finished I've usually added another few tablespoons of lemon juice and a few tablespoons of olive oil. Don't be afraid - lemon juice makes it tart, and tart, in my opinion, is good. Olive oil makes it creamy, and creamy is also good. I also recommend that hummus sits at least an hour before serving.

Food Processor Directions:
This way is much simpler and always comes out much better. Add all of the ingredients to the food processor bowl and press start. Let it mix for about 10 seconds. Stop it and scrape the sides. Process for at least 1 minute - up to 2 or 3 won't hurt.

*If you don't want to use beans from a can, use 1 1/2 cups of fresh cooked beans.

"My Little Heart"

A 52 Week poem I wrote for my niece, Rita Grace

Dawn has broke,
Here comes the sun,
The darkest hour has passed.
Flowers are blooming,
Spring rain is falling,
My heart is thawing at last.

Trees are green again,
I can breathe again,
The river finally calls.
Oh! I will answer that call
And drown these winter blues,
I'll emerge refreshed and clean.

With you comes the promise
of blessed warm moons,
The promise of hot summer suns.
With you comes the promise
Of laughter filled days
And nights filled with music and love.

Throw open the windows,
Let the light in!
Do you hear the birds singing?
They're singing for you,
They're singing for Him.
Sparkle, my little heart, and sing along.

Come purple leaves and green buds,
Come white flowers and blue skies.
Summer, fill us with color and
Bring us a playmate.
Give him dark hair and curls.
Put the wind behind us,
And shoeless we'll run,
Our faces warmed by the sun.

(week "Shoeless")

To read more about the 52-Week Club see pages 87-88

30

Hummus!

Feta

1 (15 ounce) can garbanzo beans	1 teaspoon salt
½ cup tahini	1 clove garlic, minced
⅓ cup lemon juice	1 (7 ounce) package Feta cheese
¼ cup extra-virgin olive oil	¼ cup chopped flat-leaf (Italian) parsley

Add all ingredients to food processor and process until smooth. Usually, I let it run for about 1-3 minutes. If you are using a blender, refer to directions on page 29. (The Feta will make this really thick, so a blender will require patience.)

Tabbouleh

1 (15 ounce) can garbanzo beans	½ cup chopped curly parsley
½ cup tahini	½ teaspoon allspice
⅓ cup lemon juice	¼ cup olive oil
1 teaspoon salt	½ cup finely chopped tomatoes
¼ cup chopped fresh mint	½ cup finely chopped cucumber
2 green onions, roughly chopped	

Add all ingredients, **except tomatoes and cucumbers**, to food processor and process until smooth, about 1-3 minutes. If you are using a blender, refer to directions on page 29. Just before serving, place chopped tomatoes and cucumbers on top.

Sicilian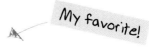

My favorite!

1 (15 ounce) can cannellini beans	***Topping:***
¼ cup tahini	1 medium vine-ripe or Roma
⅓ cup lemon juice	tomato, diced small
¼ cup extra-virgin olive oil	¼ cup chopped fresh basil (see page 18)
1 teaspoon salt	¼ cup extra-virgin olive oil
4-5 cloves garlic, roasted then minced	1-2 cloves garlic, minced
(see ***"To roast garlic"*** on page 29)	

Add all ingredients, **except for topping,** to food processor and process until smooth, about 1-3 minutes. If you are using a blender, refer to directions on page 29.

Add ingredients for topping to a small bowl and mix. Just before serving, drizzle the hummus with a little more olive oil and top with topping mixture.

Spicy Tomatillos

2-3 medium tomatillos
1 (15 ounce) can garbanzo beans
⅓ cup tahini
2 jalapenos, de-seeded* and roughly chopped

2 cloves garlic, minced
1 cup cilantro leaves
⅓ cup lime juice
1 teaspoon salt

Remove husks from tomatillos and cut in half. Place cut size down on cookie sheet. Broil for 5-7 minutes or until skins brown and juices flow. Add beans, tahini, jalapenos, garlic, cilantro, lime juice, salt and tomatillos to food processor. Process until smooth, about 1-3 minutes. If you are using a blender, refer to directions on page 29.

*For more spice, keep some seeds.

Tomato & Goat Cheese

2 Roma tomatoes
1 (15 ounce) can garbanzo beans
½ cup tahini
⅓ cup lemon juice

1 teaspoon salt
1 clove garlic, minced (or ½ teaspoon garlic powder)
5 ounces Goat cheese

Cut tomatoes in half. Scoop and discard all seeds and juices. Roughly chop what's left.

Add all ingredients to food processor and process until smooth, about 1-3 minutes. If you are using a blender, refer to directions on page 29. The tomatoes will make this more liquidy than usual. I recommend making this recipe the night before, or at least 2 hours before serving, to let it thicken up a bit.

Creamy Lebne

1 (15 ounce) can garbanzo beans
¼ cup tahini
⅓ cup lemon juice
1 teaspoon salt

½ cup Lebne (a.k.a Kiefer cheese or Greek yogurt*)
2 cloves garlic, minced

Add all ingredients to food processor and process until smooth, about 1-3 minutes. If you are using a blender, refer to directions on page 29.

*Lebne (or Lebneh) is a Middle Eastern yogurt. Use Greek Yogurt - found at places like Trader Joe's - to substitute. If all else fails use plain yogurt...

Hummus!

"Rounds Of Rum"

From 52 Week "Round Of Rum" by Tom Vanden Avond

Hush ya, buachaill,
Hush and listen to my sad and lonesome tale
About the bravest captain who ever set to sail.
His name was Sean O'Farrell:
As tough as the roughest sea
And this is how they cut him down
On a deep and lonesome sea

O'Farrell came from Galway Bay the sea was in his blood.
You can trace the sailin' Farrell men 'til the days before the flood.
So his mother didn't bat an eye when her 12 year old set sail
In the schooner *Liberty*, bound for New South Wales.

For years he sailed the mighty seas, his reputation grew.
From port to port and all the lands of Sean all brave men knew.
But he never hurt an honest man and this was his just creed,
He never stole, he never raped or was taken in by greed.

Forget about buried treasure, boyo,
Forget your rounds of rum.
O'Farrell sailed for nuthin' else
But the love of only one.
Her name was Jenny Connolly
And to her man was true;
With the blackest hair and fairest skin
And eyes of Irish blue.

It was dark one night without a moon
On a deep and lonesome sea.
The first mate and them other cowards called out "Mutiny!"
But old Sean was tough he held them off, all night they did attack,
'Till finally they took him down, five lead balls in his back.

Hush ya, buachaill,
Hush and listen, I did get my revenge.
I sailed to every end of earth and killed those wicked men.
For 30 years I roamed this world
And tonight it is complete:
For I'm starin' into the very eyes that made my Jenny weep.
May God damn your wicked eyes who made my Jenny weep.

To read more about the 52-Week Club see pages 87-88

Spinach

1 tablespoon olive oil
4 cups chopped baby spinach
1 (15 ounce) can garbanzo beans
½ cup tahini

½ cup lemon juice
1 teaspoon salt
1 clove garlic, minced

Heat oil in a large skillet over medium heat. Add spinach and toss, almost constantly, until wilted. Add to food processor, along with the other ingredients, and process until smooth, about 1-3 minutes. If you are using a blender, refer to directions on page 29.

Cilantro Lime

3 cloves roasted garlic, minced
   (see *"To roast garlic"* on page 29)
1 (15 ounce) can garbanzo beans
½ cup tahini

½ cup lime juice
1 teaspoon salt
1 bunch cilantro, chopped (about ¾ cup)

Add roasted and minced garlic, along with the other ingredients to food processor. Process until smooth, about 1-3 minutes. If you are using a blender, refer to directions on page 29.

"Music is food you can hear"

Chunky Tomato

1 (15 ounce) can garbanzo beans
¼ cup tahini
3 tablespoons lemon juice
¼ cup tomato paste

½ teaspoon salt
2 cloves garlic, minced
1-2 vine-ripe tomatoes, finely chopped

Add garbanzo beans, tahini, lemon juice, tomato paste, salt and minced garlic to food processor. Process until smooth, about 1-3 minutes. If you are using a blender, refer to directions on page 29. Pour into a bowl.

Cut tomatoes in half. Remove and discard all seeds and extra juices. Finely chop tomatoes and add to hummus. Mix well. If I were you, I'd put a bunch of crumbled Feta on top before serving.

Roasted Red Pepper

1 (15 ounce) can garbanzo beans
1 roasted red bell pepper (directions below)
½ cup tahini

¼ cup lemon juice
1 teaspoon salt
1 clove garlic, minced

To roast red pepper in oven:

Heat oven to 375 degrees. Cut peppers in half, drizzle with olive oil and sprinkle with salt and pepper. Rub oil and spices all over peppers. Place peppers cut side down on a cookie sheet and roast for 15 minutes, or until charred all over. When done, put in a zip top bag and put in the fridge until cool to the touch.

To roast red pepper on the stove:

This is the way I prefer to roast a bell pepper, if I'm in the presence of a gas range. Turn one of the burners on to high heat and place the red pepper directly on the burner. Use tongs to turn the pepper until the entire thing is black and charred. When done, put in a zip top bag, seal and put in the fridge until cool to the touch.

When pepper is cool enough to touch, remove from the bag and peel the skin off. It should come off effortlessly.

Add all ingredients to food processor and process until smooth, about 1-3 minutes. If you are using a blender, refer to directions on page 29.

Other ways to use Hummus:

- Instead of mayo, spread hummus on a sandwich, in a wrap or on a burger.

- Instead of salad dressing, I like to mix a large spoonful or so of hummus in my Tabbouleh or other chopped salads.

- Use it as a veggie dip.

- If you're having guests over and you want to get fancy, make Hummus Bites:
Layer pita chips on a serving tray, top with a spoonful of hummus, some crumbled Feta and diced tomatoes.

Add all ingredients to food processor and process until smooth, about 1-3 minutes. If you are using a blender, refer to directions on page 29.

Black Bean

2 (15 ounce) cans black beans
½ cup tahini
⅓ cup lime juice

1 teaspoon salt
1 clove garlic, minced

Kalamata Olive

1 (15 ounce) can garbanzo beans
1 cup quartered Kalamata olives
1 tablespoon olive juice from jar
½ cup tahini

¼ cup lemon juice
1 clove garlic, minced
½ to 1 teaspoon salt*

*Olives are quite salty, so start with 1/2 teaspoon.
Add more if you feel it needs it.

Sour Cream & Onion

1 (15 ounce) can cannellini beans
¼ cup tahini
½ cup sour cream
3 green onions, chopped

3 tablespoons lemon juice
1 clove garlic, minced
1 teaspoon salt

Artichoke

1 (15 ounce) can cannellini beans
2 (6.5 ounce) jars marinated artichoke
   hearts (save juice from 1 jar)
¼ cup tahini

2 tablespoons lemon juice
1 teaspoon salt
1-2 cloves garlic, minced

Hummus!

Sun-Dried Tomato

1 (15 ounce) can garbanzo beans
½ cup tahini
⅓ cup lemon juice
¼ cup oil from sun-dried tomato jar

½ cup roughly chopped sun-dried
   tomatoes
1 teaspoon salt
1 clove garlic, minced

Curry

1 (15 ounce) can garbanzo beans
½ cup tahini
⅓ cup lemon juice
2 tablespoons extra-virgin olive oil

½ teaspoon salt
½ teaspoon cumin
1 teaspoon curry
1 teaspoon garlic powder

Pesto

1 (15 ounce) can garbanzo beans
½ cup tahini
½ cup lemon juice
1 teaspoon salt

¼ cup + 2 tablespoons 'Spinach Pesto'
   (page 50)

Stop & smell the hummus!

Guacahummus

1 (15 ounce) can cannellini beans
1 avocado
⅓ cup lime juice
1 clove garlic, minced

½ cup chopped cilantro
2 tablespoons diced white onion
½ teaspoon salt

Spicy Spanish

1 (15 ounce) can garbanzo beans
½ cup tahini
⅓ cup lemon juice
½ teaspoon salt
¼ cup olive oil

1-2 cloves garlic, minced
½ teaspoon cayenne pepper
¼ teaspoon dried thyme
¼ teaspoon paprika

"Go For Broke"

by Mary Joseph

A few winters ago my sister and her husband moved into a farm house that sat on about two acres of land, surrounded by rows upon rows of almond trees. Along with the house was a beautiful, beat-up old barn that her husband had a vision of turning into a music venue. My sister and I spent a few dusty days in that barn, cleaning it out, while her husband, Willy Tea, and his friends built a stage, repaired the walls, installed a curtain that rose to reveal the stage and even hung up a spinning mirror ball. As we got everything ready for the grand opening, there was a certain electricity in the air, like there was something very special about to happen. The excitement we felt was more than for the opening of the venue, or even the show. We knew there was something important about the band we were about to meet. And, on January 24th, 2009, my life was changed forever by a band of gypsy punks from Oregon called Larry & His Flask.

While I was busy making enough pasta to feed 200 people for the grand opening of The Tea Farm, L.A.H.F. pulled up in their blue, beat up Ford van. When I had everything for the sauce in the pot and set to a simmer, I bundled up my 10 month old niece and went outside to meet them. Willy Tea, having met them weeks before, said during their show they were "jumping off the stage onto tables and sitting on peoples shoulders while they played!" I pictured obnoxious, scruffy men in their late 30's/early 40's who stank of whiskey and cigarettes, possibly missing teeth, using foul language and having heroin-skinny bodies. But instead, we met these strikingly talented musicians, all under 25, who were genuinely nice, well-mannered and played beautiful songs.

On my way out of the house I passed the back of their van. It was wide open and I could see there was a bunk built into the back. Beneath piles of blankets and pillows bright blue eyes were peering out at me, set on a face framed by a giant beard and a wild mane of hair belonging to Ian Cook. As he smiled at me and I smiled back, I immediately felt a connection with him. It was then clear to me that, from the get-go, L.A.H.F and the Tea Farm family were meant to be.

Larry & His Flask are like no band I've ever seen - which seems to be the general consensus. As soon as Jamin says "Hello everybody! We're Larry & His Flask!" and the first song begins, people are glued to the stage. Everyone is watching with smiles and wide eyes. People are looking at their friends shaking their heads with looks on their faces that say: "What the hell is this? Are these guys serious?!"

When all six members are on stage, they are truly a sight to behold. They play their instruments fast and they play them really well. It's difficult to describe the kind of music they play and they don't fit into any of the genres found in your local music store. Their music sounds like rowdy bluegrass/folk with heavy Punk Rock roots and a splash of gypsy soul. Each band member exudes super high energy. It's baffling to know that they do this nearly every night for months at a time.

Hummus!

Jesse plays the stand-up bass and is down in front of the stage using the instrument to propel him into the air as he jumps and dances around. With his long beard and the way he leaps and twirls, he reminds me of a character from Fiddler on the Roof.

Ian, sporting a magnificent beard and mustache, looks like Santa's prodigal son who left the family business to be in a band. He starts off on the stage, but half way into the first verse, he's down on the floor with Jesse, playing guitar and dancing around like you imagine boys do in their rooms alone, when no one is looking.

Kirk is on stage with the mandolin, singing along with a grin on his face and a twinkle in his eye. He rarely looks up from his mandolin, except maybe to smile at one of the boys when something unbeknownst to the crowd amuses them.

Andrew plays banjo and goes back and forth between the stage and the floor. He shreds on the banjo and rocks it like it's a guitar. With his crooked tie, upturned collar, slightly wrinkled suit, and unkempt hair, he has the look of a young, down-on-his-luck stock broker who lost millions of dollars in the market - went home to find his wife with another man - then spent the duration of the evening at the bar drinking scotch on the rocks.

Dall plays the guitar and dances all over and around everything: the stage, the floor, into the crowd, wherever he can get to. His wild black hair and long black beard contrast his suit pants, button down shirt, vest and tie perfectly. You should see him in this exact outfit riding his skateboard before a show: a wild man in a suit...beautiful. As he belts out each song his eyes remind me of the line from 'Nobody Home' by Pink Floyd: "I've got wild staring eyes." With those wild staring eyes he looks straight into the eyes of the people in the crowd, who incidentally are also all staring wildly at the dancing gypsy boys.

Jamin keeps to the stage. In front of him is a snare, a high hat and a kick drum. He invites the crowd to come closer, encourages them to drink more and to "Bring us drinks too!" During "My Name Is Cancer", the boys all begin to get down onto the ground still playing their instruments. Dall is on his back with closed eyes playing the guitar like one possessed and fighting for his soul. Jesse squats over his bass playing it like a drum. Jamin leaves his drums to come to the edge of the crowd, telling everyone to get down on the floor. People are uneasy at first, but, Jamin insists and one by one they get off their barstools or chairs, and squat down. Jamin uses the floor like a drum and some people get into it by slapping at the floor like it's their own set of congas.

This is just the opening song. After this, the crowd is theirs and mid-show Jamin has thrown the tambourine out to whoever wants to catch it. Soon people are dancing like they're at a hoe-down or a church revival - inhibitions lost, smiles all around. They've just been infected with a lovely disease called "The Flask" and they'll be all the better for it.

L.A.H.F. lives on the road with the occasional month off at home - which is in Oregon. I was lucky enough to join them on a few tours in 2009 and got a little taste of life on the road - and I loved every minute of it. The boys head out not knowing where they'll sleep, when they'll eat or if they'll get paid. They'll sleep anywhere: in the bus, on the beach, in a park...anywhere. With them, freedom has precedence over comfort.

As far as food goes, it was relatively foreign to me to shop like they do: searching for the cheapest options and passing up what they really wanted because they only had so much money. Sometimes, I would splurge and buy some good bread and cheese and treats, like birthday cookies, whiskey or grocery store sushi. Their purchases generally consisted of a few loaves of cheap white bread, lunch meat, a head of lettuce, cream cheese, fruit and always a giant jar of peanut butter. This was to be breakfast, snacks, lunch and dinner, unless someone else came along with food. I saw more random combinations of sandwiches with them than I ever thought possible. My favorite was Jamin's peanut butter, honey, Sriracha (their favorite hot sauce) and lettuce sandwich. He said it was good, but the lettuce, of all things, was "throwing the whole thing off."

These boys put Sriracha on everything. When I saw them put it on their perfectly tasty pizza I was truly astonished. "It adds flavor and spice to the flavorless and spice-less." The reason for the constant Sriracha-ing I understand, but as a cook, it slightly bothers me. I call it "defiling good food". Anyhow, they say, when you're on the road as much as they are, and when you have as little food options as they have, the Sriracha is essential.

To live this lifestyle you have to be very comfortable with the people you are traveling with. Germaphobes need not apply. They share plates, forks and giant jugs of water. Once, we used Jamin's pocket knife to spread the peanut butter. Another time we used a giant stick someone found. I had made a sandwich once while we were driving and when I was done I licked the knife clean and wiped whatever was left on my pants. Jesse laughed and said: "You're one of us now, Mary."

Something I noticed from the start that continually impresses me is the way they share things- anything and everything is anyone's and everyone's. If someone peels an orange everyone gets a slice. When we were at someone's house one morning, Jesse would wander into the kitchen, grab a bunch of grapes and then come into the living room and pass one out to each of us. Later, Jamin picked some fruit off a tree, took a bite and passed it around. Once, when down to the last piece of pizza, Andrew took a bite, handed it to Jamin and said: "Last piece, pass it around" and we all got one last bite.

Selfishness seems nonexistent with them. They have such love and respect for each other and this rambling life they live. They are married to each other and the van is their home. This must be the case in order to travel almost year-round successfully in such close quarters. Touring for such long periods of time has been referred to by other musicans as: "How to break up a band." Not so with L.A.H.F. It seems to make them stronger, which is a rare thing indeed.

L.A.H.F helped me see that life is full of magical moments and a lifetime is nothing but a series of moments strung together. You can't hold onto regret, or worry about the future. All you have is right now and this moment, and it's up to you how you spend it. The boys often say "This is the best day of my life" - and mean it wholeheartedly. I've started saying it as well. If every day is the best day of your life, how amazing will your

Hummus!

life be when you look back on it?

I can honestly say that meeting Larry & His Flask woke me up. I was stuck in a place because it was comfortable and because I was afraid to make a much needed change. When I met L.A.H.F. and saw how free they were, it inspired me to gather my courage and change my life. Shortly after meeting them, I left my job in the city where I lived alone and moved to the country to be close to my family. I got rid of nearly all of my belongings, keeping only my books, kitchen stuff, guitars, family pictures and heirlooms. I used to have 2 closets plus full of clothing. Now, I just have a couple of drawers.

I realized that what I really needed more than money and a nice apartment was the closeness of my family. Now, I have ample time to devote to them above anything else. Now, my joy comes from simple things: nieces and nephews, books, food, music, true love and motherhood. All of these things surround me now that, thanks in part to six gypsy boys, I'm finally home.

Sauces & Dressings

Roasted Tomato Feta Sauce - 44

Tomato Vodka Sauce - 45

Portabella Mushroom Sauce - 45

Spicy Sausage Tomato Sauce - 46

Moroccan Tomato Sauce - 47

Puntanesca Sauce - 48

Chunky Turkey Pasta Sauce - 49

Spinach Pesto - 50

Cilantro Pesto - 50

Parsley Pesto - 50

MAN IN DRESS

Tartar Sauce - 51

Tomato-Lime Tartar Sauce - 51

Tomato Gravy - 53

Turkey Gravy - 53

Sito's Syrian Salad Dressing - 54

Chunky Feta Salad Dressing - 57

Italian Herb Vinaigrette - 57

Creamy Herb Vinaigrette - 57

Creamy Jalapeno Dressing - 58

Caesar Salad Dressing - 58

(MARY HATES DRESSES)

Spinach Pesto - Page 50

Spicy Sausage Tomato Sauce - Page 46

Creamy Herb Vinaigrette - Page 57

Roasted Tomato Feta Sauce

(makes about 3 cups, covers 1 pound of pasta, serves 4)

5-6 (about 4 cups) medium vine-ripe
   tomatoes
2 tablespoons olive oil
¼ teaspoon salt
¼ teaspoon pepper
6 cloves roasted garlic*
1 teaspoon olive oil
1 large shallot, chopped

1 tablespoon chopped fresh oregano**
1 tablespoon chopped fresh basil**
¼ teaspoon salt
¼ teaspoon pepper
2 tablespoons tomato paste
1 (7 ounce) package crumbled Feta cheese
fresh basil for garnish

Preheat oven to 400 degrees.

**or 1 teaspoon dried

Cut the tomatoes in half and arrange them cut side down on a cookie sheet. Drizzle with olive oil and sprinkle with salt and pepper. Place unpeeled cloves of garlic in the middle of a large square of tin foil. Drizzle liberally with olive oil - about 2 tablespoons. Fold up the ends of the foil tightly, completely sealing the opening so that no air can escape. Place on cookie sheet with the tomatoes. Put the garlic and the tomatoes into the oven. Remove the garlic after 10 minutes and roast the tomatoes for 10 minutes more.

Let tomatoes and garlic cool for about 10 minutes or so before handling. Peel the tomatoes and put them in the bowl of your food processor (or blender). Cut an end off of each clove of garlic, squeeze from the shell and mince. Add to the food processor along with any oil left in the foil.

"It was 12 different kinds of awesome."
   -Timothy Burgess
     Adelaide, Australia

Heat 1 teaspoon of oil in a medium skillet over medium heat. Add shallots, sprinkle with (just a little) salt. Cook and stir for about 2 or 3 minutes or until translucent. Remove from skillet and add to food processor bowl. Process until smooth.

Pour tomato mixture into a large pot. Add oregano, basil, salt, pepper and tomato paste and bring to a boil. Immediately reduce heat to low and simmer for 10 or 15 minutes before serving.

Garnish with chopped fresh basil and crumbled Feta.

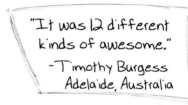
*Six cloves seems like a lot of garlic, but when roasted, it loses its bitterness and takes on a wonderful sweetness. My general rule is, if you use 2 fresh cloves, use 4 roasted.

44

Tomato Vodka Sauce

(makes about 2 cups, covers 1 pound of pasta, serves 4)

1 tablespoon olive oil
½ medium onion diced (about ½ cup)
2 cloves garlic, minced
1 (15 ounce) can diced chopped tomatoes
  (do not drain)
2 tablespoons tomato paste
¼ cup vodka

1 teaspoon honey (or sugar)
¼ teaspoon red pepper flakes
½ teaspoon salt
¼ teaspoon pepper
¼ cup heavy cream
¼ cup grated Parmesan cheese

In a medium pot, heat oil over medium heat. Add onion, cook and stir until tender, about 2 or 3 minutes. Add garlic, cook and stir for about 1 minute. Stir in tomatoes, tomato paste, vodka, honey, red pepper flakes, salt and pepper. Use a potato masher to mash tomatoes until most of the really thick parts are smooshed. Bring to a boil and reduce heat. Simmer uncovered for 15 minutes. Stir in cream and cheese. Cook and stir until heated through and cheese is melted. Serve with your favorite pasta.

This is great with gnocchi, fresh Parmesan cheese, crispy fried pancetta and fresh basil.

Portabella Mushroom Sauce

(makes about 2 cups)

¼ cup butter
1 small shallot, thinly sliced
2 cloves garlic, minced
1 large Portabella mushroom, finely chopped
¼ teaspoon salt
½ cup dry white wine
1 cup veggie stock

½ cup heavy cream
2 tablespoons flour
½ teaspoon salt
½ teaspoon pepper
2 tablespoons chopped fresh basil
1 tablespoon chopped fresh thyme

In a medium pot, melt butter over medium heat. Add shallots, cook and stir for about 2 minutes or until shallots are translucent. Add garlic, mushrooms and salt. Cook and stir for another 2 minutes, just until mushrooms begin to sweat. Add wine, cook and stir until wine is reduced by half, about 1-2 minutes.

In a small bowl add veggie stock, cream and flour. Whisk with a fork until there aren't any lumps. Whisk into the mushroom mixture. Add salt and pepper. Bring to a boil, cook and stir until sauce thickens, about 1 minute. Add basil and thyme. Stir until combined and remove from heat. Pour over pasta or use as gravy for meat or potatoes.

Substitute this for a can of cream-of-mushroom soup!

Spicy Sausage Tomato Sauce

(makes about 4 cups, covers 1-2 pounds of pasta, serves 4-6)

½ medium onion, chopped (about ½ cup)
1 medium green pepper, chopped
5 cloves garlic, minced
1 pound Hot Italian sausage
 (remove casings if using links)
1 (28 ounce) can crushed tomatoes
 (with herbs is nice)
½ cup water
¼ cup tomato paste

1 tablespoon butter
½ teaspoon salt
1 teaspoon pepper
1 tablespoon fresh thyme (or 1 teaspoon
 dried - but fresh is the best!)
½ cup chopped fresh flat-leaf
 (Italian) parsley
½ cup shredded Parmesan cheese

Start by chopping the onions, green pepper and mincing the garlic. Set aside.

In a medium pot, cook sausage over medium heat. Use a wooden spoon to break sausage into small pieces. When it's almost cooked through - about 5-6 minutes - add onion, green pepper and garlic. Cook and stir for about 3 minutes or until veggies are soft.

Add tomatoes, water, tomato paste, butter, salt, pepper, thyme, parsley and cheese. Bring to a boil, turn heat to low and simmer for about 30 minutes. Stir every few minutes or so to make sure the sauce isn't sticking to the bottom of the pan.

The longer the sauce simmers, the more the flavors will develop. Sometimes I'll cook this for up to 1 hour.

(Do not cover the sauce while it simmers.)

For those who think music isn't important, here is a short list of some ways in which music is a part of our lives:

Music is used at graduations, sporting events, weddings, funerals, religious services, opening ceremonies on TV shows, in music boxes, as ring tones, in commercials and video games. You listen while you exercise, to 'set the mood', while you clean, you sing in the shower and you use music to comfort your baby. It's the second thing you turn on in your car, on a long drive or on a short drive. It's played in stores, office buildings and restaurants. The music industry, from music stores alone, makes over 3 billion dollars a year. The average person spends between $100 and $500 a year on mp3's and concerts.

So the next time your child shows an interest in music, stop before you tell them that music will never take them anywhere. Think of all the ways music has been, and always will be, a part of your everyday life and encourage them instead.

-Mary

Sauces & Dressings

Moroccan Tomato Sauce

(makes about 4 cups, covers 1-2 pounds of pasta, serves 4-6)

1 pound lean ground lamb (or lean ground beef)
½ cup diced onion*
3-4 cloves garlic, minced
1 (28 ounce) can crushed tomatoes**
½ cup water
2 teaspoons cumin
1 teaspoon paprika
½ cup chopped flat-leaf (Italian) parsley
½ cup chopped cilantro
2 tablespoons lemon juice
2 tablespoons capers, rinsed and
  chopped***
½ teaspoon salt
¼ cup grated Parmesan cheese

*Make sure you dice the onion really small. You don't want a bunch of big chunks.

(Or maybe you do! Be free!)

Heat a large pot over medium heat and add lamb. Break it into pieces, cook and stir for about 5 minutes. If there seems to be excess juices (a little is ok), drain and return meat to pan. If you get good, lean meat, you may not have anything to drain. Add onion and garlic, cook and stir for about 2 minutes. Add tomatoes and water. Stir until combined. Add cumin, paprika, parsley, cilantro, lemon juice, capers and salt. Bring to a boil, turn heat to low, and simmer for 10 minutes.

**Use tomatoes with added herbs or garlic for extra flavor!

***To easily chop capers: Mash 'em with the broad side of your knife before chopping.

Puntanesca Sauce
(serves 2-4)

Recipe courtesy of my dad's best man, Eddie Nader

"Puntanesca means "ladies of the night" in Italian. This type of spaghetti being named that, was due to the ladies of the night coming to the bistros after they finished their biz for the night. The owners would throw together a sauce for them with what ever was left in the bins; capers, peppers, olives, etc. At least that is the rumor that I heard. Maybe as valid as the Caesar salad being named after the waiter, "Caesar", who invented the original recipe. Who knows." - Eddie

⅛ cup olive oil
2 garlic cloves, minced
¼ teaspoon red pepper flakes
1 tablespoon anchovy paste
1 (28 ounce) can whole tomatoes
  (keep juice)

3 tablespoons tomato paste
2 tablespoons capers
24 Kalamata olives, pitted and coarsely
  chopped
1 (16 ounce) package potato gnocci
Parmesan cheese to taste

Heat oil in a skillet over low heat. Add garlic and cook for one minute. Add red pepper flakes, anchovy paste, tomatoes, tomato paste, capers and olives. Simmer until the sauce thickens and is reduced to 3 cups, about 30 minutes. Season with salt and pepper.

Bring a large pot of lightly salted water to a boil. Cook gnocci in boiling water until they float. Drain and serve sauce over warm gnocci sprinkled with parmesan cheese.

Eddie

Dad

Look at all that hair!

Sauces & Dressings

Chunky Turkey Pasta Sauce

(makes about 4 cups, covers 1 pound of pasta)

2 tablespoons olive oil
1 pound lean ground turkey
½ medium yellow onion diced (about ½ cup)
½ medium red bell pepper, chopped
2 cloves garlic, minced
1 teaspoon salt
½ teaspoon pepper
1 tablespoon dried oregano
1 tablespoon dried parsley
1 (14.5 ounce) can diced tomatoes
  (basil, oregano, garlic flavored. Save juice!)
3 tablespoons tomato paste
¼ cup chopped fresh basil
½ cup (about 4 ounces) crumbled Feta cheese
1 teaspoon salt

"It was like a flavor explosion in my mouth!"

– Emily Webster
Oakdale, CA

Heat oil in a large pot over medium heat and add turkey. Cook and stir for about 3-4 minutes. Add onion, red pepper, garlic, salt, pepper, oregano and parsley. Cook and stir for another 4 minutes. Add tomatoes (and juices), tomato paste and basil. Bring to a boil then turn heat to low. Add Feta and salt. Stir until Feta is mostly melted. Simmer for about 5 minutes and serve hot.

"Guilty Pleasures"
By Micah Garbarino, Oklahoma City, OK

Chocolate, doing it on Sunday afternoon and Steam – all guilty pleasures. Music can be a guilty pleasure. I will never admit some of the stuff I listen to. When friends stumble on to something in my CD collection I wish I would have hidden better I'll say something like, "Dude, I bought that when I was like 6 years old, I didn't even know it was in there" or "That's not even mine" - nothing believable of course, but I have to say something, right? But when I was a kid, there was nothing to be guilty about. A good hook was just that…a good hook. Here's an example to get you to do some "soul" searching for your own transgressions...

Don't laugh (too hard) when I say at 11 years old I scoured the jukebox at Fenton's ice cream parlor on Piedmont Avenue in Oakland for the eternal hit from Steam "Na Na Hey Hey Kiss Him Goodbye." The day before that, I called the radio station requesting it and had a tape in my Dad's huge Teac cassette deck all cued up to record. Shoot me now, please, because that story is not so much about pleasure as it is about guilt.

Spinach Pesto

(makes about 3/4 cup)

¼ cup chopped fresh basil
2 cups chopped baby spinach
¼ cup shredded Parmesan cheese
2 tablespoons pine nuts
2 cloves garlic, minced

2 tablespoons lemon juice
¼ cup + 1 tablespoon extra-virgin olive oil
½ teaspoon salt
¼ teaspoon pepper

Add basil, spinach, cheese, pine nuts, garlic, lemon juice, oil, salt and pepper to the bowl of your food processor (or blender). Process (or blend) for about 10 seconds. Use your spatula to scrape the sides of the bowl. Process again until smooth, about 1 minute or so.

Cilantro Pesto

(makes about 3/4 cup)

3 cups roughly chopped cilantro
  (about 1 large bunch)
1 clove garlic, minced
2 ½ tablespoons lime juice
¼ cup + 1 tablespoon extra-virgin olive oil
½ teaspoon salt

This is great as a marinade or dipping sauce for chicken and fish.

Add cilantro, garlic, lime juice, oil and salt to the bowl of your food processor (or blender). Process (or blend) for about 10 seconds. Use your spatula to scrape the sides of the bowl. Process again until smooth, about 1 minute or so.

Parsley Pesto

(makes about 3/4 cup)

3 cups roughly chopped flat-leaf (Italian) parsley (about 1 large bunch)
1 clove garlic, minced
2 ½ tablespoons lemon juice
¼ cup + 1 tablespoon extra-virgin olive oil
½ teaspoon salt
¼ teaspoon pepper

Use as a dip for kabobs or put it on your burger!

Add parsley, garlic, lemon juice, oil, salt and pepper to the bowl of your food processor (or blender). Process (or blend) for about 10 seconds. Use your spatula to scrape the sides of the bowl. Process again until smooth, about 1 minute or so.

Tartar Sauce

(makes about ¾ cup)

½ cup mayonnaise
1 tablespoon olive oil
½ teaspoon honey
1 tablespoon capers, chopped and mashed
2 teaspoons lemon juice

1 teaspoon horseradish (1 ½ teaspoons if you like it spicy)
3 tablespoons dill relish (squeeze as much juice out as possible)

Add all ingredients to a small bowl and whisk until completely combined.

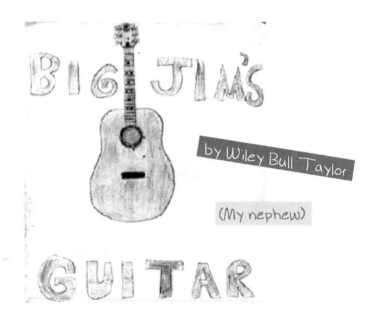

Tomato-Lime Tartar Sauce

(makes about ¾ cup)

½ cup mayonnaise
2 tablespoons finely chopped dill pickle
1 tablespoon capers, smashed and chopped
1 garlic clove, minced
1 tablespoon tomato paste

2 tablespoons finely chopped flat-leaf (Italian) parsley
1 ½ teaspoons chopped tarragon
¼ teaspoon pepper
1 tablespoon lime juice

Same as instructions for 'Tartar Sauce' above: Add everything and whisk!

An Ode to Readers' Digest
by Kim Brown - Sacramento, CA

A while back, I stumbled upon an OCD vintage treasure at a garage sale. No, really. I mean it. My clumsy ass had tripped, and rising to my feet, I spied the dusty culprit: a record collection from Readers' Digest, entitled *Mood Music for Dining*. I slid the inner box out of its green-and-white swan-adorned casing to find a filing system of sorts, with numbers carefully labeling the slip cover for each disc. Each number corresponded to a circumstance for eating: cocktails, a picnic for a summer's day, a romantic dinner for two, etc. The range of music was broad, and my interest piqued.

The best damn $2 I've ever spent.

And so, inspired by this brilliant feat of engineering melding two of my greatest loves, I've assembled a menu for your aural and oral consumption. Some are elaborate, some simple, some attempts at humor—no pattern in particular, just a list of well-known artists transformed into food counterparts. Think more the "sounds like" bit in charades, but edible. Now *there's* a dinner party idea.

Bon Appetit!

- The Frank Sinatra: prime rib, baked potato with sour cream and chives, and a seasonal vegetable medley, served aside an endless supply of very dirty martinis.

- The Leonard Cohen: the best cup of strong black coffee ever brewed with a French press—in a no-frills mug.

- The Pink Floyd: meat, followed by pudding—but only if you eat your meat.

- The Earth Kitt: vanilla sponge cake, lightly drizzled with a cardamom honey glaze and a sprinkling of cinnamon, served with a scoop of Rainier cherry sorbet.

- The Madonna: two ice cream cones, anything but vanilla, topped with hard candy and nuts.

- The Lynyrd Skynyrd: Southern fried (free-range) chicken.

- The Ozzy Osbourne: steak tartar and a bowl full of nuts.

- The Cat Stevens: spiced lentil salad with curry and coconut, washed down with a mango lassi.

- The Velvet Underground: bananas flambé.

- The Justin Timberlake: two all-beef patties with special sauce, lettuce, cheese, pickles and onions, served on a sesame seed bun—you're lovin it.

Tomato Gravy

(makes about 2 cups)

¼ cup butter
3 tablespoons flour
1 clove garlic, minced
2 cups (about 3-4) diced vine-ripe tomatoes

½ cup veggie (or chicken) broth
½ teaspoon salt
¼ teaspoon pepper
¼ teaspoon red pepper flakes*

In a pot or large nonstick skillet, melt butter. When it begins to foam - after about 1 minute or so - add flour and whisk until smooth. Cook for another minute, whisking constantly. Add garlic and stir for about 30 seconds. Add tomatoes and their juices. Use a potato masher to mash the tomatoes until there aren't very many lumps. Add broth, salt, pepper and red pepper flakes. Bring to a boil. Cook, stirring frequently, about 3-4 minutes. Remove from heat.

I originally made this recipe to go over stuffed Portabella mushrooms, but I also use this on meatloaf instead of ketchup. It's also great served with mashed potatoes as an alternative to traditional meat gravy.

*The red pepper flakes give this some bite. Use half that amount, or none at all, if you don't want the heat.

Turkey Gravy

(makes about 1 ½ cups)

2 tablespoons butter
1 clove garlic, minced
1 ½ cups turkey broth*

¼ cup flour
½ teaspoon salt
¼ teaspoon pepper

Melt butter in a medium skillet. When butter begins to foam, add garlic. Cook and stir for about 30 seconds. Whisk in just **1** cup of the turkey broth.

In a separate bowl whisk ½ cup turkey broth and flour until smooth. Add to the skillet and whisk until completely combined. Add salt and pepper. Bring to a boil and cook, stirring occasionally, until desired thickness. The gravy should only take a few minutes to thicken.

*Chicken broth will produce the same delicious result.
If you're a vegetarian, use veggie broth!

Sito's Syrian Salad Dressing

(makes about 2 cups)

This is my Syrian Grandmother's recipe. When I smell this dressing, it takes me straight back to my childhood.

½ cup red wine vinegar
1 cup vegetable/canola oil
2 cloves garlic, minced

½ teaspoon salt
¼ teaspoon pepper
1 teaspoon dried oregano

Add all ingredients to a jar with a lid. Seal and shake well. Keep in fridge and shake well before each use.

From 52 Week "Life Is Beautiful" by Bethany Taylor

A little girl said she learned a lesson, she learned that lesson well.
"Life is full of pain and sorrow" she knows how to live in hell.
Her momma says that she will be nothing
'Cuz she's got too much dirt in her ears,
A filthy pail of water and a chain tied around her heel.

I saw a pretty picture of some prairie children play.
They said the government came
And took all their daddy's axes away.
Ain't got no axes, got no fire wood to keep them warm.
They'll die come winter.
That storms gonna freeze their blood.

Gutter babies, gutter moms, poor gutter dads.
Born to a life of sin, they cant see their saviors hand.
But that don't really bother us much,
No we're much, much to busy....
Yeah we're much, much, much too busy
with our cars and colored TV's.

I think we need a, Lord, I know we need a pourin' down.

To read more about the 52-Week Club see pages 87-88

Sauces & Dressings

Writing Songs.

Here are some tips that have helped me.
— (BTW I'm a horrble speller, sorry for ~~that~~) — —

- **Imagery**; adds a power lift to any song
  develop an eye for details
  (no subject or object is too small)

- **Mining**; The songwriters words most effactivley ring
  true w/ the listener when observing un-
  important but interesting things that con-
  ~~tribute~~ to ~~the~~ atmosphere of the song

- **Notebooks**; Keep one around all the time. You will
  hear or see ~~things~~ ~~can~~ a that can
  accuratly ~~describe~~ describe ~~the~~ moment
  it is experenced.

- **Its all around you**; Look for suggestions with song titles ~~is~~ ?
  ~~newspapers~~ concepts in newspapers, conver-
  sations, store ads etc...

- **The first line**; Really good first lines ~~or~~ that have a
  ~~strong~~, captivating idea can make us
  want to listen to the song.
  It also sets the premise.

- **Rhyme**;

Single rhyme — "two — blue"
double — "funny — bunny"

,so on and so forth, ⟶

(1)

By taking time to be more innovative w/ your rhyme you show ~~say~~ ~~skill~~ ~~needs~~ consideration for your listener. It is the clearest most tangible way to prove to your listener that your song writing skills are good.
(Rhyming dictionarys are very helpful)

Try this; Get 5 colored pens and ~~white~~ circle the, single, double and triple ~~pop~~ rhymes with seperatea colors. Then ~~the~~ words with intence feelings and words with imagry. The more colorful the ~~better~~ the song.

Use :

- Alliteration - similar sounds "hollow hallway"
- Assonance - like ~~sound~~ vowels "waste, taste"
- Consonance - like sound consonants "clickity, clackity"

About the time I met Joey Eisinger, I'd just written my first song. One night we had a long discussion about song writing and the next time I saw him, he'd written this for me.

Chunky Feta Salad Dressing

(makes about 2 cups)

1 cup sour cream
½ cup mayonnaise
1 tablespoon lemon juice
1 tablespoon distilled white vinegar
¼ cup chopped fresh basil

2 chopped green onions
2 cloves garlic, minced
¼ teaspoon salt
¼ cup crumbled Feta cheese
½ cup crumbled Feta cheese

Add sour cream, mayonnaise, lemon juice, vinegar, basil, green onions, garlic, salt and ¼ cup of the Feta to the bowl of your food processor (or blender). Process until smooth and creamy. Pour into bowl and add the other ½ cup crumbled Feta. Stir until mixture is combined.

I can't repeat what my cousin Gabe said about this recipe - but trust me - he REALLY liked it...!

Italian Herb Vinaigrette

(makes about 1 cup)

¼ cup red wine vinegar
⅔ cup canola oil
2 cloves garlic, minced
3 tablespoons chopped flat-leaf
  (Italian) parsley
3 tablespoons chopped fresh basil

2 teaspoons dried oregano
1 teaspoon sugar
1 tablespoon lemon juice
1 teaspoon kosher salt
¼ teaspoon pepper
½ teaspoon onion powder

!@#$%

Add all of the ingredients to the bowl of your food processor (or blender). Process for about 30 seconds, turn off then scrape the sides of the bowl with a spatula. Process for another minute. For best results, make this a day before serving.

Creamy Herb Vinaigrette

(makes about 1 cup)

½ cup extra-virgin olive oil
½ cup mayonnaise
¼ cup red wine vinegar
½ cup chopped flat-leaf (Italian) parsley
½ cup chopped fresh basil

1 clove garlic, minced
¼ teaspoon salt
¼ teaspoon pepper
2 tablespoons shredded Parmesan cheese
½ teaspoon sugar

Same directions as 'Italian Herb Vinaigrette' above.

Creamy Jalapeno Dressing

(makes about 1 cup)

½ cup mayonnaise
¼ cup olive oil
1 clove garlic, minced
3 tablespoons crumbled Queso Fresco cheese*
2 teaspoons Worcestershire sauce

2 teaspoons Dijon mustard
1 tablespoon lime juice
1 jalapeno, diced
⅛ teaspoon salt
⅛ teaspoon pepper

Mix mayonnaise, olive oil, garlic, cheese, Worcestershire, Dijon, lime juice, jalapeno, salt and pepper in food processor until smooth. If you don't have a food processor, just chop the jalapeno as tiny as possible and whisk everything with a fork until smooth and creamy.

*Queso Fresco is a Mexican cheese usually found in most grocery stores. Sometimes it's not with the 'regular' cheese, but with the Mexican meats and cheese.

Caesar Salad Dressing

(makes about 1 cup)

½ cup mayonnaise
¼ cup olive oil
1 clove garlic, minced
3 tablespoons grated Parmesan cheese
2 teaspoons Worcestershire sauce

2 teaspoons Dijon mustard
1 tablespoon lemon juice
⅛ teaspoon salt
⅛ teaspoon pepper

Mix mayonnaise, olive oil, garlic, cheese, Worcestershire, Dijon, lemon juice, salt and pepper in food processor until smooth. If you don't have a food processor whisk with a fork until smooth and creamy. Feel free to add more or less garlic depending on how garlicy you like your dressing.

Sauces & Dressings

Soup & Salad

(and sandwiches, sort of)

Cheesy Sausage Soup – 62

Taco Soup – 63

Chicken Dumpling Soup – 67

White Chili – 68

Spicy Bite-Back Chili – 69

Tom V's Up North Stew – 71

Garlic Croutons – 72

Warm Spinach Salad – 73

Chopped Greek Salad – 74

Sunomono – 75

Thai Tomato
Cucumber Salad – 76

Tabbouleh – 79

Syrian Salad with
Lebne Dressing – 80

Chopped Caesar Salad – 81

Chopped Mexi-Caesar Salad – 81

Pesto Caesar Salad – 83

Tomato Caprese Salad
with Fried Polenta – 84

Lentil Feta Salad – 86

Three-Bean Salad – 86

Roasted Vegetable Salad – 89

Olive Pasta Salad – 90

Classic Potato Salad – 95

Mom's Potato Salad – 96

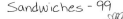

Herbed Potato Salad – 97

Baked Potato-ey
Potato Salad – 98

Sandwiches – 99

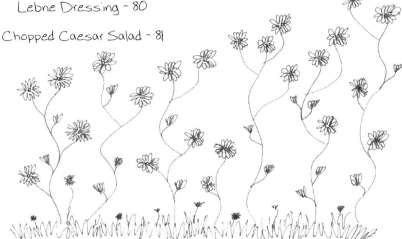

Cheesy Sausage Soup - Page 62

White Chili - Page 68

Taco Soup - Page 63

Tabbouleh - Page 79

Thai Tomato Cucumber Salad - Page 76

Olive Pasta Salad - 90

Cheesy Sausage Soup

(serves 4-6)

½ pound ground Mild Italian sausage*
½ cup chopped white onion
1 red bell pepper, chopped
2 cloves garlic, minced
½ teaspoon salt
½ teaspoon pepper
2 cups chicken broth
1 cup diced potato (about half of a large Idaho)

1 (15 ounce) can white beans (drain but do not rinse)
1 (14.75 ounce) can creamed corn
1 ½ cups shredded sharp Cheddar cheese
1 cup shredded Monterey Jack cheese
¾ teaspoon salt
¼ teaspoon pepper
chopped chives (optional)

Heat a large pot over medium heat for a few minutes. Add sausage and use a wooden spoon to break into little pieces. Cook and stir for about 5 minutes. Add onions, bell pepper, garlic, salt and pepper. Cook and stir until onions and peppers are soft and sausage is cooked through, about 5 more minutes.

Use Hot Italian for extra kick!

Add broth, potato, beans and corn. Bring to a boil. Cook, stirring occasionally for 10 minutes. Turn heat to low and add cheese, salt and pepper. Stir until cheese is melted and remove from heat. Garnish with chopped chives.

I have to say that one of my favorite parts of touring and playing music, aside from seeing new places and the shows themselves, is experiencing the hospitality of strangers. Music brings folks together in so many ways, but being offered to stay at someone's home after a show is such a genuine and humbling thing. The unique story that goes with each floor, couch, bed, lawn, window sill, boat, and wherever else I've slept on tour, has had such a profound effect on the way I see the people around me. Not to mention the many late night and early morning conversations that have taken place in the kitchens, basements, gardens, rooftops, porches, and so on, covering the widest range of topics imaginable. These moments are some of my best memories from tour.

- (Scott) McDougall - Portland, OR

Soup & Salad

Taco Soup

(serves 6)

This is my sister's recipe - she's the soup queen!

1 pound ground beef
2 teaspoons garlic powder
2 teaspoons dried onions
1 tablespoon cumin
1 teaspoon chili powder
¼ teaspoon cayenne pepper
1 teaspoon salt
2 (32 ounce) containers chicken broth
1 bunch green onions, chopped
½ cup chopped cilantro
½ cup chopped flat-leaf (Italian) parsley
½ medium chopped tomato (about ½ cup)
½ cup tomato sauce
1 cup corn (from a can or off the stalk)
1 (15 ounce) can black beans
  (drained and rinsed)
½ to 1 cup sliced olives
⅛ teaspoon cayenne pepper
½ teaspoon garlic powder
1 teaspoon cumin
½ teaspoon salt

Interesting...

Heat a large skillet over medium heat and add beef, garlic powder, dried onions, cumin, chili powder, cayenne pepper and salt. Cook and stir until browned, about 10 minutes.

Meanwhile, in a large pot, add broth, green onions, cilantro, parsley, tomato, tomato sauce, corn, beans, olives, cayenne pepper, garlic powder, cumin and salt. Cover and bring to a boil.

When the meat is done, drain and add to the pot. Bring back to a boil, remove cover, lower heat and simmer for 20-30 minutes. (The longer it simmers, the more the flavors will come out.)

Serve hot and garnished! ———▶

Garnish Ideas
tortilla chips
sour cream
cilantro
green onions
olives
cheese!!

"My Hometown"
by Casey Weber - French Lake, WI

French Lake is a small town where two roads that seem to lead from nowhere to nowhere intersect. It is a quiet little town, with a population of about 50 in central Minnesota. One of those small towns, that regardless of the year, the feeling is still that of the 40's.

Growing up in this town was an experience that I wouldn't give up for a ticket to heaven. The times I have had, stories that have been made, and the friends I have found, make this a place that I can truly call "my hometown".

My folks bought an old farmhouse on a little 6 acre lot back in 1989 that overlooks French Lake itself. Our place is about a mile east of town, but if you live within 5 miles you consider it French Lake. Growing up here sometimes seemed difficult for a kid during those most influential years. A lot of the kids our age already had their friends, and it was obvious that these were the type of kids that you almost had to be family to be "in" with them. It took a lot of time and some fights on the bus before some of them grew on me, and were people that I could actually hang out with.

French Lake consists of Lantto's gas station, a Lutheran Church, and a little beauty salon. There are about 5 houses scattered about also.

Lantto's store is a gas station that is pretty much the center of town. It is a gas station that, after all the traveling I have done, have yet to find one like it. They sell a little bit of everything there. When you walk in, there is a small little table with 4 chairs that are full every morning with farmers and locals talking weather and telling lies. If the chairs are full, there is a stack of bags of dog food to sit on right next to the table. There are some tanks in the back full of minnows, and a wall of fishing equipment for someone stopping on the way to the lake. You can go there on a Friday night and rent movies. (Likely not too new of movies, but at least they are within the last 3 years or so. I don't think Chris (the owner) keeps up too much on "New Releases"!) Right next to the liars table are racks of Red Wing Boots. Most locals will go there and buy boots even if the cost is a little more, just trying to support the locals. They make their own pizza in the back, and the rest of the store consists of the usual gas station trinkets, sodas and snacks.

Lantto's wasn't always where it is now, though. The store that is there now is only about 7 years old. The lot that the store sits on used to be an empty field that was only good for corn, beans and the occasional browsing deer. Before, it was at the opposite corner of town- across the street- kiddy korner to the Northwest.

The "old store" is a little building that looks like a painting out of the 20's. It is a little white building, with a covered porch over concrete steps out front. When the store was there it still had the atmosphere of an old convenience store. The front of the building always had stacks of rock salt under the porch. If there was ever a better place to sit

Soup & Salad

and watch a rain storm or catch up on the local gossip, I would like to find it. Usually there were the old timers and farmers sitting out front on those piles of salt just watching traffic go by and catching up on the news of the day.

When you walked into the store, you walked on an old hardwood floor that showed its years, and if that floor could talk, the stories it would tell. To the right were a couple of old wooden fold down chairs that sat on an old cast iron frame bolted to the floor. They were rarely vacant of a local just sitting around watching the world go by one patron at a time. I have heard stories that, years ago, there was even an old wood burning stove next to those two chairs.

To the right of the entrance was the counter that was usually manned by one of the Lanttos. See, there were 9 kids in all: 8 boys and 1 girl. They all put their time in at the store, and some still do at the new store. In fact, it is likely that Billy Lantto will end up inheriting the new store. I remember there being one of those neat wooden cash registers that made a lot of noise every time the drawer flew open and about knocked over whoever was running it at the time.

The ceiling was covered with those neat bronze/brass tiles that you can only find in old buildings like this one. Lining the length of the store were racks of a large assortment of food and other necessities. It was basically a small grocery store in the middle of nowhere. In the back of the store were glass coolers. Go down a few old steps in the back of the store, and there were the old steel tanks that held the assortment of minnows and a wrecked refrigerator that held little tubs of leeches and night crawlers. It was easy to buy bait from the Lanttos, but next to impossible to find out where the fish were biting.

(Ernie Lantto - 1947)

On the corner in front of the store was a gas pump. You remember the kind - the ones that had the old roll type that you always had to tell the person at the counter how much gas you pumped. But, they always still took a little look out the window to make sure- as if they were sure that you could have squeezed another gallon into that old beat up Chevy truck full of hay bales.

The parking lot out back was a hangout for the kids. Usually, on a weekend, the local kids of all ages were content with just hanging out in that old gravel lot. It made for a Monday morning story if a cop would drive by. On the real boring nights we would pour oil on the road in front of the store and have burnout contests to see who had the better $100 beater.

Ever since the new store was built, the old store has been taken over by the Lantto kids. You walk in now, and there are a couple of rooms framed and sheet rocked in. The old wooden chairs are long gone and those old floors have since been carpeted and tiled. Where the counter used to be is now an entertainment center. The spot where the coolers sat is now a fairly modernized kitchen. The same place that the minnow tanks were is now a framed-in bathroom. The spot where that gas pump sat is now just a covered-over concrete slab. The covered porch is still there, but it just doesn't feel the same to watch a storm roll in while standing there.

If there is a heaven, for me, it would be a Saturday night sitting on a pile of salt bags under that covered porch, bullshitting with the old Finnish farmers and friends of the past with an old lazy dog laying next to the door, moving only to lift an ear every time a car passed or someone came in. Sometimes, when I drive by the old store in the middle of the night, I think of the ghosts and old souls that never want to leave this place because this is their heaven - just like the old days of telling lies, fibbing about the fish they caught and how much rain was coming.

Time passes that old store now and life moves on. The hustle bustle of today may change our town, may change our lives, but there will always be the old store. There will always be the new store. There will always be French Lake. There will always be the memories of those nights drag racing from the old store to the beauty salon to see who was more of a man.

When I talk to someone and they tell me that they are from a small town of about 2,000 people, I just sit back with a grin on my face and think of my hometown. Someday I will raise kids of my own around here and I hope that the new store will give them memories, just like the old store did for me.

Casey Weber runs 'Weber's Deck' in the heart of French Lake, a small town with a population of about 22 in central Minnesota. Bands from all over the country come to play on this little deck and the crowds often number in the hundreds. Many folks travel hours each week to spend time at Weber's Deck and listen to the greatest music in the world. Weber's Deck is for the fans, by the fans. Many volunteers come together each week to make the festivities happen. No profit is made and all donations from the fans go directly to the bands.

Soup & Salad

Chicken Dumpling Soup

(serves 6-8)

1 (4-5 pound) whole chicken
14 cups (3 ½ quarts) water
2 teaspoons salt
5-6 cloves garlic, minced
¾ cup flat-leaf (Italian) parsley
2 tablespoons chopped basil
1 teaspoon chopped fresh rosemary
4 stalks celery, chopped
1 large yellow onion, chopped
1 cup frozen peas
1 large carrot, chopped
1 large potato, chopped

Dumplings:
3 ½ cups flour
1 ½ teaspoons rosemary
½ teaspoon garlic powder
¼ teaspoon salt
½ teaspoon pepper
1 cup soup broth
1 egg

Add chicken, water, salt, garlic, parsley, basil, rosemary, celery and onion to large pot. Bring to a boil, reduce heat to low-medium and cover. Simmer until chicken is cooked, about 30 minutes. To check, cut into the thickest part of the chicken. When chicken is done, take it out and place in a large dish (9x13 baking dishes work well).

While chicken cools, add peas, carrots and potatoes to the pot and continue to simmer. You may leave it uncovered at this point.

Now, make the dumplings. Add flour, rosemary, garlic powder, salt and pepper to the bowl of your standing mixer. Turn it on low and slowly add broth. In a separate bowl beat egg and add it to the mixture. Mix until combined. The consistency should be a little sticky, but not gooey. If it's too hard to get off of your fingers, it's too gooey. (Add flour or broth as needed.) Test a piece by tearing a bit off and rolling it into a ball. If you can do this without any gooey residue, it's done.

Roll all of the dough into dumplings and add to the pot. I like to make two different sized dumplings. I roll some into nickel sized balls and some into pea sized balls. This way, you'll get a dumpling with every bite with the small ones, and every once in a while you'll get a nice big one. Cook dumplings in the soup for 10-12 minutes.

While dumplings are cooking, tear chicken from the bones. Either shred it or chop it and add to the pot. When the dumplings are cooked, the soup's done. (Check a big dumpling to see if it's cooked through.)

"If food is fuel, then I'm running on mattar paneer."
- Punam Shaida - San Francisco, CA

White Chili

(serves 6-8)

2 tablespoons olive oil
1 pound ground chicken
1 pound ground sausage (try to find some that's flavored)
½ teaspoon salt
½ teaspoon pepper
½ teaspoon garlic powder
1 tablespoon olive oil
1 medium onion, chopped
4 cloves garlic, minced

1 medium green pepper, diced
2 (12 ounce) cans corn, drained
2 (15 ounce) cans Cannellini beans, (drained and rinsed)
2 (10.75 ounce) cans cream of chicken soup
2 cans milk (use soup can)
2 (4 ounce) cans diced mild green chilies
1 teaspoon cumin
¼ teaspoon cayenne pepper (optional)
2 cups shredded Pepper Jack cheese

Heat oil in a large skillet over medium heat. Add chicken and sausage. Season with salt, pepper and garlic powder. Use a wooden spoon or spatula to break the meat up as it cooks.

Meanwhile, in a large pot cook and stir onion in olive oil until it begins to soften. Add garlic and green pepper, cook and stir for about 1 minute. Add corn, beans, soup, milk, chilies, cumin, cayenne and cheese. When chicken and sausage mixture is done - about 10 minutes - drain and add to the pot with the veggies and beans.

Bring to a boil, turn heat to low and simmer for 30 minutes, stirring frequently.

Garnish ideas: Cheddar cheese, jalapenos, chives, green onions.

"This chili is beautiful...it tastes like pure love..."

- Ian Cook -
Larry & His Flask

Spicy Bite-Back Chili

(serves 6-8)

Recipe courtesy of Wayne Joseph - Northville, MI

¼ cup extra-virgin olive oil
12 cloves garlic, peeled and chopped
1 habanero pepper, de-seeded and chopped
1 jalapeno pepper, sliced in rings with seeds
1 medium onion, chopped
1 large green bell pepper, de-seeded and chopped

1 pound ground chuck (or lean ground turkey)
2 tablespoons cumin
2 (16 ounce) cans tomato sauce
1 (16 ounce) can chili beans – hot & spicy
1 tablespoon cayenne pepper
¼ cup chili powder

In a three quart saucepan add olive oil, garlic, habanero, jalapeno, onion and green pepper. Sauté over medium heat until tender, 10 minutes or so. Stir occasionally.

Drain the mixture into a separate bowl and set aside. In the same saucepan, add the meat and one tablespoon of cumin.

Cook the meat over medium heat until done, about 10 minutes. Drain the liquid off the meat and reintroduce the vegetable mixture. Stir until combined. Add the tomato sauce and chili beans. Stir until combined.

Add in the remaining cumin, the cayenne pepper and the chili powder. Stir until combined.

"Of Late"
by Wayne Joseph

I believe I am the only person left
who's unfashionably on time...

In Magellan-like style, I claim this booth.
Planting my flag of cell phone and planner, I wait -
Absently, I Gene Krupa my pen
in rhythm to the scratchy Muzak...
I practice my fake smile
pretending his poorly crafted excuses
will be tonight's tabloid headlines...

I have mastered the faces of the noon-time crowd -
I could pick them all out of a line-up
especially the Al Queada bus-boy...

69

(continued) ——▶

I observe the art museum my table has become...
The "still life cheese in silver bowl with matching spoon"
contrasts the "half-sliced semi-circle bread with diet soda"
while "bar nap hugging tablecloth under smudged water glass"
clashes with "Map of Sicily plastic ashtray"

I'm inventing stories to explain
the sorrowful eyes of the bartender...
the weight of unasked-for tales
circles in the cigar smoke of the regulars...

I busy myself in these scribbled lines
to lessen the attention
from the disingenuous maitre `d -
The waiter redundants the "can I get you anything" question...

Am I stood up?

I debate circling the restaurant
certain my party
having already entered
has been stricken with soap-opera amnesia...

Thirty minutes past post time
I'm fidgeting at the starting gate...
Should I amputate the heel of the Italian loaf
forever depriving my overdue guest of its symmetry –

Is that real butter?

I am able to recite the memorized menu
like Patrick Henry's famous
"Give Me Liberty or Give Me Dover Sole"

After much contemplation -
I settle on a five-course meal
from the wine list.

Tom V's Up North Stew

Recipe courtesy of Tom Vanden Avond - Green Bay, WI

"Man came to the door, I said for whom are you lookin'? He said "Your wife."
I said: "She's busy in the kitchen cookin'" - Bob Dylan

"I says: "Don't forget the garlic and the bay leaf and maybe
put a little brandy in my tea." - Tom Vanden Avond

1 pound beef stew meat (I prefer venison)
flour (about 2-3 tablespoons)
olive oil
4-8 cloves garlic, finely chopped
½ a yellow onion, finely chopped
½ bottle red wine (750ml)
  (preferably Benny's from up the hill)
balsamic vinegar (optional)
Worcestershire Sauce
1 packet brown gravy mix
1 huge russet potato (or 3 medium red)

2 bay leaves
salt
pepper
Cajun seasoning
½ bag mini carrots
1 package mushrooms
1 pound asparagus (cut into thirds)
1 can black eyed peas
  (regional - are not available everywhere)
1 can chopped spinach

Cover meat with some flour. Put some olive oil in a pan with 2 of the garlic cloves and yellow onion. Add meat and brown, adding splashes of red wine, balsamic vinegar and Worcestershire sauce. In a big pot throw in all that stuff, plus the gravy mix and water, according to gravy packet. Simmer for about an hour.

Add chopped potatoes, bay leaves, more garlic, more wine, more Worcestershire and spices (couple pinches salt, pepper, Cajun).

After ½ hour add carrots. Another ½ hour, add chopped mushrooms and asparagus. ½ hour later add more spices to taste, along with can of black-eyed peas and spinach. 10 minutes later, test meat for tenderness and add spice and flour for your preferred thickness.

Garlic Croutons

(makes 2 cups)

3 tablespoons olive oil
3-4 cloves garlic, minced
2 cups cubed sourdough bread

¼ teaspoon salt
¼ teaspoon pepper

These are so much better than packaged croutons!

Heat oil in a large skillet over medium heat. Add minced garlic, cook and stir for 30 seconds. Garlic will brown fast, so don't walk away from it. Add bread to the skillet. Toss bread in the olive oil and garlic until coated. Add salt and pepper and toss some more.

Cook for about 5 minutes, tossing every 30 seconds or so, until bread reaches your desired crunchiness. Remove from heat and drain on a paper towel.

Before he met my mom, my father toured Canada, the western United States, and South America playing guitar for a Bolivian folk band. After dating her for four months he decided to quit music and have kids with her (me being one of the two). My grandmother was a great piano player and her brother was jazz drummer in Hungary during the 1930's. Having said that, you could say I grew up in a musical family. There was plenty of music around the house all the time. My dad would play music with friends and family during parties. I never actually engaged in the music, but I would sit and watch, as they'd perform throughout the night.

I tried the saxophone in the 4th grade, but it never really grabbed. When I think about it now, it never really provided the sub-conscious release I'd need. Around that time my father had started playing drums with some friends of his and brought a drum set home one day. Being the curious type that I am, I fooled around with it and started coming up with stuff of my own. When I got to middle school I only wanted to play drums and chase girls. Nothing else. After school I'd skate home and play 'til the neighbors called the cops, or my parents. When high school came about, I started to take the drums more serious and started to take lessons. I never got along with the music teachers at the schools, so that was one big crap shoot for me.

I remember when I first heard Heavy Metal. I was about eleven or twelve, in my room listening to Elvis Presley. My brother was in his room and started to play Mettalica's *And Justice For All*. The first song I heard was 'Blackened'. When heard it blast all the way to my room, I ran in and asked what he was listening to. I was hooked. Since then, my musical palette has grown quite a bit. I became influenced by many different bands, not just Metal: Latin, Jazz, New Wave, Hip-Hop, Punk and Pop.

I'm glad I get to play with so many people these days. Playing drums, for me, is a way of life and I couldn't imagine doing anything else.

- Josh Schmidt - Dave Rude Band - Berkeley, CA

Soup & Salad

Warm Spinach Salad

(serves 2-4)

1 ½ cups cubed bread
1 tablespoon olive oil
⅛ teaspoon salt
⅛ teaspoon pepper
⅛ teaspoon garlic powder
2 cups (about 1 carton) halved grape tomatoes
1 cup (about ½ medium) thinly sliced red onion
⅓ cup pine nuts
4 cups fresh baby spinach
¼ cup (about 2 ounces) crumbled Feta cheese
1 tablespoon extra-virgin olive oil
¼ teaspoon salt
¼ teaspoon pepper
¼ teaspoon garlic powder

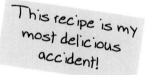

This recipe is my most delicious accident!

There are a lot of steps to this salad, but, if you time it right, each phase will be done right after the other.

Preheat oven to 350 degrees.

Cut about 3-4 slices of sourdough bread into cubes. Put bread in a zip top bag and drizzle with olive oil. Sprinkle with salt, pepper and garlic powder. Seal bag, massage oil and spices into bread and set aside.

Put the halved grape tomatoes on a cookie sheet or baking dish. Drizzle with olive oil and sprinkle with salt, pepper and garlic powder. Use your hands to rub the oil and spices all over the tomatoes. Turn them cut side down. Roast for 10 minutes or until the tops begin to shrivel. Be careful not to over cook, otherwise the skins will come right off.

Meanwhile, heat two skillets over medium heat. In one add a little olive oil, the onions and pine nuts. In the other, add a little olive oil and the cubed bread. Cook until pine nuts are lightly browned and onion is translucent and soft, tossing frequently. At the same time, toss the bread until all sides are browned.

Put the spinach and crumbled Feta in a large bowl and toss. As everything finishes, pour over spinach. Add olive oil, salt, pepper and garlic powder and toss. Serve warm.

An easier way to do the croutons is to put them in the oven on a cookie sheet for about 7-10 minutes, but I like the way they taste when they're pan-fried more.

Chopped Greek Salad

(serves 2-4)

1 cup diced English cucumber
1 package grape tomatoes, quartered
2 cups chopped lettuce
½ cup quartered Kalamata olives
¼ cup crumbled Feta cheese
¼ cup olive oil

2 tablespoons lemon juice
2 tablespoons balsamic vinegar
½ teaspoon salt
½ teaspoon pepper
½ teaspoon garlic powder

Mix cucumber, tomatoes, lettuce, olives and Feta in a large bowl.

In a separate bowl whisk olive oil, lemon juice, vinegar, salt, pepper and garlic powder until completely combined. Immediately pour over the veggies before the oil/vinegar/spices separate - it will separate quickly.

I recommend making this at least an hour before serving so the flavors can intensify.

(If you make this ahead of time, don't add the lettuce until right before serving or the lettuce will get mushy!)

The Beatles, of course, and I will tell you why. The comparison is representative of something that I see flolloping itself all over mainstream music, and our societies views towards it, today.

Elvis had a good singing voice. I think that's all that can be said of him musically. He didn't write too many songs, if any, and the ones he did sing weren't really "original" or "creative", per se. But, what he did have was style. Swagger. That "it" factor, with dollar signs, shining labels swooning, easy to swallow Swagger.

The Beatles wrote many, many very good songs, and although one might have a hard time saying whose singing voices were better between John, Paul and Elvis...I think that there existed a bit more of an unrehearsed passion in the voices of those British boys.

The Beatles vs. Elvis is a question of Imagination vs. Fashion, of Camping vs. Disneyland, The Discovery Channel vs. E! Entertainment Television. Both equally entertaining - just for completely different reasons. I think I just want to know how stuff works...

- Dean Haakenson - Be Brave Bold Robot - Sacramento, CA - When asked "Elvis or The Beatles?"

Sunomono

(serves 2-4)

2 large English cucumbers
¼ cup rice vinegar
2 tablespoons sesame oil
1 tablespoon sugar
1 teaspoon salt
¼ teaspoon soy sauce

2 tablespoons sesame seeds
1 teaspoon ginger

Sunomono is a Japanese cucumber salad that is usually found in Sushi restaurants.

Use a cheese grater with the 'slice' option to thinly slice the cucumbers. Lay down two pieces of paper towels - one on top of the other. Layer the cucumber slices on top of the towels. Put 2 more pieces of paper towels on top of the cucumbers. Roll them up and squeeze as much water out as you can. (The more the better - no one likes soggy Sunomono.) You may have to do this in batches.

In a small bowl whisk the rest of the ingredients together and pour over cucumbers. Mix well. Allow this to sit in refrigerator for at least an hour before serving. This is best if made the day before serving.

I come from a very large family and two things I remember most in my young age were music and food. A small 3 bedroom house held my parents, my grandmother, three of us kids, my teenage uncle and his girlfriend and a number of his friends. When the men were home the guitars were out. The women spent most of their time in the kitchen and taking care of us kids. My mother's beautiful voice was always singing. If music was being played, and it almost always was, you would find her dancing and singing around the house.

Now that I'm older, I find that cooking and eating are always better when music is around. I find nothing more relaxing at the end of a long day than turning on some music, pouring a glass of wine, and cooking. The music brings happiness to my soul and my soul pours itself into my food.

My most favorite is matching the music from my childhood to the recipes of my past. Nothing says fried chicken, mashed potatoes, gravy, green beans and corn bread like Lynyrd Skynyrd or Neil Young. Or my mother's sausage gravy over biscuits with pancakes paired with Carole King or James Taylor.

Life has taken me many places with different menus and play lists, but one things is for sure: music moves us, food fills us, and when the two are put together there is magic in the soul.

-Tawny Dunn - Modesto, CA

Thai Tomato Cucumber Salad

(serves 2-4)

2 vine ripe tomatoes cut into ½ inch chunks
4 inches of an English cucumber sliced about
  ⅛ inch thick
1 cup bean sprouts
½ cup thinly sliced and quartered red onion
2 tablespoons roughly chopped cilantro

3 tablespoons rice wine vinegar
1 tablespoon lime juice
¼ teaspoon sugar
½ teaspoon red hot chili oil
½ teaspoon salt

Add tomato, cucumber, bean sprouts, red onion and cilantro to a medium sized bowl. In a separate small bowl, whisk together vinegar, lime juice, sugar, chili oil and salt. Pour over veggies and toss. Allow to sit at least an hour before serving. Add more or less chili oil to make it more or less spicy.

My earliest memory of creating a dish that ventured from the recipe was when I was about 10 or 11 years old. My mom, a single working mother, spent a good part of my younger years teaching me the basics in cooking and baking, something my grandmother didn't do with her as much as she would've liked. When I was in the fourth grade, my mom began leaving the recipes for our dinner. They were hand written because it was usually a dish that we had at one time (or many) crafted together without following a recipe, only our noses and appetites. She wrote the measurements as close as she could estimate and encouraged me to "taste it to see if it needed more of anything." It was then that I began to understand the importance of flavor combinations and sampling the product over stringent calculation when it came to mastering the homemade cuisine. Subsequently, I was at a young age when I began to "cook with my nose" and create blends of flavors by being inspired with what I had to work with.

Although I grew up always admiring music and art, I never considered myself artistic. I would listen in awe to the music created by my talented friends or at the countless shows I'd attend and wonder why I was shorted the creative gene. Ironically, it was only a few years ago when it occurred to me that I am not only one who appreciates music and art, I have artistic abilities, too! My canvas is the palate, my set list depends on my appetite, and it does not take much for me to unleash the creative juices and prepare a delicious meal. I rarely follow recipes and this is how my best dishes evolve. I am thankful for the freedom my mom instilled in me in cultivating my creativity in the kitchen. Today, I enjoy creating spicy dishes with a Southwestern or Asian flare.

- Mary Silvers - Oakdale, CA

Soup & Salad

It'd take days to recount the many ways that music changed and/or diverted my life. But maybe I can more easily explain how food changed touring...for me and my band mates, at least.

Touring and playing music for a living is a true blessing for the few who are able to pull it off. And while I wouldn't say it is the easiest way of life, it definitely isn't the hardest. But after every tour, we'd all come home and start remembering the things that sucked and what we could do to help it avoid sucking next time.

When we first started out traveling as a band, we didn't really consider food much. Our individual food budgets were $2-$5 a day. We mostly ate fresh fruit and vegetables from grocery stores and for me, cold canned beans were an all-too-familiar lunch and dinner. Jim ate cans of garbanzos. Jason specialized in canned spinach. But over the years, touring for us became a full-time endeavor and livelihood and food was a constant concern. We mostly got the same thing every night. Veggie tray, candy, chips, hummus, bread, cheese, cold cuts. It soon got monotonous, although it was great to always have sustenance available at all times. Conversely, it was bad to have all that food around when you were bored after spending hours stuck at the venue. It was easy to just eat crap all day simply to ease the boredom. Restaurants were an occasional option, but the cost of eating quality restaurant food made it a very rare occurrence.

But, we came up with a solution. Everyone in the band liked to cook at home and band cook-outs were a common occurrence there as well. We decided it would be a good idea to bring along on tour a full cooking rig...a big tub with a camp stove, essential utensils, pots and pans, spices, oils...Basically a portable kitchen. We also had room enough to cart around a Weber grill. We created an identical kit for touring in Europe.

The result of this experiment were immediate and successful. Boredom was alleviated by contributing to prep work or making pre-meal snackies. Instantly, the atmosphere became more familial. Everyone had a kitchen job to do...we were all chopping, cutting, marinating, making salsa, tasting each other's work. It gave the day a lot more focus and we were always eating well and healthy. We figured out that by pre-arranging it with the venue, we could have the money meant for fulfilling the backstage rider and do all the shopping ourselves. A very valuable side affect was it allowed all us California natives a chance to eat good Mexican food in say, Ohio....or Tennessee....or Austria.

Plus, it was fun as hell.

We had BBQs in alleys behind theatres and bars, in parking lots, on sidewalks, in nearby parks, sometimes in someone's back yard. It wasn't rare for random people off the streets to join us, or fans to happen by and end up spending the afternoon eating chicken tacos and throwing a Frisbee around or playing wiffleball. Other bands we were touring with would kick in their rider money and pretty soon we'd be hosting nightly BBQs for 30 people.

I think back on those days and what a huge loss it would have been to have not followed through with the portable kitchen idea. It sure was a lot of work and clean up was never very fun, but to have relied on unhealthy "road food", or to have spent all those hours between the sound check and the show being bored, eating another damn ham and cheese sandwich, simply would have been a crime. It was a revolution to us. A way to bring a little bit of home with us no matter where we were or what time it was. And, it was definitely the only way to get good Mexican food in Ohio. Or Austria.

-Aaron Burtch - Grandaddy/The Good Luck Thrift Store Outfit - Oakdale, CA

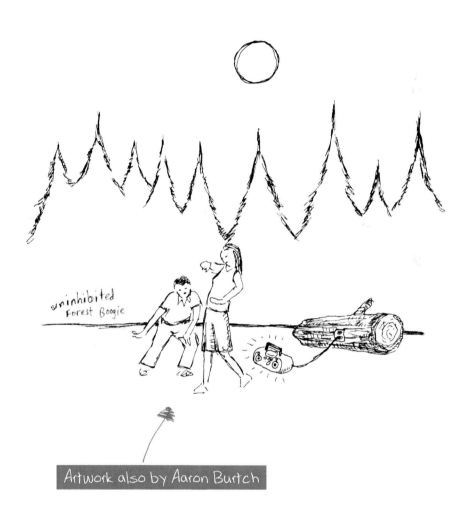

uninhibited Forest Boogie

Artwork also by Aaron Burtch

Tabbouleh

(serves 4-6)

1 bunch curly parsley, finely chopped
½ English cucumber, diced
1 package grape tomatoes, diced
3 green onions, diced
2 tablespoons fresh mint, finely chopped
⅓ cup lemon juice
⅓ cup olive oil
½ teaspoon salt
½ teaspoon pepper
1 tablespoon allspice
½ cup bulgur wheat, medium or coarse
4 ounces crumbled French Feta - the
"French" part is optional but, in my
opinion, it's the best of the Fetas

Yoseff & Banoura

My Lebanese great-great grandparents

In a large bowl toss together the parsley, cucumber, tomatoes, green onions and mint. In a separate bowl whisk together lemon juice, olive oil, salt, pepper and allspice until well blended. Pour over vegetables. Add bulgur and Feta and mix well.

This needs to sit for at least 4 hours in order for the bulgur to soften. I usually make this the day before serving. The next day, taste it before you serve it, as it might be dry. If this is the case, add alternate splashes of olive oil and lemon juice until it tastes juicy and delicious. Usually, I'll end up adding a few tablespoons of each the next day - but I like it pretty tangy, so proceed with caution.

As a young a boy growing up in Iran, I was always fascinated with noise and any random object that I could turn into a drum. From my desk at school to the pots and pans in the kitchen, I was always drumming away on something. I finally got my first real hand drum when I was nine years old. Some of my best childhood memories are from playing that drum at school and family functions. I remember my uncle would always find the most amazing street musicians and invite them to play at our parties. I'll never forget the intoxicating aroma of saffron rice and kebabs grilling on the hot fire, and the sounds of music, laughter and glasses full of homemade moonshine clinking together. Even though food and music vary in respect to their geographical locations, I truly believe that they are uniting factors in every nationality and culture, because no matter where you are, a great feast and a rockin band are sure to bring people together to celebrate life's wonderful gifts. No matter where I am in the world, food, music and family are universal truths that I hold to be self evident.

- Ray Vazira - Panhandle/Lisangaa - Modesto, CA

Syrian Salad with Lebne Dressing

(serves 4-6)

1 pita pocket
1 tablespoon olive oil
¼ teaspoon salt
¼ teaspoon pepper
¼ teaspoon garlic powder
2 medium vine ripe tomatoes, diced
½ English cucumber, diced
½ cup quartered Kalamata olives
½ cup crumbled Feta (about 4 ounces)
2 cups chopped Romaine lettuce

¼ cup chopped fresh mint
½ (15 ounce) can garbanzo beans
  (drained and rinsed)
½ cup Lebne (or Greek or plain yogurt)
¼ cup olive oil
1 tablespoon lemon juice
¼ teaspoon salt
1 teaspoon garlic powder
½ teaspoon allspice
⅛ teaspoon cumin

Preheat oven to 350 degrees.

Cut pita into ½ inch squares and put in a zip top bag. Add olive oil, salt, pepper and garlic powder. Seal bag and massage oil/spices into bread. Spread in an even layer onto cookie sheet. Bake for 8-12 minutes, depending on how crispy you want them. Allow pita to cool completely while you prepare the rest of the salad.

Add tomatoes, cucumber, olives, Feta, lettuce, mint and garbanzo beans into a large bowl and toss. Make sure there is plenty of room in the bowl, you want to be able to toss without spilling.

To make the dressing: Whisk together Lebne, olive oil, lemon juice, salt, garlic powder, allspice and cumin. It should take a few minutes of whisking to get the oil and Lebne to combine and become creamy, but you must persevere! When all is one, set aside.

Right before serving, add croutons and about half of the dressing to the veggies. Toss until combined. If you'd like, you can toss the salad and croutons and let everyone dress their own salad. If you're going to eat this the next day, don't add the dressing to the salad until ready to serve or it will become mushy.

Chopped Caesar Salad

(serves 6)

4 cups 'Garlic Croutons' (see page 72)
½ cup mayonnaise
¼ cup olive oil
1 clove garlic, minced
3 tablespoons grated Parmesan cheese
2 teaspoons Worcestershire sauce
2 teaspoons Dijon mustard

1 tablespoon lemon juice
⅛ teaspoon salt
⅛ teaspoon pepper
6 cups finely chopped romaine lettuce
1 ½ cups shredded Parmesan cheese
1 container grape tomatoes, quartered

First, follow the directions on page 72 to prepare the croutons. Next, make the dressing.

Add mayonnaise, olive oil, garlic, cheese, Worcestershire, Dijon, lemon juice, salt and pepper to a small bow. Mix in food processor or whisk with fork until completely combined. Feel free to add more or less garlic, depending on how garlicky you like your dressing.

Toss croutons with lettuce, cheese and tomatoes. Serve with dressing.

For both of these recipes: Don't add tomatoes until ready to serve or you'll have soggy salad!

Chopped Mexi-Caesar Salad

(serves 6)

2-3 medium tortillas
2 tablespoons olive oil
⅛ teaspoon salt
⅛ teaspoon pepper
⅛ teaspoon garlic powder
6 cups chopped lettuce

1 ½ cups crumbled Queso Fresco cheese
¼ cup + 2 tablespoons chopped cilantro
1 box grape tomatoes, quartered
1 recipe 'Creamy Jalapeno Dressing'
  (see page 58)

Preheat oven to 350 degrees. Cut tortillas into ½ inch squares. Toss with oil, salt, pepper and garlic powder. Place on cookie sheet and bake for about 7-10 minutes. Check after 7 minutes and every minute after until lightly browned (or darker if you prefer a crispier crouton). Set on paper towels to cool.

When cool, toss croutons, lettuce, Queso cheese, cilantro and tomatoes together. Serve with 'Creamy Jalapeno Dressing'.

"Glass & Bricks"

A girl sang me a lullaby one day on the play yard.
She said her mother knows a million or two
And she holds her in her arms.
Momma, Momma where'd you go?
Poppa, Poppa where'd you go?
These roses never smelt like you said they would,
And all the daisy's never danced like you said they could.
Why'd you say they could?

My heart is a desert,
And it's full of snakes.
Oops, one just bit me,
Guess I'm here to stay.
If these smokes don't kill me,
Maybe the drinkin' will.
At the wishing well I wished up upon a star,
But all the pennies that I threw, they never went too far.
Never went that far.

I heard there's a man from Galilee,
They say he walked on water and set captives free.
Well I'm drowning in water, and I've never been free.
Lord, won't you come and take me from this whiskey town,
So I can live with you and see the daisies dance around.
I know they dance around.

They built me a house of glass and bricks flew through it.
It got me all cut and bloody. Do you think you can fix it?
What to do, Lord.
What to do...

Artwork by Bethany Taylor

To read more about the 52-Week Club see pages 87-88

Pesto Caesar Salad

(serves 6)

Spinach Basil Pesto:
¼ cup chopped fresh basil
2 cups chopped baby spinach
¼ cup shredded Romano cheese
2 tablespoons pine nuts
2 cloves garlic, minced
2 ½ tablespoons lemon juice
¼ cup + 1 tablespoon extra-virgin olive oil
½ teaspoon salt
¼ teaspoon pepper

The rest of the salad....
½ cup 'Caesar Salad Dressing'
  (see page 58)
4 cups cubed sourdough bread
6 cups chopped romaine lettuce
1 ½ cups shredded Parmesan cheese

First, make pesto. Add basil, spinach, cheese, pine nuts, garlic, lemon juice, oil, salt and pepper to the bowl of your food processor (or blender). Process (or blend) for about 10 seconds. Use your spatula to scrape the sides of the bowl. Process again until smooth, about 1 minute or so. Measure out 2 tablespoons of the pesto and set aside.

In a medium bowl mix the 'Caesar Salad Dressing' and the rest of the 'Spinach Basil Pesto' until completely combined to create 'Pesto Caesar Dressing', set aside.

Preheat oven to 400 degrees.

Put cubed bread in a large bowl and add the 2 tablespoons of pesto. Toss until the bread is well coated. Spread evenly in one layer on a cookie sheet. Bake for 10-15 minutes, depending on how crispy you like your croutons. Remove from heat and cool for a few minutes.

Toss croutons, lettuce and cheese together. Serve with 'Pesto Caesar Dressing'.

I'll defer to Martin Scorsese and Robbie Robertson. They liked him enough to let him croon in The Last Waltz, so that's good enough for me. Although, they may have been extremely high. I had to spell check "Neil." Does that mean I don't like him?

- Micah Garbarino - Oklahoma City, OK - When asked to comment on the following: "It is said there are two kinds of people in this world: those who like Neil Diamond and those who don't....So, do you?"

Tomato Caprese Salad
with Fried Polenta
(serves 2-4)

Salad:

2 cups (about 3-4) chopped vine-ripe tomatoes

1 to 2 cups chopped Buffalo Mozzarella*

¼ cup chopped fresh basil

2 tablespoons extra-virgin olive oil

1 tablespoon balsamic vinegar

¼ teaspoon salt

Sauce:

2 cups (about 3-4) chopped vine-ripe tomatoes (keep juices)

¼ cup chopped fresh basil

2-3 cloves garlic, minced

2 tablespoons olive oil

½ teaspoon salt

¼ cup shredded Parmesan cheese

½ cup panko breadcrumbs

¼ teaspoon salt

2 egg whites, beaten

Polenta:

1 (16 ounce) tube Italian Herb flavored polenta

olive oil for frying

Add tomatoes, mozzarella, basil, oil, vinegar and salt to a bowl. Put in fridge for at least 30 minutes before serving - an hour is even better.

Next, make the sauce for the polenta. Chop the tomatoes, saving all the juices, and set aside. Chop basil, mince the garlic and set aside. Heat oil in a medium skillet over low-medium heat. Add garlic, cook and stir for about 30 seconds. Be careful not to brown the garlic - if it browns, it will taste very bitter. Add tomatoes, basil and salt. Stir until it boils. Remove immediately from heat and set aside. You don't want to cook the tomatoes too much, this is meant to be a very fresh sauce.

In a shallow dish mix Parmesan cheese, breadcrumbs and salt. (You'll probably have more of this than you need, but it's better to have too much than not enough.) In a separate shallow dish beat egg whites. Slice polenta about ½ inch thick. Cover the bottom of a medium sized skillet set over medium heat with olive oil (about ¼ cup). Dip polenta slices in egg whites, then in the breadcrumb mixture. Fry each slice for 2-3 minutes on each side or until crisp and golden brown. When done, remove from heat and rest on paper towels to drain and cool.

To serve: Top the polenta slices with some tomato sauce. Serve salad on the side.

*If you can get Mozzarella in the brine, that's the absolute best! If you can find mini-Mozzarella balls, these are also perfect. If you use them, I recommend quartering them. You should splurge on this - it'll be worth it!

I have always had a really strange relationship with music. I have no elaborate coming-of-age epiphany to share. I have no band that I grew up with and model myself after. I have a pretty normal musical genesis. My parents were both huge music buffs from the '70s, but they have always been that way, so it never crossed my mind that music could be a sub-culture. I compared music to McDonald's and Star Trek - it has always been there and it will forever remain, there is no reason to be a fanatic about them. But as I get older and my world-view slowly expands I start to realize that I do, in fact, have a very distinct relationship with music. A very violent, angry, unsatisfactory relationship.

Do you remember the old traveling fairs that used to roll through town every summer, spending three days showing us poor old country folk what we were missing in life? There was The World's Largest Rat (which we knew to be a possum), there was the Hall of Mirrors (which smelled like dirt weed and sadness), there were churros and oversized, over-stuffed animals and beer, beer, beer. It seemed like every event, ride or food stand had its own special brand of self-loathing mixed in with it. This is where I draw my music analogy from.

I am not sure if you have ever played it, but do you remember that Strong-Man-Hammer game? Step right up and see if you measure up against the other strapping men in the crowd. Sweaty teenage boys and their meaty fathers would take turns trying to impress the eager-to-be-wooed females in the crowd by swinging the hammer down with all their might, sometimes even lifting their feet off of the ground through all the effort. And yet, no one ever reached the top. To be honest, no one even came near to reaching the top. And for the first few hours of the fair there would be this line of frustrated men and boys spending their welfare checks at an alarming and exponential rate, all in the hopes of hearing what I assume to be a less-than-moving ding of a bell. Still, no winners. By the next day, there are a few new people and even fewer vengeance minded drunks. By the end of the fair, the entire town had washed its collective hands of the abomination with the bell. That right there - that is music to me.

I have spent year after year after year in search of that group or artist that rings my bell. I get closer and closer all the time. And there are a few artists that inch towards the top. But, they just don't make it. I have just as much effort trying to figure out why I am so picky. But it isn't that. I love a lot of bands. I love more bands than I can name. I just haven't found that voice. I haven't had that moment that I hear so many other people easily pull up. Seriously, everyone I know, everyone, has a great story about their favorite band and how they discovered them. Some of my friends even have more than one. So why can't I? And why the hell am I a musician? This admission alone is reason enough for me to pick up painting or writing but no... I decided a long time ago that if I couldn't find my music, then I was going to have to make it. Unfortunately, this just doubles the problem. Before, I was trying to find the perfect album. Now, I have been assigned the task of finding it and then recreating it.

In other words, I have (through over-thinking) ruined any chance I had of finding a truly pure moment within music. But I'm cool with that. I don't know anything else in my life that adds up, so why should this?

-Alexander Ayers - Sacramento, CA

Lentil Feta Salad

(serves 4-6)

1 cup lentils
½ red bell pepper, diced
2 celery stalks, diced
½ medium red onion, diced (about ½ cup)
⅓ cup chopped flat-leaf (Italian) parsley
4 ounces Feta, crumbled (about ½ cup)

2 tablespoons olive oil
2 tablespoons lemon juice
2 cloves garlic, minced
1 teaspoon salt
¼ teaspoon pepper

Put the lentils in a large pot and cover with water. The water should cover the lentils by about two inches. Bring to a boil and cook until tender, about 15-20 minutes. Check at 15 minutes, you don't want mushy lentils! Drain and immediately rinse with cold water in a colander. (This stops the lentils from cooking.)

While the lentils are cooling, dice the veggies. Put in them in a bowl and add Feta. In a separate small bowl, whisk olive oil, lemon juice, garlic, salt and pepper. Once lentils have cooled off, add them to the bowl with the veggies. (The lentils don't have to be completely cold, you just want them to be cool enough so they don't melt the cheese.)

Pour the olive oil/lemon juice mixture over the lentils and veggies and mix well. Allow the salad to sit in the fridge for a few hours before you serve it. Making this the night before serving is ideal.

"I love this so much I could spit!"
-Bethany Taylor

Three-Bean Salad

(serves 4)

1 (15 ounce) can Cannellini beans
1 (15 ounce) can black beans
1 (15 ounce) can garbanzo beans
¼ cup chopped cilantro
¼ cup chopped chives

½ cup crumbled Queso Fresco cheese
¼ cup + 2 tablespoons lime juice
¼ cup olive oil
1 teaspoon salt

Empty beans into a colander. Rinse with cold water and allow them to drain for about 1 minute. Usually, I'll get the beans draining while I chop my herbs.

Pour the beans into a bowl and add cilantro and chives.

In a small bowl whisk the Queso Fresco, lime juice, olive oil and salt until combined. Pour over beans and toss to coat. Let sit for at least an hour before serving.

Soup & Salad

The 52 Week Club

It was way back on July 4th, 2004. In the wee hours (so maybe July 5th already) there was a barbecue, beer, and a hot tub (or was it a whiffle-ball field?) Anyway, they were the necessary ingredients for coming up with hair-brained schemes and making suspect decisions. The hair-brained scheme in this case: write a song every week for one year. Our hero, Willy Tea, had been kicking this idea around for several years prior, but nobody had the wherewithal until summer 2004, when it all of a sudden seemed like the best idea ever. And who wouldn't want to embark on an adventure of such magnitude and guaranteed deliriousness? Fifty-two weeks, each week a new song based on the theme for that week, and everyone writes their interpretation of that theme. The themes would be simple words and phrases inspired by serendipitous moments, drunken ramblings, chance occurrences, late-night delusions, eureka!'s, a-ha!'s and sheer idiocy. And so, on that legendary July night, the Club came into existence with the simple word "mooner". In short, the Club is a songwriter's collective, a songwriting workshop, and a campfire sing-along, all at once. Activities consist of writing songs and then, as often as possible, performing them for each other.

Being a club there are, of course, very strict rules.

Rule number 1: Write songs. The songs can be specifically about the theme, they can mention the theme or they can work the theme word or phrase into the lyric in a way that the theme did not intend. The songs can simply be inspired by the theme and not mention the words at all. The songs can be instrumental. It really doesn't matter, as long as you write a song. One member even wrote poetry.

Rule number 2: No fair using an old (already written) song that happens to be on the same theme as a particular week. The goal of our illustrious founders was to spark creativity, not just fill out the list with old material.

The purpose of this club thing was to get our creative flows juicing, and we figured what better way than to set an oppressive deadline. But, the club is not about deadlines. Everyone who contributes even just one song in the one-year period has made the club a success.

The 52 Week Club is open to anyone. Writing just one song based off the list grants you membership and access to all the fine trappings the club has to offer. The club within the Club, however, includes anyone that finishes the task of actually writing all the songs in one year and is only reserved for people that are unemployed, can slack off at work for hours at a time or are just plain nuts. If you want to stretch your cognitive limits and improve your song-writing prowess, just see if you can do it and possibly go mad in the process, then this is the club for you.

Multiple albums were recorded, a band was started, a collective was formed, a new music venue was created, and a movement was inspired.

For more information about anything at all please visit the 52-Week Club website at www.heckabad.com.

- Chris Doud - The Good Luck Thrift Store Outfit - Oakdale, CA

Below is the 1st 52 Week Song I wrote. It's from week "Ransack" and is about my Busia ('grandma').

-Mary

The first time you saw him, did your knees get weak?
And when he said: "I love you" did your young heart skip a beat?
And did you smile?
When you stood in the chapel, all laced in white,
Did your eyes fill with tears, just at the sight of your love?
And did you smile?

Well smile now, sweet lady, rest in the arms of your Lord.
Dance in the light of the Morning Star.
Dance with your Tommy, dance with your daddy,
'Til we meet again some day.

After he drowned you in whiskey and beer,
And they ransacked your heart, wondering where they belong,
Did you smile?
And when the pain in your heart was too much to bear, did you picture his face,
Did you wish he was there?
And did you smile?

When he brought you flowers 25 years too late,
Did you know that he loved you every day of his life?
Did you smile?
Can you hear this song, are you watching me now?
Do you know that I miss you? And when I close my eyes...
...I see you smile.

Well smile now, sweet lady, rest in the arms of your Lord.
Dance in the light of the Morning Star.
Dance with your Tommy, dance with your daddy,
'Til we meet again some day.

Roasted Vegetable Salad

(serves 4)

Salad:
2 zucchinis, quartered lengthwise
2 yellow zucchinis, quartered lengthwise
2 red bell peppers, halved
½ large red onion, halved
¼ cup olive oil
½ teaspoon salt
½ teaspoon pepper
½ teaspoon garlic powder

Dressing:
2 tablespoons crumbled Goat cheese
1 tablespoon extra-virgin olive oil
1 ½ teaspoons balsamic vinegar
½ teaspoon salt
¼ teaspoon pepper

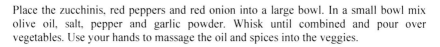

Preheat oven to 375 degrees.

Place the zucchinis, red peppers and red onion into a large bowl. In a small bowl mix olive oil, salt, pepper and garlic powder. Whisk until combined and pour over vegetables. Use your hands to massage the oil and spices into the veggies.

Place vegetables cut side down on a cookie sheet and put into the preheated oven. Roast for 10 minutes, remove zucchinis and put them on a plate to cool. Crank the oven up to 400 degrees and return peppers and onions for another 10 minutes. Remove onions only. Continue roasting red peppers until they are black and charred. Place red peppers in a zip top bag and put in the fridge until cooled.

Cut the zucchinis and onion into bite-sized chunks and put in a bowl.

When the red peppers have cooled, peel the skin off and roughly chop. Add to the bowl with the rest of the vegetables.

To make the dressing: In a small bowl whisk Goat cheese, olive oil, vinegar, salt and pepper until completely combined.

Pour the dressing over the vegetables and toss until everything is coated. I recommend making this at least an hour before serving.

Like revenge, this dish is best served cold.

Olive Pasta Salad

(serves 4-6)

Italian Herb Vinaigrette:
(makes about 1 cup)
¼ cup red wine vinegar
⅔ cup canola oil
2 cloves garlic, minced
3 tablespoons chopped flat-leaf
  (Italian) parsley
3 tablespoons chopped fresh basil
2 teaspoons dried oregano
1 teaspoon sugar
1 tablespoon lemon juice
1 teaspoon kosher salt
¼ teaspoon pepper
½ teaspoon onion powder

Salad:
½ pound tri-color rotini (corkscrew) pasta
½ cup halved Kalamata olives
½ cup halved large black olives
½ cup halved Spanish olives
1 (10.5 ounce) jar Danish Feta in oil
½ cup diced red onion
1 cup diced grape tomatoes
1 teaspoon salt

If you aren't a fan of olives, use marinated artichoke hearts, red bell peppers or tomatoes instead.

To make the dressing: Add vinegar, oil, garlic, parsley, basil, oregano, sugar, lemon juice, salt, pepper and onion powder to the bowl of your food processor. Process for about 30 seconds, or until combined. If you don't have a food processor, you can use a blender, hand mixer or whisk by hand. Allow this to sit for at least an hour before serving.

Boil pasta according to package directions. Drain and set aside in a medium sized bowl to cool.

When the pasta is cool add olives, Feta, red onion, grape tomatoes, salt, pepper, 2 tablespoons of the oil from the Feta jar (or some good extra-virgin olive oil) and all of the vinaigrette. Toss until coated and allow the salad to sit for at least an hour before serving. For best results, make the night before.

"50 Most Important Songs That Every Country Singer/Guitar Picker Should Know"

By Matt "The Gambler's Prayer" Cordano
The Good Luck Thrift Store Outfit - Oakdale, CA

50) "First Girl I Loved" (John Hartford): Another guy who checked out too soon. Too good for this world, I guess.

49) "Magdalene" (Guy Clark): This has been my favorite song since Guy Clark's new album came out last fall. Succinct and absolutely beautiful.

48) "The Malt Horse Sits Down at the End" (Chris Doud): This guy can write a !@#$% song. He's a shrewd poker player and a good friend. We're in a band. Perhaps you've heard of us.

47) "Refuse/Resist" (Sepultura): RRRARRAAAAHAHAHARRGGGGGGG!!!!!!!!!

46) "Ohoopee River Bottomland" (Larry Jon Wilson): The music industry tried to bury this guy, but that crazy right hand rhythm poppin' technique was too amazing to vanquish.

45) "Uncle Pen" (Bill Monroe): When people refer to The Good Luck Thrift Store Outfit as bluegrass and we let out that uncomfortable chuckle, it's because this is what bluegrass really sounds like.

44) "Clay Pigeons" (Blaze Foley): Classic, oft covered song about getting back on your feet. Who is Blaze Foley? See next song comment.

43) "Drunken Angel" (Lucinda Williams): Great song about great Austin, TX, songwriter Blaze Foley. The title says it all.

42) "Red House" (Jimi Hendrix—live): Jimi's rad. I'm not exactly a Hendrix worshipper, but he !@#$% nailed it on this one.

41) "Wrote a Song for Everyone" (Creedence Clearwater Revival): Awesome song hidden under an avalanche of hits. My old friend Tim and I listened to it about thirty five times in a row one night. Drew Landry covers it sometimes. Never heard of Drew Landry? Shame on you!

40) "The Four Horsemen" (Metallica): Stolen riffs from Dave Mustaine. I think I can still play the solos. One of these days, I'll plug in the half-stack.

39) "Cousin Randy" (Black Joe Lewis): He couldn't believe we brought Cyclone to Austin with us. Now that's a pair to have in the same room: Black Joe Lewis and Cyclone. Historic, indeed.

38) "Too Many Nights in a Roadhouse" (Junior Brown): Planet Earth's purveyor of the guit-steel. His genius confuses most country music fans.

37) "California Stars" (Billy Bragg and Wilco): Adapted from a Woody Guthrie poem. Pretty.

36) "Black Soul Choir" (Sixteen Horsepower): These guys scared me into believing in God. I think David Eugene Edwards inhabits several sides of the multiverse.

35) "Ace of Spades" (Motorhead): Any questions? I didn't !@#$% think so!

34) "Rue the Day" (Willy Tea): Beautiful song by my good friend, inspired by our good friend, a legend by the name of Billy Reed.

33) "Big Iron" (Marty Robbins): Cinematic western story song. Let's make a pilgrimage to the town of Agua Fria, AZ.

32) "Floater (Too Much to Ask)" (Bob Dylan): Many people do not realize that some of Dylan's best albums have come out during the last ten years. We're not just blowin' in the wind here.

31) "Guitar Town" (Steve Earle): He's got dozens of excellent songs, but there's something about his first hit that really gets me, especially the recent live version.

30) "Pukaki Joins the Goonies" (The Puffin' Billies): The only instrumental on this list. Dave Hanley and I tearing it up. Hear that nylon string guitar? That's me. Shredding. That's how I roll.

29) "Angel of Death" (Slayer): This is the blue print for death metal. It's really all you need to hear. Disturbing, nightmarish lyrics about Josef Mengele.

28) "Love Shmlove" (Built Like Alaska): Vintage BLA from the Hopalong album. I've always liked Chris Doud's guitar work on this track, and of course Neil Jackson's ethereal voice.

27) "Angel Flying Too Close to the Ground" (Willie Nelson): "I knew that someday you would fly away/ for love's the greatest healer to be found/ So leave me if you need to/ I will still remember . . ." Christ, Willie!

26) "Crossroads" (Cream—live): Some people think Clapton is overrated. I think this song has two of the best rock guitar solos I've ever heard in my life.

25) "Old Pigweed" (Mark Knopfler): Making a stew in the winter time.

24) "The Best of All Possible Worlds" (Kris Kristofferson): This guy is so clever he must have gone to Oxford

23) "Prester John in Appalachia" (The Pine Box Boys): I love these guys, especially when they sing about alcoholic preachers.

22) "Tonight, I'll Be Staying Here With You" (Afrodisiac and the Spanish Flies): Soulful rendition of the Dylan classic. Draw me a hot bath and put some Remy Martin on the rocks.

21) "Flesh and Blood" (Johnny Cash): Poignant. Spiritual. Strong. Embodies the man who wrote it.

20) "Far From Any Road" (The Handsome Family): Flawless production and arrangement. Vivid imagery. They truly take me to another place.

19) "Irish Drinking Song" (Josh Plante): When we pray, we raise our glasses and sing at the top of our lungs. Church is every Wednesday night at the Cow Track. Good song by a dear friend.

18) "Up On Cripple Creek" (The Band): Run the clavinet through the wah pedal, Garth!

17) "Rowdy Party" (The Stabone and Demar Rock Group): This may be the rowdiest song ever written. No, in fact, it does not get any rowdier than this.

16) "Murders in the Rue Morgue" (Iron Maiden): Paul D'Anno era. Edgar Allan Poe plus proto metal innovators. I prefer the live versions with Bruce Dickinson singing.

15) "Atlantic City" (Bruce Springsteen): Another "could've been a great movie but it's a song instead" vignette from the Boss's boundless imagination.

14) "Grosbec (Game Warden Song)" (Drew Landry): Hung out at Drew's place in Scott, LA, last February. The whole town turned out for a house party. Awesome zydeco band played for hours while everyone danced to kick off Mardi Gras. His folks treated us to a great Cajun dinner, jambalaya, black eyed peas, pork cracklin's, etc. Oh yeah, this song !@#$% rocks!

13) "Stay Forever" (Ween): Pretty love song by the same guys who recorded 'The Pod'.

12) "Killing Floor" (Howlin' Wolf): Woulda, shoulda, coulda.

11) "Rexroth's Daughter" (Greg Brown): Poetry. Amazing voice. This song really has beautiful lyrics. Steady, mellow rhythm with Bo Ramsey's guitar chattin' in the background.

10) "Holy Wars...The Punishment Due!" (Megadeth): They were on a mission to play guitar better than everyone else, especially Metallica. Well, they crammed more amazing riffs into this song than most bands cram into an album. Megadeth rules.

9) "Promised Land" (Chuck Berry): The first concert I ever attended was Chuck Berry at the Circle Star Theater in San Carlos, CA. I was about eight years old and obsessed with the oldies.

8) "In Dreams" (Roy Orbison): A beautiful song, but I can no longer hear it without thinking of Dennis Hopper's face in David Lynch's disturbing film Blue Velvet.

7) "7-11s Are All The Same" (Neil Hamburger): Highly perceptive lyrics sung by a true entertainer, America's funnyman, Neeeeiiiillll Haaaammmmbuuurrgerrrrrrrr!

6) "Love Song" (Tesla): A majestic accomplishment in hard rock power balladry by a little band from Sacramento, CA. Frank Hannon is butt rock's most under-appreciated fret master.

5) "Stay All Night (Stay A Little Longer)" (Bob Wills and His Texas Playboys): Everyone's done this song. I like playing it with the Plante Brothers at The Cow Track Lounge.

4) "Tennessee Stud" (Jimmie Driftwood): Cash has a great version, but if you want to talk guitar playing, check out Doc Watson's rendition. If I could pick like Doc Watson, I wouldn't be sitting around writing this bullshit.

3) "South Coast" (Ramblin' Jack Elliot): Originally written by Lilian "Bos" Ross, perfected by Ramblin' Jack. First heard this song at a concert in Berkeley. The Puffin' Billies got free tickets because we played an open mic the week before and stayed for all the performances. We got to choose any concert that month. Without a second thought, we chose Jack. That night was the first time any of us had heard this song. I was captivated by the story of old California and expanses of untamed wilderness called ranches where "the lion still rules the barranca and a man there was always alone." I met eyes with Willy Tea when the song ended, and the expressions on our faces seemed to say we had just experienced a perfect performance of a perfect song.

2) "Pancho and Lefty" (Townes Van Zandt): Alright, you don't need to tell me that Townes has dozens of other masterpieces besides the one that made a hit for Willie and Merle. I don't care. It's one of those perfect songs, and no one who has covered it has touched the way it sounds when Townes himself sings it. Also, I just love picking the chord progression. Remember, your question really asked for suggestions about what songs you could learn as a beginner. Learn this one. Learn to strum it, and as you improve, learn to pick it.

1) "Hot Rod Lincoln" (Bill Kirchen—from the album Hot Rod Lincoln Live!): A jukebox used to say a lot about a place. The Cow Track used to have a real jukebox before the Internet took over. I first heard this version of "Hot Rod Lincoln" on the jukebox at The Cow Track Lounge in Oakdale, CA. I first saw Bill Kirchen perform this song live at The Cow Track. He's the best picker to ever pick up a Fender Telecaster, and so many people have no idea who he is. Kirchen's version of "Hot Rod Lincoln" is the Gambler's favorite guitar riff of all time. Look into this guy, and try to see him live while he's still kickin'.

(Matt wrote this for the "Ask Gambler" column on The Good Luck Thrift Store Outfit's myspace blog. The original list was a top 100, then on top of that, 25 were later added as an addendum. For the complete list and to check out his band, please visit www.myspace.com/thegoodluckthriftstoreoutfit.)

Classic Potato Salad

(serves 6)

2 pounds potatoes
6 eggs
3 stalks celery, diced
3 green onions diced
2 tablespoons soybean (or canola) oil

¾ cup mayonnaise
1 to 1½ teaspoons salt (taste at 1 teaspoon
  add more if needed)
2 tablespoons lemon juice
2 tablespoons distilled white vinegar

Wash, peel and quarter potatoes. Add to a large pot, along with eggs, and cover with cold water. The water should cover the potatoes and eggs by at least 2 inches. Bring to a boil. The eggs will be done about 10 minutes **after** the water reaches a boil. Remove the eggs and continue cooking the potatoes until done, about 10 more minutes. They are done when you stick a fork or a knife into the potato and it slides right off. Drain in a colander and allow to cool. (If you don't have a large enough pot, boil potatoes and eggs separately.)

While the potatoes and eggs are boiling, chop the celery and green onions and put in a large bowl.

In a small bowl whisk oil, mayonnaise, salt, lemon juice and vinegar.

When the potatoes and eggs are cool enough to handle, chop into small pieces and add to the bowl. Add dressing and mix well. This should be made at least an hour before serving, but I highly recommend making it the day before.

From 52 Week "1987" by Chris Doud

Come on snow I can still see the leaves,
You're makin' climbin' up this mountain too easy.
My feet may be wet, but my hands are warm,
Come on God, this ain't much of a storm.
We've been walkin' this ridge since the sun woke up.
Ma, she don't fret as long as we get down by supper.
Grandpa's old watch it never worked one tick, 'cause he
Told me I was too young to worry 'bout what time it was.

To read more about the 52-Week Club see pages 87-88

Mom's Potato Salad

(serves 6)

2 pounds potatoes
6 hard boiled eggs (optional)
1 (16 ounce) jar dill pickles, diced
½ cup mayonnaise
½ cup sour cream
1 tablespoon Country Dijon Mustard
  (accept no substitutes!)
½ teaspoon salt
¼ teaspoon pepper

Mom insists on crispy pickles, but I prefer the squishy ones. I also like to use 'zesty' pickles if I can find 'em.

Wash, peel and quarter potatoes. Add to a large pot, along with eggs, and cover with cold water. The water should cover the potatoes and eggs by at least 2 inches. Bring to a boil. The eggs will be done about 10 minutes **after** the water reaches a boil. Remove the eggs and continue cooking the potatoes until done, about 10 more minutes. They are done when you stick a fork or a knife into the potato and it slides right off. Drain in a colander and allow to cool. (If you don't have a large enough pot, boil potatoes and eggs separately.)

While potatoes and eggs are boiling, chop pickles (drain all juices, big time!) and add to a large bowl. You can chop the pickles the day before - just keep them in the pickle juice and drain when ready.

In a bowl combine mayonnaise, sour cream, mustard, salt and pepper. Mix well and set aside.

When the potatoes and eggs are cool enough to touch, chop into small pieces and add to a large bowl. Pour dressing over potatoes and mix gently until just combined.

A friend of mine said this was better than his mom's potato salad. I won't mention his name because guys aren't supposed to say things like that.

Soup & Salad

Herbed Potato Salad

(serves 4-6)

6 medium red potatoes, peeled and quartered
½ cup sour cream
¼ cup mayonnaise
4 sprigs rosemary (remove leaves and chop)
1 tablespoon chopped fresh thyme

2 tablespoons chopped fresh basil
1 tablespoon olive oil
½ teaspoon salt
¼ teaspoon pepper

Wash, peel and quarter potatoes. Add to a large pot and cover with cold water. The water should cover the potatoes by at least 2 inches. Boil for 15-20 minutes. They are done when you stick a fork or a knife into the potato and it slides right off. Drain in a colander and allow to cool.

While the potatoes are boiling, in a medium bowl mix sour cream, mayonnaise, rosemary, thyme, basil, olive oil, salt and pepper.

When the potatoes are cool to the touch, chop into small pieces and add to a large bowl. Pour sour cream mixture over them. Toss gently to combine.

This should be made at least an hour before serving, but I recommend making it the day before.

There are four things that my grandparents treasured most: family, fine taste in liquor, their stereo systems with their vinyl and cassette collection and food. On one particular evening, I was about 12, they were preparing a roast, drinking Brandy and water and listening to Neil Diamond while family and friends drank and carried on. My grandfather was stuffing garlic cloves in the roast with precision and my grandma was preparing potatoes and vegetables to put with the roast later. Willie Nelson's 'Stardust' was playing on their top-of-the-line Pioneer system and Frank, their neighbor and friend, was catching a pretty good buzz along with my grandpa and grandma.

The smell of a delicious roast was in every room of the house. I was sure to devour half of it, being the growing boy that I was. Drinks were poured, Roger Whitaker hit the stereo and Frank hit the sliding glass door. (This was before my grandma put little stickers on it because of Frank running into it many times before.) Then supper was on and we would eat a full feast together at my grandparents dining room table. (The same table I now have and am writing this memoir on.) The Star Wars soundtrack was on low, one of their favorites. Everyone is stuffed full of roast and Brandy. It's getting late, 8pm, I had homework to finish. Frank leaves, my grandparents settle in for one more high-ball. As Merle and Willie sing 'Pancho & Lefty' the lights go out, the smell of supper lingers and the leftovers await my grandpa's seconds late in the night. I settle in my bed listening to the Rolling Stones hours from breakfast.

- Willy Tea - The Good Luck Thrift Store Outfit - Oakdale, CA

Baked Potato-ey Potato Salad

(serves 4-6)

2 pounds potatoes
½ pound bacon
1 cup sour cream
2 green onions, chopped

½ teaspoon salt
¼ teaspoon pepper
½ cup finely shredded Cheddar cheese

Wash, peel and quarter potatoes. Add to a large pot and cover with cold water. The water should cover the potatoes by at least 2 inches. Boil for 15-20 minutes. They are done when you stick a fork or a knife into the potato and it slides right off. Drain in a colander and allow to cool.

Chop bacon and cook in a large skillet until desired crispiness. Set aside on paper towels to drain. Set aside just a bit of the bacon, cheese and green onions for garnish.

While potatoes are boiling, mix sour cream, green onions, salt and pepper.

When potatoes are cool enough to handle, chop into small pieces and add to a large bowl. Pour sour cream mixture over them. Add bacon and cheese and mix well. Garnish with bacon, cheese and green onions.

This should be made at least an hour before serving, but I recommend making it the day before.

by Shelly Cimoli

Sandwiches

Even though I'm a big fan of sandwiches, I almost left this section out. Writing a sandwich recipe is tricky. Who measures mayonnaise before they spread it on bread? I'm assuming everyone knows how much mayo, cheese and other such foods they like on their sandwiches. My job is to share different sandwich ideas that I've come up with. Your job is to decide how much of the different ingredients you want to use.

Grilled Portabella Mushroom
Sauté Portabellas (whole) in olive oil. *Season with* salt and pepper.
Serve on: sliced sourdough bread with sliced tomatoes,
fresh basil leaves and sliced Muenster cheese.
Grill these like a grilled cheese sandwich!

Italian Chicken Salad
Boneless, skinless chicken breast* *cooked with* olive oil and
seasoned with salt and pepper. *Mix with* chopped grape tomatoes
mayonnaise, fresh basil. *Serve on* sliced focaccia with
mozzarella cheese and butter lettuce.

Monterrey Chicken Salad
Boneless, skinless chicken breast* *cooked with*
canned, diced, mild green chilies and diced onion.
When cooled, shred and *mix with* mayonnaise and *serve on*
sourdough bread with Monterey Jack cheese. Then grill it!

Here's a Willy Tea special:
Turkey breast, green chilies (diced from can), mustard, mayo,
bacon, Monterey jack cheese.

Thanksgiving Delight
Leftover turkey, hot melty Brie, toasted bread and salted!

Grilled Ham & Cheese
Spread some Salsa Verde on 2 slices of sourdough bread.
Layer ham, Pepper Jack cheese, and tomatoes - grill until cheese is melted.

*Or use a few cans of chicken.

Mashed Potato Sandwich!
Take leftover mashed potatoes, **add** a bunch of flour and make them into patties.
Fry patties in butter until crispy and brown on both sides.
Once flipped, put shredded Muenster cheese on top and let it melt.
Spread sour cream on sliced sourdough bread. Put the potato pancake
between the bread and **grill** the sandwich in the butter left in the pan.
This is soooo good!

Salami Delight
Spread mayonnaise and mustard on, you guessed it, sourdough bread.**
Layer salami (splurge on this folks, don't get the cheap stuff!), Provolone
cheese and peperoncinis. (This may be one of my favorite sandwiches.)

Adding different flavors to your mayonnaise
is a great way to kick-up any sandwich.
Here are some flavor ideas:

Basil Pesto
Add: fresh basil, garlic, grated parmesan,
diced green onions, pepper and salt

Tomato
Add: tomato paste, minced garlic, fresh chopped basil

Roasted Garlic
Add: roasted garlic, salt and pepper

Sun Dried Tomato
Add: sun-dried tomatoes, salt and pepper

Greek
Add: diced Kalamata olives, minced garlic, salt and pepper

Spicy-Mexi
Add: diced, fresh cilantro and diced jalapenos

Lemon Herb
Add: chopped fresh rosemary, minced garlic, a very small tiny bit of
dried thyme and fresh, chopped flat-leaf parsley

**As you can see, I love sourdough. But be
free, use any kind of bread you want!

"Deeds Just Died"
By Heaven Lindsey-Burtch, Turlock, CA

My eyes are closed as I curl my toes around the freshly planted mountain grass, feeling the coolness that I am unused to in my valley home. I open my eyes in time to see a glistening purple and green beetle scuttle into the cracks between the wooden boards that I myself am seated Indian style upon. I gaze upward to the patch of sky visible between the numerous surrounding pine trees and find a wispy white frog leaping across the expanse of blue, but in only a few short seconds he has metamorphosed into Captain Call's Hell Bitch mare, and with another whistle and a "Hey, fellas!", she, too, is gone. I imagine that if I were paying any attention to the sounds of the mountains, I would most likely be able to pick out a mockingbird's siren, a jay's scream, and the sound of cars rushing down highway fifty to get to goodnessknowswhere.

But I do not hear any of those things.

Instead, I opt to listen to the beautiful voice of the first person that ever gave me chickenskin just by the way she sings, one of the first women who has made me want to close my eyes and feel the music rather than watch it be made. She and many more have made me realize just how important music is and has always been in my life.

My dad, Aaron Burtch, gave music to me when I was two years old, and he has stuck by my side ever since. Growing up, Aaron was constantly quizzing me as to what classic rock song was playing on the radio and what it was (for years, I could not tell the difference between Led Zeppelin and Pink Floyd, although the indifference has since left me). When the time came, I graduated from rock school and proceeded on to my country lessons-- Merle Haggard, Loretta Lynn, George Jones-- all the real men and women who could tell it with three chords and the truth. They are the ones who have struck me the most, the ones who shake me awake, in a different way than rock music ever could.

More specifically, though, is The Good Luck Thrift Store Outfit, the band that my dad plays drums with and to whom Bethany Taylor, the beautiful woman previously mentioned, lends her vocals. Here I sit in my moma's mountain town, and the first music I choose to listen to after ten days of silence is them. I suppose it's a longing for Home that strikes me to do it. Here I am, with my family, and yet I still find myself Homesick. The warmth and belonging I have felt because of this band is quite unbelievable, nearly unexplainable. It makes me smile, makes me know that as long as I have these memories I will be able to outlive even the worst loneliness. Because of them, I know I have a Family, one that I was not born into but have grown into. And, in some ways, that is the best kind there is.

"1987" starts playing as I look up from my writing, only to find a silent white giraffe making his way across the great blue savannah, making his way Home.

Mujahdrah (Lentils & Rice) - 105

Creamed Cauliflower - 106

Baked Zucchini - 106

Pierogies - 109

Bacon Stuffing - 111

Mushroom Rice - 112

Garlic Red Pepper Rice - 112

Greek Rice - 113

Corn Cilantro Rice - 114

Syrian Rice - 114

Tomato Rice Pilaf - 115

Spinach Basil Orzo - 115

Lemon Feta Risotto - 116

Simon & Garfunkel Risotto - 116

Pesto Risotto - 117

Patatas Bravas - Page 118

Cheesy Garlic Mashed Potatoes - 124

Spicy Corn Mashed Potatoes - 125

Baked Potato-ey Mashed Potatoes - 126

Corn Cilantro Rice - Page 114

Greek Rice - Page 113

Simon & Garfunkel Risotto - Page 116

Patatas Bravas - Page 118

Pierogies - Page 109

Baked Potato-ey Mashed Potatoes - Page 126

Mujahdrah
(Lentils & Rice)
(serves 4-6)

Recipe courtesy of George Joseph - Las Vegas, NV

"This is an ancient food staple. My Sito (Arabic for grandmother) told us that Jesus ate Mujahdrah as a boy. As kids, we never thought to ask how she knew that, but we had Mujahdrah every Friday I can remember growing up. Mujahdrah has an infamous history in modern times as well. If you ever speak to anyone held hostage in the Middle East, they'll tell you that this is the dish their captors served almost exclusively. The original recipe calls for white rice, lentils and very little spice. I've changed the recipe to a more health conscious balsamic brown rice and added several spices. If you're brave of heart, you can double up on the cayenne pepper and cumin."

1 medium onion (Bussell)
2 tablespoons olive oil (Zyte Zythoon)
6 cups water
1 cup of brown rice (Riz)
1 cup lentils (Ahddas)
1 teaspoon salt (Milah)
½ teaspoon black pepper (Fliflee)
½ teaspoon cinnamon (Erhfah)
½ teaspoon allspice (Elfahrat)
½ teaspoon cayenne pepper* (Baharh)
1 teaspoon cumin (Cahmoon)
¼ teaspoon garlic salt (Toom)

> Mujahdrah can be served as a side dish or as an appetizer. A unique preparation is to make Mujahdrah into a paste using a blender. This is typically served with pita bread.

Chop the onion and brown (almost blacken) in olive oil in a large skillet. Add water to a large pot and bring to a boil. Add brown rice to the boiling water and turn heat to low. After 20 minutes add the lentils and browned onion to the rice.

Add salt, black pepper, cinnamon, allspice, red pepper, cumin and garlic salt. Cook on low for one hour.

> *Spicy! If you'd prefer, leave the cayenne out or use only ¼ teaspoon.

Creamed Cauliflower

(serves 4)

1 large head cauliflower (about 3 pounds before greens and stems are removed)
3-5 cups chicken broth, depending on size of the cauliflower
¼ cup shredded Gruyere or Parmesan cheese
¼ cup cream cheese
¼ cup diced chives
½ teaspoon salt
¼ teaspoon pepper

This is a healthier alternative to mashed potatoes. You may be amazed by the flavor!

Cut the stem from the cauliflower and discard it. Cut the cauliflower into 2 inch chunks. In a large pot add the cauliflower with enough broth to cover. Turn heat to high, bring to a boil and reduce heat to medium. Cook until the cauliflower is soft, about 10-15 minutes. Cauliflower should break apart slightly when you stick a fork in it, and slide right off of the fork without hesitation.

Remove from the heat and drain. Allow to sit in a colander for about 1 minute to make sure any excess liquid has drained off. Put cauliflower into a food processor and process until smooth. Add cheese, cream cheese, chives, salt and pepper. Process until creamy and serve hot.

Baked Zucchini

(serves 2-4)

2 medium zucchinis, quartered
¼ cup olive oil
2 teaspoons lemon juice
½ teaspoon salt
¼ teaspoon pepper

1 teaspoon ground ginger
1 clove garlic, minced
2-3 tablespoons shredded Parmesan cheese
2-3 tablespoons sesame seeds (optional)

Wash and quarter zucchinis, put in a large zip top bag and set aside. In a small bowl whisk olive oil, lemon juice, salt, pepper, ginger and garlic. Pour over the zucchini and seal the bag while squeezing as much air out as you can. Massage marinade into zucchini. Place in fridge and marinate for at least an hour.

Preheat oven to 350 degrees.

Pour zucchini and marinade into a baking dish making sure all pieces are cut side up. Sprinkle with Parmesan cheese and sesame seeds. Bake for 15 minutes.

Side Dishes

"The Barn-Againers"
By "Uncle Bob" Meisenbach

No gables, no cupola, no weather vane with a rooster atop, forever spearing the wayward wind; no fresh paint. Nope, from the outside it didn't look like much: just another old barn like others that you often see as you drive through the Central Valley. Only this one was in fairly good repair, not like many that are neglected: ramshackle ex-'animal places' from the past; held together by faith and rusty 16 penny nails. Some even listing like ships about to sink into the endless ocean of time. I've seen them propped up with two by sixes, their roofs a tatter of shingles, riddled with shafts of light; making a last valiant defense against unremitting gravity that in the end pulls us all down into the soil we sprang from. It is but the returning to Mother Earth: the minerals and elements we borrowed to clothe our souls while we walked in mystery and wonderment, the labyrinth and wrinkled surface of this old rolling globe we call our home. Yes, we all are eventually brought down by gravity: whether it's an old barn leaning on two by six boards, or an old man leaning on a cane.

When I was a boy I lived for a year with my grandparents on a farm in Nebraska. While I had many chores and often did the work of a man, that year was the happiest time of my life. I loved every waking hour of it and many of those hours were spent exploring the barn which contained more treasure than farm animals and hay. There were pigeon nests, a half full, or if you wish, half empty bottle of my granddad's whiskey, hidden from grandmother's prying eyes. Naturally I sampled it. Got a buzz, too (and that bottle was definitely on the empty side). I stayed away from the house for a couple hours, even though my grandmother called me three or four times. There were boxes of pictures of family: people I didn't recognize but identified with because they were family. A sense of family was what I was developing thanks to the love of my grandparents that I experienced that year on the farm. Then there were miscellaneous articles of junk, some on the verge of being useful, and two small bore pistols that didn't fire, until I got one of them to shoot. Which, thank God, got confiscated by the cops when that damned Leon stole it from me and was shooting too close to town. When the family would visit relatives with farms near Red Cloud or Arapaho or Naponee, the first thing I'd explore would be the barn. They were never quite the same but all were interesting in their way. I remember one in particular where I got my first roll in the hay with a distant cousin of mine. Don't misconstrue me, all we did was roll around in the hay.

To this day I love to see an old barn. They stand as wooden monuments to the past, a time that seems idyllic, less crowded, quieter, slower paced and more peaceful...that is if you exclude the little matter of the two worst wars in history. We view the past through the rose colored glasses of nostalgia. Nostalgia aside, they don't build barns like that anymore. What we now have are metal boxes that are so square and so aesthetically lacking, it's a wonder that we are able to convince cows and pigs and horses to live in them. O tempes, O mores! Or as Jimmy Buffet might say: "They looked a lot better as garbage cans."

So you can see I have a fondness for barns. I like the silence they pose as you enter them out of the howling wind or the husky, pungent smell of animals and hay. It's like a deep drag of an unfiltered Camel cigarette. But the barn that now impresses me is the barn that sang at the Tea Farm of Willy Tea. Oh, it was a magical barn. A barn that would ooze music every month: from virtuoso musicians like the big Tea himself to the Candle Man, up to whom few guitarists can hold a candle. What a deal it was: unmitigated, hella, hecka good. For a small donation you got live music, skits, poetry and a meal of chili prepared by Mary, the sister of Willy Tea's wife Bethany. Mary is a gourmet cook. She can not only prepare a dish, she is a dish. Those beans were so delicious that you ate them regardless of consequences. Ah, beans in a barn! They're called the musical fruit, dude, it's a musical barn. What could be more fitting, proper and down-right down-home than a fart in a barn?

I had the privilege of inserting poetry in the proceedings, for what is poetry but lyrics without music and besides, the word poetry is close to poultry so it may be suitable on a Tea Farm. The poetry was Willy's idea. I tell you, that guy is a one man Renaissance. He and his wife, Bethany, helped me get my butt out of neutral and start writing lyrics and even singing and I thank him for that. Him, Bethany, The Candle Man and The Professor. It is as if they had read W.B. Yeats poem: "Sailing to Byzantium":

> *An aged man is but a paltry thing*
> *A tattered coat upon a stick*
> *Unless soul sing and louder sing*
> *For every tatter in its mortal dress*

The passage has inspired me to finish my first album of twelve songs. I'm thinking about a title, maybe "The Candle Man and The Other Guy" or "Chandler and the Old Guy" or "Things Are Gonna Be"

I was leery of becoming some sort of barnyard bard, reciting poetry in a barn, but one couldn't ask for a better audience than the folks who came to the barn. It's not clear to me whether the good music was made for the good people who shared the barn, or the good people made the music good. Probably a mixture of both. But no matter, the end result is what is important: good people and good music, good food, good wine...good God! What a combination! Al this and heaven too. I loved that old barn. Too bad the cops shut it down. They claimed that is posed a traffic problem. Hell, most of the major cities of California pose a traffic problem and they don't shut *them* down. I think those cops suspected there were too many illegal smiles surrounding the place. Sometimes cops remind me of H.L. Menkin's comment about how the puritans go to bed every night worried that regardless of what they do, someone, somehow, somewhere is having fun. Still I have faith that barn will be back. It'll be 'a born-again barn' and it will sing, and we will all be 'barn-againers' and we will sing.

Carpe Diem, friend
"Uncle Bob" Meisenbach

Pierogies

(serves 4)

2 cups flour
¼ cup sour cream
1 egg, beaten
¼ teaspoon salt
2 teaspoons softened butter
¼ cup warm/hot water
1 pound mashed potatoes

I'm half Polish and we grew up with Pierogies.

This is my ultimate comfort food.

I recommend using a standing mixer for this, unless you're an expert kneader. So, assuming you have a standing mixer, put all ingredients into the bowl and, using the hook attachment, mix until a soft ball of dough forms. This should take anywhere from 2-3 minutes. Be patient - just let the mixer do its job. If it's too wet, add a little bit of flour. If it's too dry add some warm water. The dough should be really soft and pliable.

Roll dough out on a lightly floured surface until it's about ¼ inch thick. For larger pierogies use a round cookie cutter that's about 3 ½ inches in diameter. Use a rolling pin to roll them to about 4 inches. (For smaller pierogies, use a 2 ½ to 3 inch cookie cutter and roll to about 3 ½ inches.)

Bring a large pot of water to a boil and add about 1 tablespoon of salt.

You can use any mashed potatoes recipe to stuff these, the cheesier the better, in my opinion. My 'Cheesy Garlic Mashed Potatoes' recipe (page 124) is what I usually use. You can really get creative with these by adding onions, garlic, sun dried tomatoes or anything else you think sounds good. For large pierogies, fill with 1 tablespoon of mashed potatoes. For the smaller ones, about ½ a tablespoon. Place the potatoes in the middle of each circle and fold the dough over, making a half moon shape. Press the edges very firmly together and try to squeeze any air bubbles out. It is very important that the edges are completely sealed. Otherwise, when boiled, the filling will come out.

Place pierogies on a heavily floured dish. By the time you're done making all of them the bottom ones will want to stick to whatever you put them on, so be liberal with the flour.

Add about 3-5 pierogies (depending on the size of your pot, you don't want to crowd them) to the salted, boiling water. (Make sure you shake off excess flour.) As soon as you put them in they'll sink and want to stick to the bottom, so get down there with your spoon to loosen any stuck ones. Once they float to the top give them another minute or so - they'll end up taking a total of 3-5 minutes to cook. Use a slotted spoon to remove from water and place in a colander to drain. As soon as you place them in a colander, rub some butter on them so they don't stick together.

For an extra kick, you can fry these in butter with onions after you boil them.

(continued)

Another option is to bake these. It's not the traditional way, but it's much less time consuming.

To bake: Preheat the oven to 350 degrees. Place the pierogies on a lightly oiled baking sheet. (They can be close to each other because they won't expand.) Bake them for 5 minutes, flip them over and bake for another 5 minutes. You can also toss these in a frying pan with butter and onions, or just brush them with butter and serve hot.

Pierogies are best served smothered in sour cream!

My mom and her siblings in Michigan in the 60's

My mom is up front with the curlers in her hair

Side Dishes

Bacon Stuffing

(serves 6)

8 cups soft garlic sourdough bread, cubed
1 teaspoon ground thyme
1 teaspoon ground sage
½ teaspoon salt
1 pound bacon, chopped very small

1 cup diced onion
1 cup diced celery
2 cups chicken broth
¼ cup chopped flat-leaf (Italian) parsley
2 eggs, beaten until frothy

Preheat oven to 400 degrees.

Mix bread cubes, thyme, sage and salt. Spread in an even layer on a cookie sheet and put in oven until toasted, about 10-15 minutes. Remove from oven and set aside in a large bowl.

Turn oven down to 375 degrees. Lightly coat a large casserole dish with non-stick cooking spray.

In a large skillet begin to brown the (already chopped) bacon. Cook until dark brown and crispy, about 10-15 minutes. Remove bacon from skillet and drain on paper towels.

Pour out all but 2 tablespoons of the bacon grease and re-heat skillet over medium heat. Add onions and celery, cook and stir until soft, about 5-7 minutes. Remove from heat.

Add the bread, semi-cooled bacon, onion and celery mixture, broth and parsley to a large bowl. Add the beaten eggs, mix well (very gently) and pour into prepared casserole dish. Bake for 30 minutes covered. Remove and fluff with a fork. Leave uncovered and bake for another 30 minutes.

To prep the night before serving: Toast the bread and allow to cool ***completely***. Place in a zip top bag and put into the fridge. Cut up veggies. Place onion and celery in one zip top bag and parsley in another. Keep in fridge. This is especially helpful if you have a big holiday dinner to prepare the next day.

Air. Family. Music. Water. Food.

As far as I'm concerned, all these fancy shows about cookin' with all these fancy chefs is a little like going to a Toby Keith concert. You can't feel the love and all you smell is money. There's more substance in a cheeseburger.

Just sit me at the kitchen table with my family all around while grandma cooks chicken fried steak. That's hangin' out with Ramblin Jack and Guy Clark on a deserted island and all we have is a guitar and a song.

- Willy Tea - The Good Luck Thrift Store Outfit - Oakdale, CA

Mushroom Rice

(serves 4)

1 tablespoon soy sauce
1 tablespoon olive oil
4 green onions, chopped
1 cup roughly chopped button mushrooms (about 4)
1 cup roughly chopped Portabella mushrooms (½ a large or 1 medium)
1 cup roughly chopped cremini mushrooms (about 3-4 large)
1 ¾ cups beef broth
1 cup uncooked long-grain rice
1 teaspoon salt
¼ teaspoon pepper

In a medium pot heat soy sauce and olive oil over medium heat. Add green onions to the pot. Cook and stir for about 1 minute. Add mushrooms. Cook and stir for about 3 minutes or until they begin to brown. Add broth, rice, salt and pepper. Bring to a boil then turn heat to low. Cover and simmer for 15-20 minutes or until all liquid is absorbed. Serve hot.

Garlic Red Pepper Rice

(serves 2-4)

1 tablespoon olive oil
1 red bell pepper, diced small
½ cup pine nuts (optional)
2-4 cloves garlic, minced
1 tablespoon fresh thyme*
1 teaspoon salt
½ teaspoon pepper
2 cups vegetable (or chicken) broth
1 cup rice

*Remove leaves from the stem, measure, and chop small.

If you don't want to deal with fresh thyme, use 1 teaspoon dried.

Heat oil in a medium pot over medium heat. Add red pepper, cook and stir for about 2 minutes. Add pine nuts, cook and stir until lightly brown, about 3-4 more minutes.

Add garlic, cook and stir for 1 minute. Add thyme, salt, pepper and stir.

Add broth and scrape the bottom of the pan a bit in case any of the red pepper has stuck. Add rice. Bring to a boil and turn heat to low. Cover and simmer for 15-20 minutes or until all liquid is absorbed. Serve hot.

Greek Rice

(serves 2-4)

2 tablespoons olive oil
¼ cup finely diced red onion
1 clove garlic, minced
1 cup short or medium-grain rice
1 ½ cups chicken broth
2 lemons, squeezed
  (or about 2 tablespoons lemon juice from jar)
¼ teaspoon salt
¼ teaspoon pepper
⅓ cup quartered Kalamata olives
4 ounces crumbled Feta cheese*
¼ cup finely chopped flat-leaf (Italian) parsley

*I prefer French Feta because it has more of a mild, sweet flavor. For a sharper flavor, try Bulgarian or Greek.

Heat oil in a medium pot over medium heat. Add onion. Cook and stir for about 3 minutes or until onion begins to soften. Add garlic. Cook and stir for 1 minute.

Add rice, broth, lemon juice, salt and pepper. Bring to a boil and reduce heat to low. Cover and simmer for 15-20 minutes or until all liquid is absorbed.

Add olives, Feta and parsley. Stir until combined and serve hot.

From 52 Week "Let It Lie" by Bethany Taylor

"Always love mercy" is what he tells me.
"Just let it lie and wait for what God sends."
Baking bread in the family kitchen
And strong black coffee is all I need to live.

Well they don't make 'em quite like they used to,
Like the big gray castle he built in our city yard.
You can have your money, friend, that don't make a man,
My father's got more wealth in the lines of his hands,
And he holds us all together with those hands.

To read more about the 52-Week Club see pages 87-88

Corn Cilantro Rice

(serves 4)

1 tablespoon butter
1 (12 ounce) can corn (set aside juice for later)
1 cup rice
½ teaspoon chili powder
1 cup chopped cilantro
1 tablespoon butter
½ teaspoon salt

Melt butter in pot over low-medium heat. Add corn, rice and chili powder. Cook and stir for about 4 minutes. Pour the corn juice into a 2 cup measuring cup. Add water to corn juice until you have 2 cups of corn juice/water mixture.

Add corn juice/water to pot. Bring to a boil and turn heat to low. Cover and simmer for 15-20 minutes or until all liquid is absorbed. Remove from heat and add butter, cilantro and salt. Stir until combined and serve hot.

Syrian Rice

(serves 4)

½ pound ground beef
½ teaspoon salt
¼ teaspoon pepper
¼ teaspoon allspice
⅓ cup butter
½ cup pine nuts
½ cup Fideo (or vermicelli) noodles*
½ cup long-grain rice
2 cups chicken broth
½ teaspoon salt

*If you'd prefer, leave out the noodles and use a total of 1 cup of rice instead.

Heat a medium skillet over medium heat. Add beef, salt, pepper and allspice. Cook until brown, about 5-7 minutes. Drain and set aside.

Melt butter over medium heat in a medium sized pot. Add pine nuts and noodles. Cook, stirring constantly, for about 3 minutes or until pine nuts and noodles begin to brown. Don't walk away, they will burn quick! Add rice and stir until rice is a creamy white. color. Add meat mixture and broth. Bring to a boil. Mix and turn heat to low. Simmer until liquid is absorbed, about 20 minutes. Add ½ teaspoon salt and stir. Serve hot.

Side Dishes

Tomato Rice Pilaf

(serves 6)

¼ cup butter
¼ cup pine nuts
1 cup long-grain rice
1 (14 ounce) can diced tomatoes (save juice)
1 ½ cups chicken or vegetable broth

1 teaspoon dried mint
¼ teaspoon allspice
1 teaspoon salt
¼ teaspoon pepper

Melt butter in a medium sized pot over medium heat. Lightly brown pine nuts in butter, about 2 minutes. Add rice and stir frequently for 2 minutes. Add tomatoes (and juice), broth, mint, allspice, salt and pepper. Bring to boil, cover and simmer about 15 minutes. Remove from heat. Remove lid, cover top of pot with a clean dishtowel and replace lid. Let stand in warm place for 10 minutes. Fluff with fork and serve hot.

Spinach Basil Orzo

(serves 4)

1 cup uncooked orzo
¼ cup pine nuts
1 tablespoon olive oil
2 teaspoons lemon juice
¼ cup chopped fresh basil

1 cup chopped spinach
2 cloves garlic, minced
¼ cup shredded Parmesan cheese
½ teaspoon salt

Cook orzo in a medium pot according to package directions. While orzo cooks, heat a small skillet over medium heat and add pine nuts. (The pine nuts brown quickly, so don't walk away!) Toss pine nuts in skillet until light brown and set aside on paper towels. When orzo is done, drain and return to pot. Add pine nuts, olive oil, lemon juice, basil, spinach, garlic, Parmesan cheese and salt. Mix until spinach is wilted. Serve hot.

From 52 Week "Take The Bottle" by Mary Joseph

Right now I'm missing a guitar string,
so I can't tell you how I feel.
That missing note is my missing part,
so I can't tell you how I feel.

To read more about the 52-Week Club see pages 87-88

To read more about the 52-Week Club see pages 87-88

Lemon Feta Risotto

(serves 4-6 as a side dish)

3-4 cups chicken broth 1 tablespoon butter
2 tablespoons olive oil ¼ teaspoon salt
½ cup diced red onion ¼-½ cup crumbled Feta cheese
1 cup Arborio rice 2 tablespoons lemon juice
½ cup dry white wine ¼ cup chopped flat leaf (Italian) parsley

...depending on how cheesy you like it.

In a medium pot bring broth to a boil. Simmer and maintain over low heat. Set aside ¼ cup for later.

In a medium to large pot heat oil over medium heat. Add onion, cook and stir until soft. Add rice and stir until grains are well coated with oil and translucent, about 3 minutes. Add wine and stir until absorbed.

Add one ladleful of broth and stir. Once the rice absorbs broth, add another ladleful, stirring constantly. Repeat until you have added about 3 cups of broth. Check to see if the rice is done - it should be firm but chewy. If rice is still firm, add another ladleful of broth and check again. When done, stir in butter, salt, Feta, lemon juice, parsley and reserved broth.

Simon & Garfunkel Risotto

(serves 4-6 as a side dish)

3-4 cups veggie broth 2 tablespoons flat-leaf (Italian) parsley
2 tablespoons olive oil ⅛ teaspoon ground sage
1 medium shallot, chopped 1 tablespoon chopped fresh rosemary
1 cup Arborio rice 1 tablespoon chopped fresh thyme
½ cup white wine 2 tablespoons shredded Parmesan cheese

In a medium pot bring broth to a boil. Simmer and maintain over low heat. Set aside ¼ cup for later.

In a medium to large pot heat oil over medium heat. Add onion, cook and stir until soft. Add rice and stir until grains are well coated with oil and translucent, about 3 minutes. Add wine and stir until absorbed.

Add one ladleful of broth and stir. Once the rice absorbs broth, add another ladleful, stirring constantly. Repeat until you have added about 3 cups of broth. Check to see if the rice is done - it should be firm but chewy. If rice is still firm, add another ladleful of broth and check again. When done, stir in parsley, sage, rosemary and thyme. Try not to get the song stuck in your head as you add cheese and reserved broth.

Side Dishes

Pesto Risotto

(serves 4-6 as side dish)

...depending on how garlicy you like it.

1 teaspoon olive oil
2 tablespoons pine nuts
3-4 cups chicken broth
2 tablespoons olive oil
½ medium yellow onion, diced
1 cup Arborio rice

½ cup dry white wine
1 tablespoon butter
½ teaspoon salt
½ cup chopped fresh basil
1-3 cloves garlic
2 tablespoons shredded Parmesan cheese

Heat 1 teaspoon olive oil in a small skillet over medium heat. Add pine nuts and toss until lightly browned. (Don't walk away for too long, the pine nuts will burn fast.) Set aside on paper towels.

In a medium pot bring broth to a boil. Simmer and maintain over low heat. Set aside ¼ cup for later.

In a medium to large pot heat oil over medium heat. Add onion, cook and stir until soft. Add rice and stir until grains are well coated with oil and translucent, about 3 minutes. Add wine and stir until absorbed.

Add one ladleful of broth and stir. Once the rice absorbs broth, add another ladleful, stirring constantly. Repeat until you have added about 3 cups of broth. Check to see if the rice is done - it should be firm but chewy. If rice is still firm, add another ladleful of broth and check again. When done stir in butter, salt, basil, garlic, Parmesan, pine nuts and reserved broth.

There are two ways to learn an instrument and I have tried both. When I was about 10, I started learning the trumpet. I sweated through my grade exams, perspired through my weekly lessons, braved endless brass band rehearsals (sometimes on Saturdays!), dutifully practiced my scales every night and put in the hours in the church band. I don't regret all the hard work - I learned a lot about music, which was not a bad thing. But, when I was 14, I had a shiny set of train tracks on my teeth which made playing painful, so I stopped. It was the dentist's fault. That was the official line. Unofficially, I was learning the guitar. After I saw a friend, with almost no musical knowledge, pick out the chords to R.E.M.'s "Everybody Hurts", I knew I wanted to get me a six string. And, I did. Like Bryan Adams, I literally played the clumsy thing until my fingers bled - every night. Because I wanted to. After six months or so I had reached a point where playing became fun and my fingers had chunky calluses on their tips. The pain seemed worth it at the time because I was reproducing the music I loved to listen to. I never had lessons. I learned from people who were better than me and I never looked back. I might pick up the trumpet again one day. But if I do, it will be in my own time, under my own terms.

- Dave Maclure - Natal, Brazil

Patatas Bravas
(Spicy Spanish Potatoes)
with Sun-Dried Tomato Aioli
(serves 4-6)

(I am deeply and madly in love with this recipe)

Aioli:
1 cup mayonnaise
2 tablespoons tomato paste

½ teaspoon white pepper
¼ teaspoon salt
¼ cup chopped sun-dried tomatoes

Add all ingredients to the bowl of your food processor. Mix until smooth and creamy. If you don't have a food processor...go buy one. You could probably use a blender, but unless you have a *really* good one, I don't think it'd reach the smooth consistency of a traditional Aioli. Garnish with some finely chopped parsley.

Potatoes:
2 pounds red potatoes

Spice Mixture:
¼ cup + 1 tablespoon olive oil
1 tablespoon sherry vinegar
½-1 teaspoon cayenne pepper
 (1 teaspoon will be really spicy!)

2 teaspoons paprika
1 tablespoon dried thyme
2 teaspoons sweet paprika*
2 teaspoons cumin
2 teaspoons garlic powder
½ teaspoon salt
2 teaspoons black pepper

Chop potatoes (skins on) into approximately 1 inch cubes. Set aside in a large bowl.

In a separate bowl, whisk all ingredients for 'spice mixture' until combined. Pour over potatoes and toss until completely coated. Pour into a zip top bag. (Use a spatula to scrape every bit of the spice mixture in there as well.) Seal and put in the fridge. Allow to sit for at least an hour before cooking - 24 hours is ideal. Take potatoes out of the fridge about 10 minutes before you cook them so they come back to room temperature.

Preheat oven to 350 degrees. Pour the potatoes into a bowl. Add ½ cup of the aioli and toss to coat. Add potatoes in one even layer to a 9x13 baking dish. Cover with foil and bake for 20 minutes. Remove foil and bake for another 20 minutes.

Use the rest of the aioli to dip the potatoes in.

If you'd prefer to fry 'em: First, briefly boil the chopped potatoes for 5-6 minutes - you just want to soften them a bit. Drain potatoes and add to a bowl. Add spice mixture and ½ cup of the aioli. Mix until potatoes are completely coated. Fry them in about ¼ inch of hot peanut or vegetable oil (don't use olive oil) for about 10-15 minutes.

*If you can't find sweet paprika, double the amount of regular paprika. Don't use smoked paprika - it will totally change the flavor!

"Soda"

by Mary Joseph

Soda was 3 years old the first time he left home. The small town he lived in outside of Chicago sent out a search party to look for this little, wandering boy. Like most of us, Soda (real name withheld to protect the not-so-innocent) felt different growing up. He always looked older than his age and he used this to his advantage. He remembers once he went out with his parents to a restaurant and the waitresses there knew him. When his parents asked how, he said, "Because I sneak out of the house every night and eat here and drink coffee." Soda doesn't like real food. "I eat like a 5 year old" he says. He has never had soup, Mexican or Chinese food in his entire life. I asked him what he ate when he was a kid and he said, "I ate diner food, same as I do now."

At 13, he stopped mowing lawns and delivering newspapers. He used his dad's ID and traded a guitar for a car. He got jobs building guitars and working as a dressmaker for a design firm. He said he liked Singer sewing machines because they rumbled in B-flat. "B-flat is the only sound that can make an alligator and crocodile bellow" he says. "They have to be on a hard surface when they feel it, then they bellow. Some people say B-flat is the sound the earth is tuned to. Don't matter to me, B-flat's easier for the horn section to play in."

As soon as he found out that there were places where it was warm in the winter, he wanted to get to them. When he was 14, he hopped on a plane and went to meet a pen pal he had in San Jose, California. Back then, the airports had ticket dispensers like bus stations and they didn't check your identification. Although he frequently left home, this time it would be for good. It wasn't an unhappy family or rebellion that compelled him to go. It was, simply put, his destiny.

Years later, Soda ended up in Los Angeles and lived in an apartment building that used to be Charlie Chaplin's house. While living there, he played a piano that he bought for $100. Some tenants would complain about the noise, so he gave them instruments and they soon became his Million Piece Band. Even the cross-dressing apartment manager learned the auto-harp and joined up.

"I'm probably really schizophrenic and I hear a bunch of shit, so instead of being all messed up from it, I gave each of those noises to someone in the band and they'd play it. Therefore, all the voices had jobs. It's cheaper than medication. Sometimes you can find me on a bus bench talking to myself and doing math equations." Over the years The Million Piece Band constantly rotated and consisted of over 80 different people. At one point he had 19 people on stage at once.

It was then that his friends nicknamed him Soda. "Everyone had a nickname. No one ever called anyone by their real name." He was named after a teenage prostitute from an after-school special. The show was filmed in the apartment building where they lived, and as he would disappear all of the time, he was dubbed "Soda".

How I came to know him seems serendipitous. A few years before I met Soda I was living in Vegas and a friend gave he a copy of his CD. I immediately became a huge fan. Based on the quality of his music, I assumed he was big time. When I moved back to California I gave a copy of Soda's CD to my sister and her husband. That summer our friend from Texas, Tom Vanden Avond, was visiting. When Tom heard the CD he mentioned that he knew Soda and that they played music together in Austin. I was a bit star-struck to say the least. When Tom left I told him, half-joking, "Don't come back unless you have Soda with you!" Later that year when Tom came back he was accompanied by Soda.

Soda stands a bit over 6 feet tall with slicked back black hair. When he's really rockin' out, his hair sticks up and falls over like a whiskey-bent and road-tired Elvis and plays music that tends to be hard to describe. "I was nominated once for 'best un-categorizeable music'. It's un-categorizeable, which means it'll never make money because you don't know who to sell it to. So, I just give it out for free." His music is less Rock-a-Billy and more Psycho-Billy. Less roll, more rock. It's Hank Williams and Johnny Cash mixed with Punk and Blues. It's timeless and raw and his voice is reminiscent of Tom Waits. There is something for everyone – from the melancholy "Lakeshore", where he sings:

I'm goin' back home, back where I come from,
The prairies tall as the sky is blue.
And there ain't nuthin' here as far as I can see.
I'm goin' home now to Illinois".

To the more playful "Whiskey not Wine":

Well the uptown girls they always look fine
But the downtown girls drink whiskey not wine.
And the ones in the middle just can't decide
And I've always liked whiskey better than wine.
Treat a lady like a whore and she'll say she loves you.
Treat a whore like a lady and she'll always be true
And the ones in the middle end up wives.
And I've always liked whiskey, better than wine.

Two of the biggest artists I've seen live are Paul McCartney and The Who. Standing in that audience, singing along with those songs I knew by heart, goose bumps a-plenty, they seemed like gods. I was in the presence of legends and I knew it. This is the same way I feel each time I see Soda perform. I always get a sense of awe, a sort of "you-are-standing-on-holy-ground" feeling. I tend to look around to see if anyone else seems to be feeling this. When I see people who aren't paying attention I want to go up to them, shake them and yell: "Pay attention! This is a historical event!"

When Soda first became interested in music, it wasn't the music as a whole that drew him in, but the individual sounds. He says he never listened to music, he listened to sounds. When you ask him what kind of music he listens to now, he often says "I don't listen to music. I don't listen to talk radio either. Talk radio is for Socialists. I'm 100% Republican and mean." But when pressed, he'll admit that he does have favorite musicians, including Pablo Casals, Bilixa and Townes Van Zandt. "I don't like music and I don't *not* like music. There is no good music or bad music. As long as somebody lived it and they wrote it, then it's good to whoever can relate to it."

Soda is not stingy or selfish with his music. When in the presence of other musicians, he will sometimes invite them to play with him. Whether it's one guy and his guitar, an entire band or a mix of musicians, Soda, like many other musicians I've come across, enjoys the comradery of mixing it up, adding other elements, instruments and textures to his music. He claims it's only out of necessity that he does this, but I think he truly enjoys it.

I've always been very impressed by musicians who can just hop on stage with anyone and play along as if they're a regular part of the band. All the front-man has to do is give them a run-down of the chord progression and they jump right in flawlessly - as far as the crowd can tell. This, to me, is definitely a trait of a good musician. To be able to blend, play something other than your own songs, understand a melody enough to anticipate its direction and go with the flow. I'm lucky enough to be surrounded by people who do this effortlessly, and it never ceases to amaze me.

Soda will stay up late around the bonfire sharing songs with the rest of us and when he's in town, sometimes we're his million piece band. I told him once "I like to think that my sister and I are the only girls you invite to sing with you, but I imagine you have 'girls in every port'." He replied: "It's just you guys, that's all!" as he winked at his fiddle-player and mouthed the words "Don't say anything!"

From what I've seen, Soda seems to play mostly with younger musicians. To me, it's almost as though he's the wise instructor and they are his 'young grasshoppers'. This is not to say that these younger folks aren't good - they're usually great. There are exceptions of course: "If someone's playing on stage with me that sucks, I just unplug them or let them suck. Then the audience thinks we're playing experimental music."

The musician aside, it's not easy to get to know Soda as a person. His songs are personal but Soda himself is an enigma. You can know him, but it's impossible to *know* him. He's mysterious, initially intimidating and, some are convinced, he's a vampire. I was nearly convinced of this myself when I heard the following story.

A mutual friend told me that, at one point, Soda was having some health issues. He went to a doctor and they said he had the heart of an 80 year old man. They probably told him to settle down, stop drinking, stop smoking and generally clean up his act. This not being something Soda was willing to do, he got a second opinion. The next doctor said he had the heart of an 18 year old. "He regenerated! He's a vampire!" my friend said, completely convinced. I couldn't argue, I didn't want to argue. I want Soda to be a vampire. It makes him make sense.

"As far as knowing Soda, I don't think that I can give you much," says Dall from Larry & His Flask. "For me, personally, I feel like he is one of those special people that I understand quite well without knowing much about him. There are not many people that I feel this way about. His music is one thing, being very autobiographical in nature, but knowing him on a personal level just confirms everything that the music tells me. 'Sleight of Hand', 'You Cheat', 'Moonlight Drive', 'Whiskey Not Wine', and 'Bad Luck & Trouble' - I feel like that is the Soda that we usually see. That is the Soda that I usually see at least. Rockin', road hardened and mischievous. Knowing when to be heard and what to say in those moments. Always knowing that there are good times to be found, with mostly good intentions, in any given situation. It just seems like there is more that I never see."

Dall continues: "'New Orleans Dirge', 'Left Me', 'Gutter Queen', 'Pills For The Pain', 'Dirty Old Town', 'California Wine' - that part of Soda is something that I think isn't expressible except through song. Both of these sides of him speak to me, especially this other side. I'm not sure that I'm ready to commit to words what this side of me is, and I'm also not going to try and say that this is who he is when it's only speculation. But, with the music that he makes, this is who he is to me. And perhaps it is just me shaping him into what I can understand, while at the same time, maybe that is what and who he is: a chameleon who has learned to adapt to every situation that you come across on the road."

Decades after leaving home, Soda is still on the road. He lives in hotel rooms and occasionally friends put him up. He often travels alone or sometimes with another rambling musician. It's in his blood. He was born that way. "You are the way you come out" he often says. He finds sitting in one place for more than a few days at a time "boring" and "weird". He needs an almost constant change of scenery and when asked if he'll ever stop he says, "Stop what? Working? No, I'm a good Republican, I'll always work. I'm a good citizen. You can print that."

Soda works 18 hour days which include driving from town to town, playing shows, answering emails and sending music to fans. "I don't have CD's. No one uses them anymore. At shows I tell people to email me if they want music, then I'll send them a file." How does he afford to constantly move around? He jokes that he "probably owes people money...I have to keep moving" and he offers the following advice: "Keep your expenses low and don't be a !@#$ baby."

Soda has stories that will keep you captivated for hours, or at least until the whiskey is gone. When I interviewed him for this book we were sitting at Rick's Saloon in Knights Ferry. Soda was chain-smoking and sipping whiskey. He ended the interview, and I'll end this story, with the following Soda Fun-Facts, in his own words:

"Once I was playing at the Double-Down in Las Vegas with the Million Piece Band. John Fogerty was there and he came up to me, with his little kerchief on, and asked me to be in his band. I said "No". He asked me 3 times and I said "No, we don't know your songs". I don't like him very much; he's a Socialist. I also hate politicians; they're all thieves and liars. I liked Reagan though, because he had jelly bellies on his desk. My favorite color is chalkboard green, I'm allergic to cats, and I wish I was a Sagittarius. I once had a pet ferret, I don't remember his name. I'm working on getting the key to Waco, Texas. The S.W.A.T. team likes me there."

Just when I thought he was going to talk more about the S.W.A.T. team in Waco, the musician who doesn't like food or music quietly says: "It's good to play music for people - they need it. Without music you'd be totally unhappy" as he contentedly munched on his grilled cheese sandwich.

Soda - Live in Redmond, Oregon

Cheesy Garlic Mashed Potatoes

(serves 4-6)

5-6 cloves roasted garlic
  (see *"To roast garlic"* on page 29)
2 pounds potatoes
1 tablespoon salt
¼ cup butter
½ cup heavy cream
1 teaspoon salt
¼ teaspoon pepper

Wash, peel and quarter potatoes. Add to a large pot and cover with cold water. The water should cover the potatoes by at least 2 inches. Boil for 15-20 minutes. Check at 15 to see if they're done. They are done when you stick a fork or a knife into the potato and it slides right off.

While the potatoes are boiling, melt butter in a small pot. Add cream, roasted garlic, salt and pepper. Whisk until combined. Bring to a boil and immediately remove from heat. Cover to keep warm.

When potatoes are done, drain and put them back in the pot. Pour cream mixture over potatoes. Add cheese and beat with an electric mixer until creamy.

You can also use your standing mixer or a potato masher to mash the potatoes.

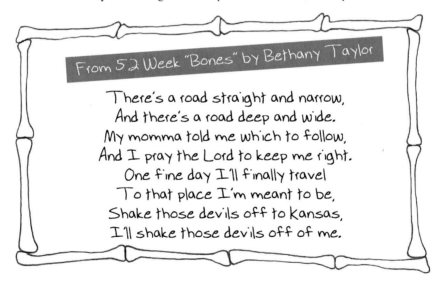

From 52 Week "Bones" by Bethany Taylor

There's a road straight and narrow,
And there's a road deep and wide.
My momma told me which to follow,
And I pray the Lord to keep me right.
One fine day I'll finally travel
To that place I'm meant to be,
Shake those devils off to Kansas,
I'll shake those devils off of me.

To read more about the 52-Week Club see pages 87-88

Side Dishes

Spicy Corn Mashed Potatoes

(serves 4-6)

2 pounds Yukon gold potatoes (peeling is optional, I like the skins on)
1 tablespoon olive oil
½ large red bell pepper, diced
2 diced jalapenos*
2-3 cloves of garlic, minced
½ (15.25 ounce) can corn
¼ cup softened butter
½ cup sour cream
½ cup chopped fresh cilantro
'Taco Seasoning' (recipe below)

*If you'd prefer something not-so-spicy, use one jalapeno.

Wash and quarter potatoes. Add to a large pot and cover with cold water. The water should cover the potatoes by at least 2 inches. Boil for 15-20 minutes. Check at 15 to see if they're done. They are done when you stick a fork or a knife into the potato and it slides right off.

While potatoes are boiling, heat oil in a large skillet over medium heat. Add red peppers, jalapeno, garlic and corn. Cook and stir until soft, about 3-5 minutes.

When potatoes are done, drain and put them back in the pot. Add butter, sour cream, corn mixture, cilantro, taco seasoning and salt. Beat with an electric mixer until creamy.

You can also use your standing mixer or a potato masher to mash and mix the potatoes.

Taco Seasoning:
1 tablespoon minced dried onions (or onion powder)
1 tablespoon chili powder
½ teaspoon salt
1 teaspoon garlic powder
1 teaspoon paprika
1 teaspoon cumin
½ teaspoon cayenne pepper

For less heat add only 1/4 teaspoon (or none at all).

Add all ingredients to a small bowl and mix!

I like Elvis better. The Beatles were pretty good, but they're also British. Elvis is all-American and he sang some good, old stars and stripes Rock 'n' Roll. He also brought international attention to the Blues. It's sad about his later years. He maybe would have been better off going out James Dean style, but, even with the giant burns and the lycra, he still out-cooled The Beatles any given day.

- Gabriel Garbarino - Loma Rica, CA - When asked "Elvis or The Beatles?"

Baked Potato-ey Mashed Potatoes

(serves 4-6)

½ pound bacon, chopped small
4 green onions, chopped
2 pounds potatoes
¼ cup butter
1 teaspoon salt

½ teaspoon pepper
½ cup sour cream
1 cup shredded Cheddar cheese
chives, finely diced (optional)

Heat a large skillet over low-medium heat. Add chopped bacon and cook until brown. When they are almost done add the onions. Remove from heat to drain on a paper towel.

Set aside some cooked bacon and onion for garnish.

Wash, peel and quarter potatoes. Add to a large pot and cover with cold water. The water should cover the potatoes by at least 2 inches. Boil for 15-20 minutes. Check at 15 to see if they're done. They are done when you stick a fork or a knife into the potato and it slides right off.

In the meantime, melt butter in a small pot. Add salt and pepper. Remove from heat. Add sour cream and whisk until completely combined.

When potatoes are done, drain well then put them back in the pot. Pour butter mixture over the potatoes and add the cheese and bacon/ onion mixture. Beat with an electric mixer until creamy.

You can also use your standing mixer or a potato masher to mash and mix the potatoes.

I went to visit an old woman, soon to die. I brought my guitar along and it made her smile. I had to introduce myself and she asked why we had never met. She said that she loved meeting musicians, and I think that made me want to cry. I couldn't agree more, I love meeting music lovers and musicians. I played her a few songs and talked for a little longer. Two weeks later I went to the funeral for Elda Dodds and wept. She was a Mother, Grandmother and a Great Grandmother who loved music - my Grand-mom. That was the best concert I have ever had.

I hate lemon bars, but she made them all the time when I was a kid. If I had liked them as much as she did, I might be a better person. I always wished that she had a secret hatred of lemon bars as well.

- John Dodds - Tater Famine - Santa Cruz, CA

"And Juan Makes Three"
by Kona Morris, Denver, CO

Ristorante Giannino's. Harvard Square. Set back in the glorious courtyard of the four-diamond Charles Hotel. The off-street location especially ideal for the frequent business of famous persona. No sidewalk passerby's or paparazzi to worry about. Also intended for the illustrious patronage, a wait staff manager adamant on forcing her employees to pretend like they don't even notice (other than the hand over foot slave servitude) when they're waiting on someone who carries a buzz. No chatting, no questions, and absolutely NO AUTOGRAPHS. Ever.

Of course, it's understandable why. Brenda (bitch manager) did have a point that it's only because of the no hassle service the eminent guests receive with their gourmet Milanese cuisine that they keep coming back for more and spreading the word within their highly acclaimed circles. Perfectly sensible, perfectly respectable. Right.

I never had a problem with it. Rather, I actually enjoyed the practice of speaking with the rich and famous as if they were no more special than any of my other "guests" (as Brenda forced us to call the customers). The only problem with this protocol, being the undying love and adorable fanaticism of a young bus boy named Juan.

He was a thin, baby-faced teenager from Brazil whose mother, Fatima, worked in the kitchen. Juan had an explosive infatuation with all things U2. Everyday sporting his black baseball hat with the oversized picture of Bono's face in mid-sing, wearing the spacey Star Trekian shades that seem to have been glued to his face for the last four decades.

And so (as you may have expected) one bright Sunday morning, who should stroll into Giannino's for an early afternoon brunch, but Bono, his wife, and a small entourage of important U2nian faces.

Bono and his wife were the nicest couple ever. He didn't want tomatoes on his Frittata del Giorno and one of his legs was noticeably longer than the other (made apparent by the different size heels of his platform sandals). She didn't wear any make-up and helped to bus the table after each course. He ate with his shades on. They were casual, friendly, and as sharp as the cheddar they grew up on. Completely unpretentious and engaging and promptly caused me to stop any and all shit talking about U2 I might have been inclined to indulge in considering I hadn't listened to anything they'd put out since Achtung Baby about eight years before.

Anyway, Juan wasn't there that day—the cruel plight of humanity—but every one of us knew simultaneously that someone had to call him. Hell or high water. As a matter of fact, about two seconds after Bono and company walked in, were seated and brought specials and menus and fizzing glasses of Pellegrino, all on-duty wait staff and busers met together in an empty side room.

Nearly in unison, "Oh my god! We've got to call Juan!"

Manager bitch knew right away what was happening. An instant later she found us. "If any of you call Juan, that will be your job. I mean it." Evil serious eyes scanning all of our faces until satisfied with her imposing threat. Exit Brenda.

"To hell with her, we've got to." We were all in agreement. Quickly deciding that there was no question about it, he had to be called. We made a pact that when confronted we would each say we did it. Like in a scene from some heart-tugging high school drama where a bunch of students join forces to overcome the corrupt fascist authority. There was absolutely no way she could fire all of us. She would be forced to swallow her own ugly foot.

So we did the deed and less than five minutes later Juan shows up. Bouncing with joy. Complete with his hallmark Bono hat, Bono t-shirt, rolled-up Bono poster, and ridiculously large camera hanging from around his neck. I'd never seen anyone gleaming with more excitement in my entire life.

But Brenda saw him coming. She met him in the doorway with a broiling glare and grinding teeth. Smoke escaping through reddening ears. "Go away Juan." Through the tightness of her clenched jaw, "Go away right now or YOU ARE FIRED."

His face filled with terror. Mouth dropped. Eyes frantically searching the dining room for just one tiny glimpse of his long time hero. "Go away *NOW* Juan," she repeated.

With panic and agony he turned himself around like a kicked puppy, continuously looking back over his shoulder for any possible sign of pity. But there was none. Not from Brenda. Rejected, he had no choice but to retreat. Forcing his deflated cheer to walk back across the vast courtyard. All of our hearts sank.

After a long and leisurely brunch, the Bono party finally finished. They playfully bickered for a moment over who was going to pay the bill and then, after one of the managerial men won the battle and an excessively generous tip was left for yours truly, they headed for the door. Myself, Brenda, and several other starry-eyed wait staff casually walked them out of the restaurant and across the outdoor patio. They turned around to wave one last goodbye and six of us stood there smiling, waving, happy family back at them.

We all watched as they made their way across the fifty or so yards of exquisite flowerbeds and exorbitant roman pillars of the courtyard. And then, just as they were almost to the end, only ten or so yards to go, out from behind a large well-pruned bush, pops our beloved little Juan. We could hear Brenda boiling under her skin. Mumbling curses and threats under hot held breath. Every one of us stunned by his audacity.

But, after leaping out, Juan does nothing. He stands in utter shock of his own impulsiveness. Staring. Wide-eyed frightened fawn.

Then suddenly, aggressively, Bono steps forward and tears the camera out of Juan's trembling hands. And he looks pissed. I imagine Daddy Warbucks violently hurling the camera of his rookie reporter into a cold marble stairwell. I am so appalled by Bono's hostile behavior. We all are. Poor Juan. Out a job and a hero the same day.

Bono holds the camera high over his head and looks as if he's two seconds away from throwing it onto the ground. But instead, he pulls the neck hole of his shirt open with his other hand, and, much to all of our surprise (especially Juan's), he shoves the camera down his shirt and begins snapping away. He takes a couple more shots of his naked chest and then throws an arm around Juan to bring him in for a picture of them together. Bono takes it at arms length. He takes all of them. His wife joins in on the other side of elated Juan. Speechless elated Juan. They do a series of pictures with Juan in the middle, including one with both of them kissing his cheeks. Then they all shake his hand. Hugs and signatures and witnessing heaven on earth for this little bus boy angel.

Brenda lets out a deep and constipated sigh followed by a few more breathy grumbles before she turns herself around to go back inside. After a few more minutes of jovial attention, the celebrity bows his goodbye and continues on his way. Juan looks up at all of us watching him, his face white and exuding shock, and then, he leaps off of the ground. Entire body. Both feet. Smiles with an oversized open mouth and pounds thumb-up fists into the air in sailing victory. Long live U2. Long live the sunglasses.

"And Juan Makes Three" reprinted from Monkey Puzzle Volume 6, published by Monkey Puzzle Press (2009) and copyright (2009) Kona Morris.

Pasta & Pizza

Creamy Basil Chicken Pasta – 133

Lamb & Black Olive Pasta – 134

Pappardelle with Sausage & Mushrooms – 134

Creamy Orecchiette with Spicy Sausage – 136

Mushroomy Meatballs & Angel Hair
with Creamy Shallot Sauce – 137

Garden Veggie Pasta – 138

Pesto Pasta with Artichokes & Olives – 138

Sausage & Three-Cheese Manicotti – 139

Poor Man's Alfredo – 140

Chicken Alfredo Orzo – 141

Orzo with Chorizo & Manchego Cheese – 142

Nacho Mama's Mac 'n' Cheese – 143

Mexi-Mac 'n' Cheese – 144

Pizza Dough – 146

Herbed Pizza Dough – 146

Red Pizza Sauce – 147

White Pizza Sauce – 147

Lamb & Goat Cheese Pizza – 148

Sausage & Portabella Pizza – 149

Chicken Pesto Pizza – 151

Buffalo Chicken Pizza – 152

Buffalo Shrimp Pizza – 153

Spinach and Feta Pizza – 154

Veggie Pesto Pizza – 155

Lamb & Black Olive Pasta - Page 134

Creamy Orecchiette with Spicy Sausage - Page 136

Creamy Basil Chicken Pasta - Page 133

Chicken Pesto Pizza - Page 151

Buffalo Chicken Pizza - Page 152

Veggie Pesto Pizza - Page 155

Creamy Basil Chicken Pasta

(serves 6)

1 pound champanelle noodles*
1 pound (about 2 large) boneless, skinless chicken breasts, cubed
½ cup breadcrumbs
¼ cup olive oil
6-8 cloves garlic, minced
2 cups chicken broth
1 ½ cups heavy cream
1 teaspoon salt
½ teaspoon pepper
2 cups finely shredded Fontina cheese
1 cup chopped fresh basil

*If you can't find champanelle, use gemelli or fusilli (corkscrew) noodles.

Boil pasta according to package directions. Drain (do not rinse!) and put back into pot. Add about 1 tablespoon of olive oil, stir and cover to keep warm.

While the pasta is boiling, chop chicken and place in a zip top storage bag. Add breadcrumbs and shake. Use your hands to press crumbs into chicken until completely coated and there are no more loose crumbs.

Heat ¼ cup of oil over medium heat in a large skillet. Add chicken and toss occasionally until all sides are nicely browned. About 7 minutes into cooking the chicken, add garlic and toss. Try to toss the chicken instead of 'stirring'. This will help the breadcrumbs to stay attached to the chicken. Cook for about 3 more minutes. Check largest piece to make sure it's done, and remove chicken from pan.

If there is a lot of oil left in the pan, pour most of it out, leaving about 1 tablespoon. Add broth, cream, salt and pepper. Bring to a boil and add cheese. Bring back to a boil and cook, whisking occasionally, for 5 minutes. Add basil and boil, whisking occasionally, for another 5 minutes.

Pour over pasta and stir until combined. Garnish with basil.

The Blues are swamp water and calluses - 200 years of lashes and bowed back, bloody palms with cotton thistles. Deals with the devil, bad whiskey, shadowy women in the live oak and Spanish moss. Good dogs, bad trucks, brutal foreman, best friends and murder.

They are American. 100%.

- Gabriel Garbarino - Loma Rica, CA

Lamb & Black Olive Pasta
(serves 2-4)

½ pound orecchiette* pasta
½ pound ground lamb
¼ teaspoon salt
¼ teaspoon pepper
3-4 cloves garlic, minced
¼ cup heavy cream

1 cup sliced large black olives
2 cups roughly chopped baby spinach
¼ teaspoon salt
¼ teaspoon pepper
2-3 ounces (¼ - ½ cup) crumbled Feta cheese

Boil orecchiette according to package directions.

While pasta is boiling, heat a medium skillet heat over low-medium heat. Add lamb, salt and pepper. After about 4 or 5 minutes add the minced garlic. Cook and stir until all of the pink in the lamb is gone - about 3 or 4 more minutes. Add cream, bring to a boil and cook for 3 minutes. Remove skillet from heat (keep the meat in the pan).

When pasta is done, drain and add back to pot. Immediately add the meat mixture, olives, spinach, salt and pepper. Toss constantly until spinach is wilted. Add Feta and stir until combined. Serve hot.

*Orecchiette is sometimes hard to find. If you can't find it, I recommend using gemelli, fusilli or large shells.

Pappardelle with Sausage & Mushrooms
(serves 4)

8 ounces pappardelle (or fettuccini) noodles
2 tablespoons olive oil
1 pound ground Italian sausage (links or bulk)
8 ounces cremini (or button) mushrooms, chopped

4-6 cloves garlic, minced
½ cup chopped fresh basil
1 teaspoon salt
1 teaspoon pepper

Boil pappardelle according to package directions. Drain and drizzle with olive oil. Put back into the pot (remove pot from heat) cover it and let it be.

While the pasta is boiling, heat the oil in a large skillet. If you're using sausage links, peel the skins off before cooking. Add sausage and break it up into little pieces with a wooden spoon or spatula. When the sausage is just starting to brown, after about 5 minutes or so, add mushrooms. Cook until mushrooms are moist and browned, about 2-3 minutes. Add garlic, basil, salt and pepper. Cook for another few minutes until sausage is cooked through. When done, add the cooked noodles to the sausage and mushroom mixture. If the skillet isn't large enough, add the sausage/mushroom mixture to the noodles. Toss until combined and serve immediately.

Pasta & Pizza

"Somethin' Special"

From 52 Week "Butter" by Amber Cross - Jenner, CA

(Copyright © 2009)

Clothes stained blue, clothes stained blue
If you raked berries you'd be too
Down to the lake two by two
Raked all day and we're all stained blue
In the fields at dawn just me and you
Close my eyes and I still see blue

Do you see that red bird through the kitchen window
He's something special, he's called a cardinal
He comes in the winter to the red leaf maple
Don't let go of something so special

Big yellow Rider next to my papa
These 18 wheels can't go no faster
Sweet rotten smell of the ripe blueberries
I ride beside him, he thinks I'm special

Down to Helen's Restaurant for a piece of pie
No one makes 'em better, Helen's home made pies
They got cherry, strawberry, chocolate cream and apple
But I want rhubarb because it's special

Going deep sea fishing, what we wants mackerel
Little orange life jacket and a box of tackle
My mom's fish chowder with saltine crackers
Big pad of butter makes it taste better

Little green Opal, now we're leaving Sebago
It's Halloween morning, wave Sherry goodbye
There's a black and white kitten and he wants my ice cream
I'll let him have it, I want rhubarb pie

Clothes stained blue, clothes stained blue
If you raked berries you'd be too
Down to the lake two by two
Raked all day and we're all stained blue
Carry my buckets two by two
Rake my berries faster than you

To read more about the 52-Week Club see pages 87-88

Creamy Orecchiette
with Spicy Sausage
(serves 4-6)

1 pound orecchiette pasta (or large shells)
1 pound ground Hot Italian sausage
3 medium vine-ripe tomatoes, chopped (save seeds and juices!)
1 teaspoon salt
½ teaspoon pepper
1 teaspoon garlic powder*
½ cup heavy cream
1 tablespoon flour
¼ cup grated Parmesan cheese

This is probably my favorite pasta dish.

Cook orecchiette according to package directions. Drain, put back in the pot, drizzle with olive oil and stir.

While pasta is cooking, heat a large pot over medium heat for about 1 minute. If you are using sausage links, peel skins off before cooking. Add sausage and use wooden spoon or spatula to break it up into pieces. Cook for about 7 minutes. Add tomatoes, salt, pepper and garlic powder. Cook for another 3-4 minutes or until sausage is cooked through. Do not drain excess juices. Use a potato masher to crush the tomatoes a bit. Whisk cream and flour together in a small bowl until smooth. Add to the sausage and tomato mixture and whisk. Bring to a boil and cook, stirring frequently, for about 3 minutes until thick and creamy. Add cheese and cook until it's melted.

When orecchiette is done, drain and add to sausage mixture. Stir until completely combined and serve hot.

*This recipe was something I just threw together one day, based on what I had in my kitchen. That said, at the time I made this I didn't have any fresh garlic or I would have used it. If you'd prefer, use 2-3 cloves of minced, fresh garlic instead of powder.

Also, if you have any fresh herbs, like basil or Italian parsley, chop some up and toss it in near the end for extra flavor.

Mushroomy Meatballs & Angel Hair
with Creamy Shallot Sauce
(makes about 15 1½ inch meatballs)

2 teaspoons olive oil
½ large shallot, diced
1 ounce thin-sliced pancetta, diced
2-3 cloves garlic, minced
½ medium Portabella mushroom, diced
2 large cremini mushrooms, diced*
½ pound lean ground beef
1 egg, beaten
¼ cup seasoned breadcrumbs
¼ cup chopped flat-leaf (Italian) parsley
2 tablespoons heavy cream
¼ cup grated Parmesan cheese

½ pound (8 ounces) angel hair pasta
1 cup chicken broth
1 cup heavy cream
3 tablespoons flour
½ teaspoon salt
¼ teaspoon pepper
½ teaspoon paprika
¼ cup butter
1 large shallot, diced
2 teaspoons lemon juice
¼ cup chopped flat-leaf (Italian) parsley

Preheat oven to 350 degrees.

Heat oil in a large skillet over low-medium heat. Add shallots, pancetta, garlic and mushrooms. Cook and stir for 2 minutes. Remove from heat and put in a large bowl. Once mixture is cool to the touch, add beef, egg, breadcrumbs, parsley, cream and cheese. Use your hands to mix well. Spray a cookie sheet with cooking spray. Form the meat mixture into 1½ inch balls and place them on the cookie sheet. Bake for 20 minutes, remove and drain on paper towels.

In a large pot, cook the angel hair according to the package directions. When done, drain pasta and put back into the pot. Drizzle with a little olive oil and toss until all noodles are well coated. Cover and set aside.

Meanwhile in a small bowl, whisk broth, cream, flour, salt, pepper and paprika. Set aside.

In a medium skillet melt the butter over low-medium heat and add diced shallot. Cook and stir for 2 minutes. Add the broth/flour mixture and bring to a boil. Add lemon juice. Cook, whisking often, for about 4-6 minutes or until sauce thickens. Remove from heat and stir in parsley. Pour the sauce over the pasta and toss until combined. Cover and allow the sauce to soak into the noodles for about 5 minutes. Serve with meatballs.

*If you can't find cremini mushrooms, you can use one whole Portabella. If you can't find a Portabella, move to a city with better stores. You can also use an 8oz package of button mushrooms - dice 'em up good...

Garden Veggie Pasta

(serves 4-6)

½ pound tri-color pasta
1 tablespoon olive oil
1 medium zucchini, chopped
1 medium red bell pepper, sliced thin and
  cut into ½ inch strips
4 green onions, chopped

2 vine-ripe tomatoes, diced
2-4 cloves garlic, minced
¼ cup + 2 tablespoons chopped fresh basil
½ - 1 teaspoon salt*
¼ teaspoon pepper

Cook pasta according to package directions. Remove from heat, drain and put back into pot. Drizzle with 1 tablespoon of olive oil, stir and cover.

I like this with 1 teaspoon of salt - but start with 1/2 and add more to taste.

While pasta is boiling, heat oil over medium heat in a large skillet. Add zucchini, red pepper and onion. Cook, tossing/stirring occasionally, until zucchini softens - about 4-5 minutes. Add tomatoes and garlic. Cook and stir about 1 minute. Add basil, salt and pepper. Toss and remove from heat. Pour veggie mixture over cooked pasta, toss and serve hot.

Garnish with fresh basil, shredded Parmesan or crumbled Feta.

As an after-thought, I really wanted to add mushrooms to both of these recipes. You should try it!

Pesto Pasta with Artichokes & Olives

(serves 4)

½ pound whole wheat rotini pasta*
'Spinach Pesto' (page 50) - all of it!
2 (6 ounce) jars marinated artichoke hearts,
  drained and chopped
1 (4.25 ounce) can diced black olives
¼ cup grated Parmesan cheese

This recipe is quick, easy, and delicious!

Make 'Spinach Pesto' according to directions on page 50. Set aside.

Boil pasta according to package directions. Remove from heat, drain and pour back into pot. Add 'Spinach Pesto' and toss until pasta is well-coated. Add artichoke hearts, olives, salt and pepper.

If you don't like whole wheat pasta but want to eat healthier, this is the perfect recipe. The pesto totally masks the whole wheat flavor. You won't even notice!

Toss until combined. Serve hot!

Sausage & Three-Cheese Manicotti

(serves 4-6)

10 manicotti shells

Filling:
1 pound ground Mild Italian sausage
1 teaspoon garlic powder
1 teaspoon dried basil
1 teaspoon dried oregano
½ cup Ricotta cheese
½ cup shredded Mozzarella cheese
½ cup shredded Fontina cheese*
1 egg, beaten

Sauce:
2 tablespoons olive oil
3-4 cloves garlic, minced
1 (28 ounce) can crushed tomatoes
¼ teaspoon salt
½ cup chopped fresh basil

Top with:
¼ to ½ cup shredded Fontina cheese
¼ to ½ cup shredded Mozzarella cheese

*If, for some reason, you can't find Fontina, a decent substitute would be Provolone, Gouda, or worst case scenario, Monterey Jack.

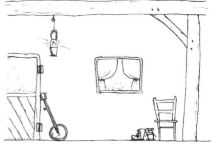

Preheat oven to 350 degrees.

Boil the manicotti shells for 7 minutes (don't salt the water). Use tongs to carefully remove from water. Drain in a colander and place in an even layer on a cutting board or tin foil. Allow shells to cool completely.

Heat a large skillet over medium heat. Add the sausage and break up into small pieces. After 5 minutes add garlic powder, basil and oregano. Cook until sausage is done - about 10 more minutes. Remove from heat, drain briefly and allow mixture to cool in a bowl. Add Ricotta, Mozzarella and Fontina. Mix well and set aside.

To make the sauce: Heat olive oil in a large pot over medium heat. Open the can of tomatoes and have it ready. Add garlic to pot. Cook and stir for 20-30 seconds and add tomatoes. Bring to a boil then turn heat to low. Simmer for 15-30 minutes (depending on how much time you have before serving!) Add cheese and stir until melted. Add basil, stir and remove from heat.

Spread about ¼ of the sauce into the bottom of an 9x13 baking dish. Divide the sausage and cheese mixture evenly and stuff into shells. Place shells in dish and top with the rest of the sauce. Top shells with remaining cheese and bake for 20 minutes.

If you don't want to make the sauce yourself, use 2-3 cups of marinara sauce from a jar.

Poor Man's Alfredo

(serves 6)

Always on a budget and with more than one mouth to feed, I invented this Alfredo using budget friendly ingredients like evaporated milk and grated Parmesan. Call me crazy, but it works. My husband, Eddie, still swears it is the best Fettuccini Alfredo to ever hit his lips. So, see for yourself. Mangiare, piace e prendere grasso!

½ cup (1 stick) butter
1 clove garlic, minced
1 pint of half and half
1 (12 ounce) can evaporated milk
1 pound fettuccini
1 (8 ounce) container Parmesan cheese

Melt butter in medium saucepan. Add minced garlic and let marry together for a few minutes. Add your half and half and evaporated milk. Cook at a medium heat until it heats through and you reach a soft simmer. (You don't want to let this boil.) Cook fettuccini according to package directions. Drain and return to pot. Add sauce to noodles and set burner to a low heat. Add half the cheese and stir occasionally until cheese is melted. Add the rest of the cheese and stir occasionally on low heat until all the cheese is melted and you have reached your desired consistency. You will want the consistency to be a little runny, because as the pasta sits, it will continue to thicken up.

If you place sliced grilled chicken on top, it is amazing:

olive oil drizzled over 4 chicken breasts
4 cloves of garlic, minced
salt and pepper (a dash to each breast)
Parmesan cheese lightly shaken over each breast
1 fresh squeezed lemon

Let sit for at least an hour, flipping over in marinade once. It can marinate up to 24 hours if you like - the longer the better. Grill on the BBQ, or if you are short on time, broil on high, 10 minutes per side.

Recipe and artwork
courtesy of Anna Cecil
Fort Benning, GA

Chicken Alfredo Orzo

(serves 2-4)

½ pound orzo pasta
2 tablespoons olive oil
2 pounds boneless, skinless chicken breast,
   chopped into bite-size pieces
½ teaspoon salt
½ teaspoon pepper

3 ounces prosciutto, chopped
1 medium shallot, finely diced
3-4 cloves garlic, minced
¾ cup heavy cream
¼ cup + 2 tablespoons grated Parmesan
   cheese

Cook orzo according to package directions. Drain and set aside.

For added color and flavor, add fresh chopped basil!

While orzo is cooking, heat olive oil in a large skillet over medium heat. Add chicken and season with salt and pepper. Cook and stir for about 4-5 minutes. Add prosciutto, shallots and garlic. Cook until chicken is done, about 4-5 more minutes. When done, use a slotted spoon to remove chicken. Set aside.

Add cream to the same skillet used for the chicken. When cream begins to boil, add the cheese. Cook and stir until thick and creamy, about 1-3 minutes. Pour cream over cooked orzo and add chicken mixture. Mix well and serve immediately.

Mother Earth continues to birth an abundance of beauty while nurturing her life with food crop, as well as humankind. With that being said, I would like to mention one of the many unsung heroes who has nurtured my survival through music. His name is Alex Safi, and he is my father.

He has performed with some of the best musicians in Detroit, including the Funk Brothers and Mitch Ryder. He played conga drums for Jackie DeShannon while opening up for Neil Diamond at Michigan's famous Pine Knob Amphitheatre. He also did a show with Edwin Starr and played with flamenco guitarist Juan Serrano.

His talents were discovered at age 3 when he was taught to play the derbucki, a Middle Eastern drum. At age 9, he began playing accordion and writing music. Over the years he developed his skills in the Joseph Family Band. He focused on singing and teaching himself to play the piano. In his early 20's he played in several rock bands including "Poor Man's Pride", "One Way Taxi", and "My Cousin and I". In the 80's he broke away as a solo artist, and continues performing live today. Alex is also an accredited actor who continues to follow his dream of touching people's hearts through his art.

I look forward to the day my dad is recognized by audiences coast to coast. Meanwhile, he has made his breakthrough in the mainstream of my heart.

- Maria Safi - Detroit, MI

Orzo with Chorizo & Manchego Cheese

(serves 2-4)

½ pound orzo pasta
1 tablespoon olive oil
½ pound ground pork (or beef) chorizo
1 cup quartered cherry tomatoes
½ cup finely shredded Manchego* cheese
¼ cup finely chopped flat-leaf (Italian) parsley
¼ teaspoon salt

*Manchego is like the Spanish version of Parmesan. Use Parmesan to substitute.

P.S. Chorizo is kinda spicy!

Cook orzo according to package directions. Drain and pour back into the pot. Drizzle with 1 tablespoon of olive oil, toss and cover.

In a medium skillet cook chorizo over low-medium heat, breaking it up with a wooden spoon as it cooks. When done - about 10-15 minutes** - drain in a colander and add to the orzo. Add tomatoes, cheese, parsley and salt. Gently toss and serve immediately.

**Chorizo should be cooked slowly on low heat. Once it's cooked it'll burn fast, so pay attention!

by Jamin Marshall

JRM

Pasta & Pizza

Nacho Mama's Mac 'n' Cheese

(serves 6-8)

1 pound small pasta shells
1 pound lean ground beef
1 (1.25 ounce) packet taco seasoning
  (or use mine on page 125*)
½ cup butter
3 tablespoons flour
1 (12 ounce) can evaporated milk
  (substitute with cream or milk)
1 (15.5 ounce) Salsa Con Queso
  (nacho cheese sauce/dip)
8 ounces shredded Monterey Jack cheese
0-2 (4 ounce) cans diced jalapenos**
  (depending on how spicy you prefer)
1 teaspoon salt
1 teaspoon pepper
¾ cup (gently) crushed tortilla chips

*If you use my taco seasoning recipe, add the seasoning as the beef browns and do not add water! Drain off any excess juices when it's done.

Preheat oven to 350 degrees. Lightly butter a 9x13 baking dish and set aside.

Bring a large pot of salted water to a boil. Add noodles and cook until just barely tender, about 10 minutes. (The pasta will cook a bit more as it bakes. For this reason, you want to just barely undercook the pasta, or else once baked, it will be too mushy.) Drain well, rinse, drain again and pour into buttered baking dish. Add a little butter and stir every once in a while so the noodles don't stick together.

While pasta boils, cook ground beef according to directions on the taco seasoning packet. Set aside.

In a medium pot add butter. Heat over low-medium heat until butter melts and begins to foam. Add flour and whisk, almost constantly, for 30 seconds. Add evaporated milk and whisk until combined. When mixture begins to boil, turn heat to low and add the Salsa Con Queso and Monterey Jack. Stir until melted. Add salt and pepper, mix well and pour over pasta. Add beef and jalapenos and mix well. Sprinkle crushed tortilla chips on top. Pat the crackers into the cheese a bit and bake for 20 minutes or until hot and bubbly. Serve hot.

**If you'd prefer, use fresh jalapenos. You can roast 'em first or simply dice 'em up and toss 'em in!

Mexi-Mac 'n' Cheese

(serves 6-8)

1 pound small pasta shells
½ cup crushed corn chips
2 tablespoons butter, melted
1 pound boneless, skinless chicken breast, cooked and shredded
2 (7 ounce) cans mild diced green chilies
2-3 jalapenos, finely diced (optional, depending on how spicy you want it)
½ cup chopped cilantro
½ cup butter
3 tablespoons flour   ...I didn't win...
4 cups milk
8 ounces (about 2 cups) shredded Cheddar cheese
12 ounces (about 4 cups*) shredded Pepper Jack cheese
1 ¼ teaspoons salt
1 teaspoon pepper   ...but I should have!

Preheat oven to 350 degrees. Lightly butter a 9x13 casserole dish and set aside.

In a large pot bring salted water to a boil. Add noodles and cook until just barely tender, about 10 minutes. (The pasta will cook a bit more as it bakes. For this reason, you want to just barely undercook the pasta, or else once baked, it will be too mushy.) Drain well, rinse, drain again and pour into a very large bowl. Add a little butter and stir every once in a while so noodles don't stick together.

Mix crushed corn chips with 2 tablespoons of melted butter and set aside.

Add (cooked and shredded) chicken, chilies, jalapenos and cilantro to the bowl with the noodles. Mix and set aside.

In a medium pot add butter. Heat over low-medium heat until melted. Add flour and whisk almost constantly for about 30 seconds. Add milk and whisk until combined. Bring to a boil and add cheese. Stir until melted and immediately remove from heat. Add salt and pepper and stir. Pour cheese mixture over the chicken/pasta mixture. Mix well and pour into buttered casserole dish.

Cover the top with crushed corn chips and lightly pat into the pasta.

Bake for 30 minutes or until bubbly. Serve hot.

*I know it's a lot of cheese, but this isn't supposed to be good for you, it's supposed to be delicious...

Felix the cat. Take half now, half later. I think there were about twelve of us squashed in the room together. The walls were splattered with paint and graffiti, a couple of box spring-less beds were planted catty-corner from one another, and a clay red, round mound of a chair was shoved up against the corner farthest from the door. This is the spot where I chose to start the night. As the night progressed into morning, the seat became less of a purposeful resting area and more of a safe-haven; and a kind of cell. I was like a beached whale who chose to shimmy out of the sea but could not leave once on shore. Felix kicked in.

It was silly goofy fun at first; the trails from the pager were especially swell. I was pretty shy and couldn't help but be a thousand times more so feeling this way. I sucked it up, felt uncomfortable, and smiled like my life depended on it. "Riders On The Storm—it's like us." Yeah, I get it: The Doors are trippy. Jim Morrison is a teenage poet, mad, psychedelic scientist helping take us through this dangerous rain storm. Storms are frightening and exciting and dark and shocking and all these obvious metaphors, but they are beautiful, and that is the point. We're riders on the storm. Play it again. And then again. And then again. And then they played that song again. "Riders On The Storm, like us...you know??" I get it. I totally get it. How could I not get it? How obvious, how shallow. Wait a second....The Doors? I love The Doors right? And then I got it, and I mean I really, really got it. I knew at that moment what music meant to me. I knew that it meant something different to me than anyone else in that cool, sticky room. Heck, maybe more than anyone I knew in any fashion at that strange point in my little life. Because I discovered that night what I cannot stand about music.

Music is a sacred trust made between the maker and the taker. I will buy every syllable you are singing, every noise that you are ringing, if you promise to me that you will be honest to me - but the second I question your motives, the second you weigh down a song with politics of the age or the popular teenage fads or your strategically placed messages, I will stop listening. Don't tell me how to feel, tell me how *you* feel, and I will feel however I choose. "Riders On The Storm" seemed to me to be nothing more than a commercial jingle, selling a canned version of an interesting, vital and valid culture. It was a song rich kids would play to upset their parents, but really it was barely more challenging and difficult than your run-of-the-mill Sonny and Cher tune. Thanks Lizard King, but no thanks. "Riders On The Storm" continues to sort of haunt me, as some bizarre moment in time when I threw out the trivial and opened my ear to the subtle.

It continued to play for what seemed like hours anyway. Eventually the plant on the window sill went from black to orange to green, the storm was over and it was time to leave. So I stumbled off the dune and made my strange way out of the house. On the way back to my room I stopped at McDonald's for cheeseburgers, but I don't think I even ate anything. I got home sometime late in the morning and dove into my bunk, hit play on the stereo and turned up some Frank Black. It was like returning to sea.

- David Burtch - Turlock, CA

Pizza Dough

(makes 1 large or 4 small pizzas)

1 cup warm water (110 degrees)	1 tablespoon salt
1 teaspoon sugar	2 tablespoons extra-virgin olive oil
2 ¼ teaspoons active dry yeast	3 cups bread flour (all-purpose will also
(or one 1.25 ounce packet)	work, but bread flour is best)

Mix sugar and warm water in the bowl of your standing mixer. Add yeast. Let sit for 5-10 minutes or until frothy.

Add salt, olive oil and flour. Attach your dough hook and start out on the lowest speed (so the flour doesn't go everywhere). Increase the speed one notch and let it ride until dough forms into a ball. Don't mess with it, just walk away. If you have a good mixer, it will grab every bit of dough from the sides and bottom of the bowl. If the dough is too sticky you may have to add more flour.

While the dough is mixing, lightly oil a glass or metal bowl. When the dough is done, take if off of the hook, work it back into a smooth ball and put it into the bowl. Cover with a damp towel and put in a warm, dark place for an hour, or until doubled in size. Punch dough down and form back into a ball before rolling.

If you don't need to use the dough right away, it can sit for hours and be fine. It'll raise a little more, but that doesn't really matter.

> Dough experts might argue this, but no one has complained about my pizza dough yet...

Herbed Pizza Dough

Make the dough as instructed above except, after you add the flour, add 1 teaspoon dried, crushed rosemary, 1 teaspoon dried oregano and ½ teaspoon garlic powder.

> If you aren't feeling ambitious enough to make your own pizza dough, I highly encourage you to make a trip to Trader Joe's and buy theirs. The dough you buy at "normal" grocery stores is usually frozen and isn't even CLOSE to being what I'd call "good". Sometimes pizza parlors will sell you theirs, so call around and go the extra mile. Pizza is only as good as the dough it's made with!

Red Pizza Sauce

(makes a little over 1 cup, enough for two or three 14 inch pizzas)

2 tablespoons olive oil
3-6 cloves garlic, minced
1 (15 ounce) can tomato sauce
2 teaspoons chopped fresh thyme
2 teaspoons chopped fresh oregano

⅛ teaspoon salt
⅛ teaspoon pepper
¼ teaspoon onion powder
¼ teaspoon red pepper flakes*

In a medium pot, heat oil over low-medium heat. Add garlic and cook about 30 seconds, just until fragrant. You don't want the garlic to brown, which can happen fast. Add tomato sauce and whisk until combined. Add thyme, oregano, salt, pepper, onion powder and red pepper flakes. Bring to a boil, turn heat to low and simmer for 30 minutes, stirring occasionally. This is really, really good if you let it sit in the fridge overnight.

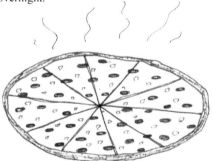

*The red pepper flakes give the sauce a bit of a kick. If you'd prefer a less spicy sauce, leave the flakes out.

White Pizza Sauce

(makes about 1 cup, enough for two or three 14 inch pizzas)

2 tablespoons olive oil
2-3 cloves garlic, minced
1 cup heavy cream
1 teaspoon dried oregano

½ teaspoon dried thyme
½ teaspoon garlic salt*
½ cup shredded Parmesan cheese

Heat olive oil in medium pot or non-stick skillet over low-medium heat. Add garlic, cook and stir for about 30 seconds. Add cream and whisk until oil and cream are completely combined, about 30 seconds. Add oregano, thyme and garlic salt. Whisk until combined. Add cheese and bring to a boil. (At this point the sauce should be pretty hot, so it won't take long to boil.) Turn heat to low and whisk frequently for 5 minutes. Don't allow sauce to boil over or stick to the bottom. Remove immediately from heat.

*If you don't have garlic salt, you can substitute with ¼ teaspoon each of salt and garlic powder.

Lamb & Goat Cheese Pizza

(serves 4-6)

1 recipe 'Pizza Dough' (page 146)
½ large roasted red bell pepper (for directions see 'Roasted Red Pepper Hummus' on page 35)
1 tablespoon olive oil
½ small onion, chopped (about ¼ cup)
3 cloves garlic, minced
1 (14 ounce) can chopped/diced tomatoes (garlic, oregano and basil flavored is nice)
1 tablespoon tomato paste
1 tablespoon butter

¼ teaspoon salt
½ pound ground lamb
3 tablespoons chopped fresh mint
¼ teaspoon garlic powder (or 1 clove fresh garlic, minced)
¼ teaspoon salt
¼ teaspoon pepper
½ medium red onion, thinly sliced (about ½ cup)
2 to 4 ounces crumbled Goat cheese
¼ cup shredded Parmesan cheese

Preheat oven to 400 degrees.

In a medium pot or large non-stick skillet heat oil over low-medium heat. Add onion and garlic. Cook and stir for 1-2 minutes. Add tomatoes, cook and stir until mixture begins to boil, about 2-3 minutes. Add tomato paste, butter and salt. Bring back to a boil, turn heat to low and simmer for 15-20 minutes. Remove from heat and allow sauce to cool. Add to the bowl of your food processor (or blender) and process until pureed.

Mix together lamb, mint, garlic powder, salt and pepper. Heat a medium skillet over medium heat. Add lamb mixture, cook and stir for about 5 minutes, breaking it up as you go. Add sliced red onion, cook and stir for another 4-5 minutes. Remove from heat and set aside.

To roll dough: Place on a lightly floured surface. Making sure that the thickness of the dough is even, roll into a 12-14 inch circle. Place on a pizza pan or large cookie sheet. (If you feel crazy, you can make it into a square.) I like to roll the edges of the dough in a bit to make the outer crust thicker and prettier. Use a fork to stab the dough all over its surface*. If you don't do this, the dough may balloon up in the oven.

Pre-bake the crust for 7 minutes. Remove and layer sauce, lamb/onion mixture, red pepper, goat cheese and Parmesan. Bake for 10-15 minutes, remove pizza from pan and place directly on oven rack for 5 more minutes. Let this cool for at least 5 minutes before you cut it.

*In the industry this is called "docking."

Pasta & Pizza

Sausage & Portabella Pizza

(serves 4-6)

1 recipe 'Pizza Dough' (page 146)
½ cup - 1 cup 'Red Pizza Sauce' (page 147)
½ pound ground sausage*
2 teaspoons olive oil
1 medium Portabella mushroom,
   roughly chopped**
2 cups shredded Mozzarella cheese
2 tablespoons shredded Parmesan cheese

Preheat oven to 400 degrees.

Look for flavored sausage, such as Sage and Fennel or Italian, at specialty stores.

I like to use Hot Italian sausage on mine.

If you are using sausage links, remove casings before cooking.

Heat medium skillet over medium heat. Add sausage and use a wooden spoon or spatula to break up into little pieces. Cook until done, about 10 minutes. Drain sausage in colander and set aside. Return skillet to stovetop (do not wipe clean). Add olive oil and heat for about 1 minute. Add mushrooms and cook just until they start to sweat, about 1-2 minutes. Remove from heat and put on paper towels to drain.

Roll dough according to instructions on page 148.

Pre-bake the crust for 7 minutes. Remove from oven and layer sauce, Mozzarella, sausage, mushrooms and top with Parmesan.

Bake for 10-15 minutes. Remove pizza from pan and place directly on oven rack for 5 more minutes.

Let this cool for at least 5-10 minutes before you cut it.

Feel free to use any kind of mushroom you prefer! Good ol' button mushrooms would work just fine.

I fell in love with music the first time I fell in love with a girl.

I can remember the smoky flicker of candles across a dimly lit room. Furnished with only a mattress on the floor, drying flowers hanging in every corner and posters upon posters of immortal groups like The Stones and Fleetwood Mac covering the walls. The room was somehow alive. It breathed.

While whimsy thoughts of love filled my head and the drowsiness of love filled my body, The Beatles *White Album* played from start to finish. A vast mosaic of sound, atmospheric and heavy, I let them take me on a journey that would forever change my views on music.

I seemed forever polarized from that moment on between two distinct groups: bands which sucked and bands which didn't. Somehow, in that evening, I realized what separated the two.

All the music I had heard before was but an echo of greatness, a mere reaching for, where this band so obviously succeeded in grasping. It forever changed me. Forever altered my journey. Forever cemented love on a transcendental plane. And while the relationship with the girl would eventually end, my love affair with music would only strengthen. I would go on to play guitar, grow my hair out, join a band and make a record.

I was hooked.

Story and artwork by Octavio Hernandez
Hot Pistol - Sacramento, CA

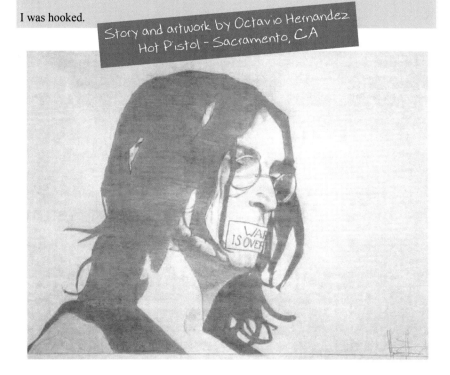

Chicken Pesto Pizza

(serves 4-6)

1 recipe 'Pizza Dough' (page 146)
1 recipe 'Spinach Pesto' (page 50)
½ pound (about 1 cup) chopped boneless, skinless chicken breasts
1 tablespoon olive oil

½ medium red onion, thinly sliced
1 (2.25 ounce) can sliced black olives
1 (4 ounce) container crumbled Feta cheese (about ½ cup)

Preheat oven to 400 degrees.

Heat a large skillet over medium heat. Add chicken and 2 tablespoons of the pesto. Toss until chicken is completely coated. Cook and stir until done, about 10 minutes. Remove chicken from skillet and set aside.

Keep the skillet on the heat and add olive oil and red onions. Cook and stir for about 1 minute, until onion begins to soften. Remove from heat and set aside.

Roll dough according to instructions on page 148.

Pre-bake the crust for 7 minutes. Layer pesto, chicken, red onions, olives and Feta. Bake for 10-15 minutes, remove pizza from pan and place directly on oven rack for 5 more minutes.

Let this cool for at least 5-10 minutes before you cut it.

From 52 Week "Mayor" by Bethany Taylor

Well, they found us in a bloody mess,
I swore that it was all self defense.
But they said "It don't matter! You
Messed with the wrong boy."
You see, it turns out the boy I messed...
It turns out the boy I messed with
Was the mayor's one and only son.
So, one more shot of whiskey please,
One more shot of whiskey please,
Before I die...before I die

To read more about the 52-Week Club see pages 87-88

Buffalo Chicken Pizza

(serves 4-6)

1 recipe 'Pizza Dough' (page 146)
1 stick butter
2-3 cloves garlic, minced
½ cup hot sauce
½ pound (about 1 cup) chopped boneless, skinless chicken breasts
1 tablespoon olive oil
½ medium red onion, thinly sliced (about ½ cup)
½ teaspoon salt
1 cup shredded Muenster cheese
1 (4 ounce) container crumbled Feta cheese (about ½ cup)

In a large pot melt butter over medium heat. Add garlic, cook and stir for about 30 seconds. Add hot sauce and whisk until combined. Add chicken, cook and stir until done, about 10 minutes. Remove from heat and allow chicken to soak in the sauce for about an hour. If you are making this ahead of time, put chicken and sauce into a zip top bag and keep refrigerated until you're ready to serve. (This can be done the day before serving.)

Preheat oven to 400 degrees.

Heat oil in a medium skillet over medium heat. Add red onions and salt. Cook and stir until soft, about 1-2 minutes. Remove from heat and set aside.

Roll dough according to instructions on page 148.

Pre-bake the crust for 7 minutes. Layer Muenster, chicken (hot sauce juices and all), red onions and Feta. Bake for 10-15 minutes. Remove pizza from pan and place directly on oven rack for 5 more minutes.

(It's a buffalo doing the chicken dance on a pizza!)

Buffalo Shrimp Pizza

(serves 4-6)

1 recipe 'Pizza Dough' (page 146)
¼ cup butter
3 cloves garlic, minced
¼ cup hot sauce
½ pound jumbo shrimp, peeled and
  de-veined*

½ large vine-ripe tomato, diced
1 cup shredded Fontina or Gouda cheese
1 (4 ounce) container crumbled Feta
  cheese (about ½ cup)

Preheat oven to 400 degrees.

*You can buy 'em this way. Don't forget to cut the tails off!

In a large skillet melt butter over medium heat. Add garlic, cook and stir for about 30 seconds. Add hot sauce and whisk until combined. Add shrimp. Cook and stir until shrimp is pink all over - about 2 minutes. Remove the skillet from heat and let sit, stirring occasionally, while you prepare the rest of the pizza.

Roll dough according to instructions on page 148.

Pre-bake crust for 7 minutes. Layer shrimp, tomatoes, Fontina and Feta. Bake for 10-15 minutes. Remove pizza from pan and place directly on oven rack for 5 more minutes.

Let this cool for at least 5-10 minutes before you cut it.

From 52 Week "Southern Girls" Chris Doud

Just one morning in New York town,
Eat in' New York bagels with a New York frown.
Too many people with too many dreams,
Lincoln Tunnel take me outta here, I gotta leave.
Just one night in Baton Rouge,
Sippin' coffee gone cold and full of chicory root.
Wondering why I keep a ramblin' around,
And don't just find some nice southern girl
To settle down with.

To read more about the 52-Week Club see pages 87-88

Spinach & Feta Pizza

(serves 4-6)

1 recipe 'Pizza Dough' (page 146)
½ to 1 cup 'White Pizza Sauce' (page 147)
1 tablespoon olive oil
4 cups chopped spinach

1 cup shredded Mozzarella cheese
1 (4 ounce) container crumbled Feta
cheese (about ½ cup)

Preheat oven to 400 degrees.

Heat oil in a large skillet over low-medium heat. Add spinach and toss until spinach begins to wilt, about 1 minute. Remove from heat and set aside.

Roll dough according to instructions on page 148.

Pre-bake the crust for 7 minutes. Layer 'White Pizza Sauce', Mozzarella, spinach and Feta. Bake for 10-15 minutes. Remove pizza from pan and place directly on oven rack for 5 more minutes.

Let this cool for at least 5-10 minutes before you cut it.

Me and my niece, Rita, making bread

Veggie Pesto Pizza

(serves 4-6)

1 recipe 'Pizza Dough' (page 146)
½ cup 'Spinach Pesto' (page 50)
1 (2.25 ounce) can sliced black olives
1 medium tomato, diced

½ medium red onion, thinly sliced
1 (4 ounce) container crumbled Feta
cheese (about ½ cup)

Preheat oven to 400 degrees.

Roll dough according to instructions on page 148.

Pre-bake the crust for 7 minutes.

Layer pesto, olives, tomatoes, red onion and Feta. Bake for 10-15 minutes. Remove pizza from pan and place directly on oven rack for 5 more minutes.

Allow pizza to cool for at least 5-10 minutes before you cut it.

I'm not going to sit here and say that "Music is like my air, maaaan" or "I can't live without music, maaaan" because I didn't really have to try to breathe. I kind of just popped out and the doctor sucked the snot out of my nose and there it went. I *can* live without music because, quite frankly it's the air I breathe and nourishment I give my body that keeps me alive.

I had to *learn* music. I had to train myself how to do what I was hearing in my head and feeling in my bones. To this day that process has not changed.

But I do get sick of it. There are times when I'm playing so much music or working around it or listening to it that I just have to give my soul a break and go plant some flowers or make some biscuits and gravy or, God forbid, take a long drive in silence....no radio, no iPod, no CD's, nothing...just wind, road, coffee and smokes.

I'll have to say that I have definitely lived an extraordinary life because of music. I remember telling my mom about 5 years ago, "Even if I never reach the notoriety required to be considered a 'successful' musician, my quality of life has been successful." I've done more, met more interesting people and felt the most incredible feelings– the kinds of feelings only experienced when harmony, heart, beats, interaction and truth collide - feelings that are set aside by God, I believe, just for creative people. I think that's what King David must've felt when he'd write hymns all day.

-Dave Hanley - Dave Hanley Band - Modesto, CA

155

Main Dishes

Spanish Lamb - 159

Herbed Lamb with Rosemary Gravy - 160

Lamb Meatloaf - 163

Kofta (Fried Lamb) - 164

Sito's Grape Leaves - 165

World's Best BBQ Lamb-Chops - 166

Stuffed Kofta Loaf - 167

Dad's Sloppy Yoseffs - 168

"There's-Nuthin-To-Eat" Shepherds Pie - 169

Italian-Swedish Meatballs - 171

Mom's Beef Enchiladas - 173

Dad's Lebanese Chicken - 177

Chicken with Mushroom & Olive Cream Sauce - 178

Garlic Herb-Butter Chicken - 179

Creamy Lemon Rosemary Chicken - 180

Ginger Chicken with Summer Rice - 181

Mom's Chicken & Rice Casserole - 182

Chicken Artichoke Casserole - 183

Cheesy Chicken Enchiladas - 184

Sausage & Tomato Rice - 187

Lamb Risotto - 189

Spicy Poblano Chicken Risotto - 190

Chicken & Sun-Dried Tomato Risotto - 191

Quiche Lorraine - 192

Mexican Quiche - 192

Veggie Herb Quiche - 194

Turkey Pot Pie - 195

Green Chili Turkey Taco Melts - 196

White Meatloaf - 197

Mexican Veggie Rice - 198

Veggie Enchiladas - 201

Spinach & Rice Stuffed Zucchini Boats - 203

156

Green Chili Turkey Taco Melts - Page 196

Cheesy Chicken Enchiladas - Page 184

Creamy Lemon Rosemary Chicken - Page 180

Spanish Lamb - Page 159

Sausage & Tomato Rice - Page 187

Turkey Pot Pie - Page 195

Spanish Lamb

(serves 2-4)

½ small yellow onion, chopped
4 cloves garlic, minced
2 tablespoons chopped fresh mint
  (stems removed)
3 tablespoons chopped flat-leaf
  (Italian) parsley
¼ cup olive oil
1 teaspoon salt
1 teaspoon pepper

1 teaspoon paprika
1 pound lamb, cubed (about 1 inch in size),
  trimmed of fat

Serve with
Patatas Bravas - page 118.

In a medium bowl mix onion, garlic, mint, parsley, olive oil, salt, pepper and paprika. Add cubed lamb and mix until lamb is well coated. Pour into a zip top bag. Squeeze as much air out as you can and put bag in fridge. Marinate over night (or at least 8 hours).

Remove bag from fridge 10 minutes before cooking to bring meat to room temperature. (Meat will cook more evenly if at room temperature as opposed to being cold.) Heat a medium-large pot over medium heat. Pour entire contents of bag into heated pot. Cook about 8 minutes for rare, about 10 minutes for medium. Stir occasionally to make sure all sides are browned. Save the liquid for dipping bread in.

From 52 Week "Stuff To Sleep On" by Willy Tea

There's something buried deep down in my dreams.
All I need is a pallet on your floor,
Friends and enough gasoline,
Then I'll go give it another shot.
Might not turn out like I thought, but I'll give it all I got.
Been a while since I been out your way,
I'll call you when I get to Salinas,
Gonna take a little break.
I'm a little bit of a mess, I could use a little rest,
Then I'll get back to my best.
It's the wind that I rode on,
It's the wind that'll take me away.
All I can do is pray, all I can do is pray
That it blows me back through one day.

To read more about the 52-Week Club see pages 87-88

Herbed Lamb with Rosemary Gravy

(serves 2)

2 tablespoons olive oil
½ teaspoon dried basil
½ teaspoon dried thyme
½ teaspoon salt
¼ teaspoon pepper
1 pound boneless leg of lamb, trimmed of fat and cut into 1 inch cubes
½ cup chicken broth
¼ cup heavy cream
½ teaspoon salt
⅛ teaspoon pepper
2 teaspoons flour
1 tablespoon olive oil
½ large shallot, diced
2 tablespoons chopped fresh rosemary*
1 tablespoon fresh squeezed lemon juice (about ½ a lemon)

*First, remove leaves from the stem. Next, chop leaves and measure.

Mix oil, basil, thyme, salt and pepper in medium bowl. Add cubed lamb and mix until meat is coated. Pour meat mixture into a zip top bag. Squeeze the air out, seal and put in the fridge. Marinate for 1-2 hours before cooking. Remove bag from fridge 10 minutes before cooking to bring meat to room temperature. (Meat will cook more evenly if at room temperature.)

In a small bowl whisk broth, cream, salt, pepper, flour and set aside. Heat olive oil in a medium skillet over medium heat. Add shallots, cook and stir for 1 minute. Add rosemary, cook and stir for 1 minute. Add broth and cream mixture to the pan. Whisk until combined and bring to a boil. Cook and stir frequently for about 2 minutes or until thick. Add lemon juice, stir, remove from skillet and pour into a gravy boat (or some other such contraption).

There are a few ways you can cook the lamb but I prefer it pan-fried.

To pan fry: Heat 1 tablespoon of olive oil in a large skillet over medium heat. Cook about 8 minutes for rare, about 10 minutes for medium. Stir occasionally to make sure all sides are browned. Serve with rosemary gravy.

Another delicious option is to skewer the lamb and grill it!

Main Dishes

Mama used to sing around the house with the radio. Sometimes she would turn up the volume when a song came on that she liked. That song would stick in her head and she would sing it all day. She liked Patsy Kline, Loretta Lyn, Roger Whitiker, Lawrence Whelk, Nat King Cole and Frank Sinatra. Some of what she liked didn't do it for me, while other songs moved me into profound states of mind. I noticed early that music affected all people differently. I wanted to find my own collection of music that rhymed with my life and feelings. And so I began a sojourn into my own musical wilderness. I listened to everything. I learned all the words, even to songs that I did not like. I listened to the feeling of each song and opened myself to the vast world of expression.

The old time radio on my grandma's refrigerator would fill the long afternoons with Willie Nelson, Waylon Jennings, Jim Reeves and Charlie Rich. Really old school country is what grandma liked. These songs still remind me of playing freely and carelessly in her back yard. If we weren't at grandma's, my oldest brother would baby-sit us while my single mom worked. He would take us to the local ice rink and we would skate around to his choices of music: Chicago, Three-Dog Night, Gordon Lightfoot, Jim Croche, David Gates and Bread, John Lennon, Neil Diamond and Deep Purple. His music shaped a part of mine.

One day I was flipping trough the AM dial and came across some Blues. Not just any Blues, but Howlin Wolf and Hubert Sumlin, Robert Johnson, and Honey Boy Edwards, Lead Belly and Ruth Brown - to more current artists like Clapton, Hooker and BB. I was blown away! I never heard so much emotion in music before. The common thread of all the music that moved me was the story telling. Speaking of struggle and heartache seemed to be the driving motives. It too shaped how I hear music.

I began playing horns in elementary school. I tried them all: French, Alto, Cornett. But they just seemed emotionless. Watching Lawrence Welk one night with my mother, I heard the tenor sax come out of the TV and it hit me! Blowing like the autumn winds! Cool and moving one moment then crying and screaming the next. So the next day in school I traded in my loaner French horn for a loaner Tenor sax and off I went to destroy the peace in my neighborhood. I had to go out and away from my southern California desert community so my squeaking would only harm cactuses and |rattlesnakes.

As I was getting better playing in the marching band, Prop 13 took away the music program from our school, thus leaving me with no sax and no music lessons. My family was too poor to buy lessons for me. With my paper route money I bought a garage sale electric guitar for $82 - a little beat up and pieced together, but it worked o.k. I asked the garage-sale-man to show me three chords. He did and I went on down my musical road at age 16. My neighbors had a Hard Rock and Blues band and needed a sound system for the practice room. Since I was hanging around trying to learn guitar by watching, and begging for help, they voted me to be the guy who had to learn the sound system so they could have monitors and could hear the vocals.

I learned to engineer sound, which lead to a career in mixing live shows. As a sound engineer I was near enough musicians to learn from. I'd watch their fingers so at the end of the night I would play what I learned.

Now the music I make is influenced by everything from Modern Rock and Blues to early acoustic Folk and Bluegrass with a touch of jazz and Spanish classical.

I frequent musical festivals to share in the camaraderie and learn new things. If you have never bathed in three thousand acoustic instruments played by kind musicians willing to share knowledge and songs, you can't imagine how amazing that is.

From homegrown pickers and storytellers like Dave Hanley and Willy Tea, to big timers like Tim O'Brien, Emmy Lou, Alison Krauss and Steve Earl we all learn from each other. Not a day goes by that I don't play my guitar and try to emulate my mentors and express myself.

I had often asked myself "Where does this inner quest for music come from?" One day my mother told me. It turns out that my absentee father was a musician. Mom says he played several instruments, guitar and vibes being his mainstay. He traveled around North America playing in bands and living like a rebel... I had no idea... I guess some things are genetic.

My soul is full of music inspired by everyone else's musical expressions of their life experiences. The words I write are words my own life experiences and those words are

- T.J. Birman - Jenner, CA

T.J. drew this in my notebook at the 2008 Strawberry Music Festival

Main Dishes

Lamb Meatloaf

(serves 4)

2 teaspoons olive oil
½ medium red bell pepper, diced
½ cup diced yellow onion
2 cloves garlic, minced
½ pound ground lamb
½ pound ground turkey
¾ cup quick oats
½ cup chopped flat-leaf (Italian) parsley

½ cup finely shredded Gruyere (or Parmesan cheese)
1 egg plus 1 yolk, beaten
1 teaspoon salt
½ teaspoon pepper
'Tomato Gravy' (page 53) or use plain ol' boring ketchup

Preheat oven to 350 degrees.

Save egg white for the next morning's breakfast

Heat olive oil in a medium skillet over medium heat. Add peppers and onion. Cook and stir until they begin to soften, about 2 minutes. Add garlic, cook and stir for about 1 minute. Remove onions and garlic from skillet. Drain and allow to cool for a few minutes. When cool, add mixture to large bowl. Add lamb, turkey, oats, parsley, cheese, egg, salt and pepper. Mix well with your hands until completely combined. Either press mixture into loaf pan or form by hand into a loaf shape and place on cookie sheet. Rub the top with some of the gravy (or ketchup), just enough to cover. Cook for 60 minutes. Serve with the rest of the tomato gravy.

All you need is love? No thanks. Music is the muscle that keeps me moving. It's so much more than melody and counterpoint, rests and time signatures. It is the manifestation of life. It can touch you gently, it can hammer you over the head, it can start you up, it can knock you out.

Who needs caffeine? I'll give you a triple shot of The Stones to start you up. Who needs smack? Nick Drake's *Pink Moon* will lull you into a dreamy dreariness your dear life has never seen before. Who needs blow? The cocaine cowboys from Aerosmith have all the lines your beak could handle.

So what about love? Throw down your Dr. Phil book and listen to The Beatles, people. They'll be the first to tell you that in the end the love you make is equal to the love you take.

- Anastüblychin - Petrol/The Aktion/DEFACED/Bright Feathers & Electric Beach/ The ONS - Mill Valley, CA

Kofta (Fried Lamb)

(serves 4)

1 cup coarse bulgur wheat
¼ cup water
½ medium white onion, quartered
½ medium green pepper, quartered
1 teaspoon cumin
¼ teaspoon allspice

1 tablespoon salt
1 teaspoon pepper
1 pound ground lamb
½ cup pine nuts (optional)
olive oil (or vegetable oil) for frying

Put the bulgur wheat into a large bowl. Add water until it comes to about ½ inch above the wheat. Soak for 30 minutes.

In a blender add water, onion, green pepper, cumin, allspice, salt and pepper. Blend until liquefied with as few lumps as possible.

> Pause a moment, breathe deeply and enjoy this mouth-watering aroma. What you smell is one of the reasons why this cookbook is in existence.

Place the lamb in a bowl and pour the onion/pepper/spice mixture over it. Add the wheat and use your hands to mix well until all ingredients are completely combined. (Add pine-nuts here, if desired.) I recommend mixing the meat and spices at least an hour before you cook it so that everything can marinate together. (This tastes especially good if it sits over night.) Take mixture out of the fridge about 10 minutes before cooking so it comes back to room temperature.

Add 3 tablespoons of olive oil (my grandma used vegetable oil) to a large skillet over medium heat. Let oil heat up for 1-2 minutes. In the meantime, make the meat mixture into patties. I recommend shaping them into ovals as opposed to circles (they will need to fit into a pita that has been sliced in half). I wouldn't make them any fatter (pre-fried) than a ½ inch. Fry about 4-5 minutes, flip and fry for another 4-5 minutes. They should be really dark brown when they are done. Set on paper towels to drain excess oil.

To serve: Slice pita bread in half and open the pocket. Spread some hummus and Lebne (or Greek yogurt/plain yogurt) inside. Next, layer lamb patty, sliced tomatoes and sliced Feta cheese.

> My dad likes to slice up some red onions and put them in the pan as the lamb is frying, then adds the sautéed onion to the halved pita.

Main Dishes

Sito's Grape Leaves

Recipe courtesy of Wayne Joseph - Northville, MI

(serves 4-6)

1 (64 ounce) jar grape leaves*
2 fresh lemons
2 cups white rice
2 pounds ground chuck
½ stick of unsalted butter
2 teaspoons allspice
2 teaspoons cinnamon
2 teaspoons dried mint
1½ teaspoons salt
1 teaspoon black pepper
1 teaspoon cayenne pepper

*You can usually find these at your local grocery store, and most definitely at Mediterranean markets.

Line the bottom of a five quart saucepan with unrolled grape leaves and squeeze one-half (½) of a fresh lemon over the leaves.

Parboil rice for 10 minutes and drain. In a large mixing bowl add raw meat, parboiled rice, butter, allspice, cinnamon, mint, salt, black pepper and cayenne pepper. Mix by hand until all ingredients are combined. (You might need to use clean kitchen gloves, as rice will be hot.)

Set mixture aside and lose the gloves. Prepare each grape leaf by clipping off any remaining stem. With the point of the leaf facing the top and the vein-side of the leaf facing up, place some of the mixture at the bottom-middle of the leaf with a minimum of one-inch of leaf on either side of the mixture. (The amount of stuffing you use depends on the size of the leaf.) Roll from the bottom up, folding and tucking the corners as you go. When completed, the final roll of the leaf should be in the middle and none of the stuffing should be visible.

Place the completed leaf in the lined saucepan, starting with the outside circle working in. Once one layer is complete (usually 15-20 rolled leaves) squeeze one-half (½) of a fresh lemon over that layer and begin the next layer. You should have enough mixture and grape leaves for three layers.

Once you've completed the third layer, squeeze one-half (½) of a fresh lemon over that layer and gently add water until it just covers all the layers of leaves. Do not add water too quickly, as it can cause some of the leaves to unravel before cooking.

Cover the top with a layer of unrolled grape leaves. Now take a glass or ceramic dinner plate and invert it over the grape leaves to hold them in place while cooking. The less area between the edge of the plate and the side of the saucepan, the better

(continued)

(this will also help keep the leaves in place during cooking). I place a large rock (old country tradition) on the plate to help hold it down during cooking.

Now, turn the heat to medium. Once the water starts to gently boil, set time for 20 more minutes.

Remove the rock and plate. Test for doneness. Gently remove grape leaves and let stand on paper towel to drain off any excess water.

Here's another recipe from cousin Wayne....

World's Best BBQ Lamb-Chops
(serves 4-6)

6 loin lamb chops
1 (4 ounce) package Char-Crust Roasted Garlic & Peppercorn Rub
1 cup mesquite smoking chips

In a small mixing bowl pour in 2 ounces of Rub. Prepare each lamb chop by cutting off all visible fat and scraping out the matter from the top center of the bone.

Start the barbeque (you want a very hot fire). Completely dredge all sides of the lamb chops in the Rub. When the fire is ready, spread the mesquite chips over the coal. Replace the grill. Place the lamb chops on the grill.

Cook for 3 minutes on each side. This will make a perfect medium rare lamb chop. For medium, spend 4 minutes per side. Rub blackens while sealing in the juices of the meat. Don't worry, this is what you're looking for.

Main Dishes

Stuffed Kofta Loaf

(serves 6-8)

2 cups coarse Bulgur wheat
1 medium white onion, cut into eighths
1 medium green pepper, cut into eighths
2 teaspoons cumin
1 tablespoon salt
2 teaspoons pepper
½ teaspoon allspice

¼ cup water
2 pounds lean ground lamb (or beef)
1 cup pine nuts (optional)
2 eggs, beaten
½ cup panko breadcrumbs
8 ounces Feta cheese, crumbled
'Lebne Sauce' (recipe below)

Preheat oven to 350 degrees.

Put the bulgur wheat into a large bowl. Add water until it comes to about ½ inch above the wheat. Soak for 30 minutes.

In a blender add the onion, green pepper, spices and water. Blend until liquefied with as few lumps as possible.

Put the lamb in a bowl and pour the onion/pepper/spices mixture over it. Add the wheat, pine nuts, egg and breadcrumbs. Use your hands to mix well until all ingredients are completely combined.

Put half of the meat on a large cookie sheet and shape into a long, flat rectangle about an inch thick. Sprinkle the cheese down the middle of the meat. (Make sure there's about ½ to 1 inch space between the Feta and the edges of the meat.) Put the rest of the meat on top, completely covering the Feta. Use your hands to mold the top meat and the bottom meat into each other, forming a long loaf. Make sure the meat is sealed on all sides so the cheese doesn't melt out.

Bake for 1 hour. While meatloaf is cooking, prepare the 'Lebne Sauce' below.

Remove the meatloaf and spread all of the Lebne Sauce evenly on the loaf. Place back in oven for another 15 minutes. Remove and allow to sit for about 10 minutes before serving.

Serve with Tabbouleh (page 79),
Syrian Salad (page 80)

Lebne Sauce:

½ cup Lebne (or Greek or plain yogurt)
2 tablespoons chopped fresh mint
  (or 2 teaspoons dried)
2 teaspoons olive oil

2 tablespoons tomato paste
¼ teaspoon salt
1 clove garlic, minced

Whisk all ingredients together in small bowl until creamy.

Dad's Sloppy Yoseffs
(serves 4-6)

2 pounds lean ground lamb (or beef)*
1 medium red onion, diced
3-4 cloves of garlic, minced
1 teaspoon allspice
2 teaspoons salt
1 teaspoon pepper
⅓ cup dried mint
1 (28 ounce) can crushed tomatoes
pita bread
Lebne** (a.k.a Kiefer Cheese or Greek Yogurt)

*If you'd prefer something a little healthier, use ground chicken or turkey.

Heat a large pot over medium heat. Add lamb and use a wooden spoon or spatula to break into little pieces. After about 5 minutes, add onions, garlic, spices and mint. Continue to cook, stirring often, about 3-5 more minutes. Add tomatoes, turn heat to medium-low and cook for 25 minutes. Every 5 minutes or so, give it a stir. Most of the tomato juice should be absorbed. If it seems to be too juicy, cook for a few more minutes.

To serve: Cut the pita bread in half and carefully open the pocket. Spread some Lebne on one side of the bread and stuff it with some of the meat mixture. If you haven't guessed, based on the name of this dish, these are sloppy - so proceed with unrestrained caution.

**You can use regular plain yogurt if you can't find either of these.

Dad's poker face

Main Dishes

"There's-Nuthin'-to-Eat" Shepherd's Pie

(serves 6 hungry musicians (barely) or 12 regular people)

Read about how this dish came to be

2 pounds mashed potatoes
2 cups uncooked rice
2 pounds ground beef
5 celery sticks sliced into half-moons
1 cup frozen (or canned) corn*
1 cup frozen peas*
1 (8 ounce) package mushrooms, chopped
5 cloves garlic, minced
1 teaspoon salt
1 teaspoon pepper

1 bunch flat-leaf parsley, chopped small
¼ cup butter
¼ cup flour
6 cups broth made with tomato bouillon
(or chicken or beef bouillon)
½ teaspoon salt
½ teaspoon pepper
1 cup heavy cream (or milk)
3 tablespoons flour
¼ cup seasoned breadcrumbs

Pre-heat oven to 350 degrees.

Make 2 pounds of mashed potatoes. I recommend my 'Cheesy Garlic Mashed Potatoes' on page 124.

If you have less people to feed, this dish can easily be cut in half.

Cook 2 cups of rice according to package directions. (2 cups of uncooked rice makes about 4 cups cooked.)

Heat a large skillet over medium heat. Add beef and break up with a wooden spoon. When meat begins to brown (after about 3 minutes) add celery, corn, peas, mushrooms, garlic, salt and pepper. Cook and stir until meat is cooked through, about 5-6 more minutes. Remove from heat and set aside. Do not drain.

In a medium pot melt butter. When butter begins to foam, add flour and whisk until smooth. Slowly whisk in broth. Continue to whisk until all lumps are gone. Add salt and pepper. In a small bowl whisk 3 tablespoons of flour into cream until there aren't any lumps. Whisk into broth mixture. Bring to a boil and turn heat to low. Cook, stirring occasionally, until mixture thickens, about 3-5 minutes.

When the rice is done, mix in parsley and divide evenly. Spread into the bottom of two 9x13 casserole dishes. Divide the beef evenly and spread over the rice. Next, pour and spread a little gravy over beef. Spread mashed potatoes evenly over the beef. (This will be easier if potatoes are hot.) Divide the rest of the gravy and evenly pour over the potatoes. Sprinkle potatoes with bread crumbs. Bake for 35 minutes and serve hot.

*If you don't have corn and peas, any combination of mixed veggies will work fine!

On November 11th, 2009, high atop Mt. Shasta at the northern most part of California, my sister, her husband and Larry & His Flask sat stranded in a 1991 Bluebird school bus. I was safe and warm at home preparing enough pasta to feed the 8 weary travelers upon their return home. Bethany called me to tell me they wouldn't be home that night, since they couldn't get help until the next morning. Not only were they stranded, but they had very little food, and since they were on the top of a mountain, they were nowhere near a grocery store.

Luckily, somewhere in the middle of their 2009 summer tour, the Larry boys had bought a little camp stove. Bethany, determined to feed the hungry men, rummaged around the ice chest and found some rice, an onion, some garlic, some beans, a few corn tortillas and a gravy packet. From that she managed to make a most delicious pot of food.

The next night I met them in Stockton with the giant tin of pasta I cooked the night before. The pasta was cold, but they didn't care. They immediately dug in and by the end of the night every trace of it was gone. They didn't come home that night, but the next day they planned on coming over for lunch.

When morning came, it dawned on me that we didn't have any food. When they arrived I told Bethany we had "nothing to eat," but after what she'd been through - making something out of nothing - she knew better. We had rice, potatoes, ground beef, a plethora of spices, random frozen veggies and random fresh veggies (well, just look at the recipe - you'll see what we had). We also had bouillon - so that meant gravy. As I looked at all we had, I thought "Well look at that! That's practically the makings of a Shepherd's Pie!"

And a delicious pie it was! I've made a lot of food - more than I could include in this book - but I knew this recipe had to be squeezed in. Needless to say, both 'pies' were devoured before I could get a decent picture. But honestly, a Shepherd's Pie isn't the prettiest picture...and when it comes to hungry Larry's, they just don't care how it looks.

-Mary

Main Dishes

Italian-Swedish Meatballs

(makes about 24 -1 ½ inch meatballs)

½ pound bacon
2 teaspoons olive oil
½ medium white onion, diced
2 cloves garlic, minced
½ pound ground beef
½ pound ground pork
½ cup chopped fresh basil
¼ cup chopped fresh oregano*
½ teaspoon salt
½ teaspoon pepper

1 egg, beaten
½ cup shredded Parmesan cheese
1 tablespoon olive oil
¼ cup + 1 tablespoon flour
3 cups beef broth
¼ cup heavy cream
½ teaspoon nutmeg
½ teaspoon allspice
½ teaspoon salt

For all of you half Italian, half Swedes out there...

Dice bacon and cook until crisp. Drain on paper towels and set aside. Pour grease from pan, wipe with paper towel and return to stove.

Using the same skillet, heat olive oil over medium-low heat. Add onions, cook and stir for about 3 minutes. Add garlic, cook and stir for another minute or so. Remove onions and garlic from skillet and place in a medium bowl. Add the beef, pork, basil, oregano, salt, pepper, egg, Parmesan cheese and bacon to the bowl. Mix with your hands until completely combined. (I like to let any meatball or meatloaf mixture sit for at least an hour or overnight, but it'll still be good if you make the meatballs right away.)

Form meatballs into 1½ inch balls and set aside. Heat oil in large skillet over low-medium heat. Add meatballs and cook until brown, about 5 minutes each side. Once browned, remove from skillet and set on paper towels to drain.

Now, depending on your meat, you'll either have a whole lot of grease or just a tiny bit. If you aren't sure how much is too much, take a second and pour grease into a glass measuring cup. Pour ¼ cup back into the skillet and discard the rest.

Add flour to the grease in the skillet and whisk until lightly browned. Gradually add broth, constantly whisking. Use a spatula to scrape up any bits stuck to the pan. If there are any burnt pieces that are big and obvious, remove them using a slotted spoon. Add cream, nutmeg, allspice and salt. Whisk until combined. Bring to a boil and cook, stirring frequently, until sauce reaches a thick consistency. Add the meatballs back to the skillet, turn heat to low and simmer for about 5 more minutes.

Serve over rice or pasta.

*Sometimes, depending where you live, it's hard to find fresh oregano. You can either double the basil or substitute with flat-leaf (Italian) parsley.

"Basking in the Cold Concrete"

From 52 Week "Basking In The Cold Concrete"
by Jason Turner

Apple orchard is so familiar from where I am,
Secret grove's about a stone's throw away.
Smashin' leaves with my feet out in that pourin' rain,
I can hear that wood stove whisper my name.
Black oaks rise up all painful and wretched like,
They follow the creek up all the way.
That's where that rope swing is knotted and tied up high,
'Cause it's secret and that's the way it'll stay.

I wore a smile as I hunted, oh so skillfully-
Chasing White Tail as they bound away.
Hold a tree frog and cradle him so delicate.
Can you hear that squirrel chippin' up that tree?
Grab a root to pull yourself out of this dry creek bed
Before the flood comes and washes you away.
Overcome a cord of wood and stand up straight and tall,
Spread your arms like you're gonna fly away.

I'm so tired when that full day has wrapped into night,
Hot supper has warmed me from within.
Face in hands we play Checkers under yellow lights,
When he tells one I laugh at him again.
Climb in bed with those clean and flat-pressed linen sheets,
Pulled so tight I can hardly move my toes.
He comes in and sits there by my small twin bed,
Leaves his love and tells me one more joke.

Grandpa's shirt didn't fit the best,
That straw hat always hooked a branch.
"Use your fist to thin 'em well."
The air's so clean!
Motherlode was my Grandpa's home,
Lush Meadows where his ashes roam.
I'll never make a place like this in history...
...If I'm basking in the cold concrete.

FOR
HARVEY B. LANCASTER

To read more about the 52-Week Club see pages 87-88

Main Dishes

Mom's Beef Enchiladas

(serves 8 comfortably)

1 cup sour cream
1 (28 ounce) can red enchilada sauce
1 pound ground beef
½ cup finely diced yellow onion
1 teaspoon salt
2-3 cups shredded Cheddar cheese (for filling)
8-10 burrito size flour tortillas
1-2 cups shredded Cheddar cheese (for topping)
1 cup sliced olives

Preheat oven to 350 degrees.

In a medium bowl whisk sour cream and enchilada sauce and set aside.

Heat a large skillet over medium heat. Add beef, onions and salt. Cook until beef is cooked through, about 10 minutes. Use a colander to drain the meat/onion mixture. Place in a bowl and allow mixture to cool. When beef has cooled off a bit (about 5 minutes) add cheese for filling and mix well.

Pour about ¼ of the sauce into a 9x13 inch baking dish and spread it around so it covers the bottom. Spoon about ⅓ to ½ cup of the meat/cheese mixture into the middle of each tortilla and fold like a burrito (folding ends in first and rolling tightly).

Place enchiladas flap side down in the baking dish. Pour the rest of the sauce over them and top with the rest of the cheese and olives. Bake uncovered for 30 minutes or until hot and bubbly.

These enchiladas make the best leftovers! The flavors really develop after sitting in the fridge overnight.

To prepare these the day before serving, simply assemble the enchiladas and pour the sauce over them. Cover with foil and put in the fridge. The next day simply uncover them and bake at 350 degrees for 30 minutes.

Some of my food testers said this had too much cheese. I say there's no such thing...

...I think this recipe is perfect...

...so proceed with caution!!

"The Tender Dance of The Entertainer & The Entertained"
By Dean Haakenson - Be Brave Bold Robot - Sacramento, CA

Relationships are a responsibility/necessary pleasure/casualty of being alive. The price we pay for having other entities in our shared space-time to help create the atmosphere that ultimately feeds our minds and bodies the nutrients they need to Rock. Alas, it is an inevitable human trait to neglect or ignore this great responsibility--that much appears certain to me (and perhaps the greatest human tragedy, or at least the provenance of many other great human tragedies). We see what we want to see. But! Let us not forget. Not that we must "be nice" or have any sort of required modes of behavior within all of our countless relationships, but, simply, let us not forget that they exist. I know. Duh.

My point. My point is that "Rock Shows" [the name I will give for any sort of situation where you have one group of people (or person) who are paying deliberate attention to another group of people (or person), the latter group being aware of the former's gift of attention, and taking advantage of it in one of many different ways]...Rock Shows are relationships. More accurately, Rock Shows are our gift for having to deal with relationships that really matter, or moreover, relationships that last longer than Rock Shows. Please don't get me wrong! My point (if I ever come to it...how's that for a long relationship!) lies mostly in my contention that they matter most righteously, these relationships that we have with Rock Shows. It's just that the self-contained nature of a Rock Show, premeditated or otherwise, ensures that there is an end* and it will be no further than a few days away. You embrace, you part ways, and in between you experience the relationship that is a Rock Show. The relationship ends because the rock show, relationship Entity A to your Entity B, stops making noise and becomes a memory (the intensity of which depending on how much "fun" you actually had at the Rock Show).

*Let us assume that this writing's definition of a relationship notes a distinct "end" to such a thing as a relationship and is not in consideration of the very real phenomena of a lasting relationship with a memory or any other sort of idea or representation of an expired entity (that once existed but now does not).

So. We have established (or maybe just I have...are you following me?!...I know, I'm easily misunderstood...so I lead myself to believe...) that being at a Rock Show is like being in the middle of a relationship, and relationships are a thing not to be neglected and active attention must be paid by all parties during the course that the relationship runs. Good.

Now, Rock Shows take on two basic forms: big ones and little ones. If performing music has not become a career for you and you don't tour incessantly, then you probably play mostly little shows. And we have all attended both little shows and big shows (I say this realizing that maybe there are some people who take zero interest in local music, and only go to "big" Rock Shows when the last American Idol winner comes through town...and I say THAT instantly feeling a small pang of guilt for the fact that I don't go to as many local shows as I should...lazy Dean...). The relationship dynamic at big shows is different than the dynamic at little ones, but there exists the relationship, to be sure.

I play music in Sacramento. I really haven't played in too many other cities and have never played to more than around a hundred people (except the 2006 SAMMIES, Rock!). Sacramento shows are intimate, little shows. Always. I don't think shows exceed more than a hundred people, commonly, and it's usually more like 40, or 7. As the Entertainer in the relationship that is a Rock Show, I realize that I have the easy job. I speak my mind and sing my songs and do some practiced "skitting" or "soap-boxing" once in a while. At both little shows and big shows, whatever the Entertainer says (necessarily into the microphone at the big shows), people will hear and relate to in whatever way, and hopefully absorb, and possibly be moved to act upon. To a smaller audience, the Entertainer will be able to be more aware of the audience's subtle nuances, thus adding a whole new dynamic, and, really, making little shows a bit more full of accountability than big shows. The responsibility of the Entertainer is to pay attention to this relationship. Say "hi" to the person on the other end.

For the Entertained, (the audience being half of the Rock Show relationship), things are a bit more tricky. The Entertainer must know how you feel. The success of any relationship hinges upon communication. The question is "what do you expect me to do?!" Big Shows. With Big Shows, unless you are right up in front of the stage, amongst the area of the massive "Entity of the Entertained" that does the verbal communicating with the Entertainer, you don't have the option of dialogue. 'Tis a shame, but you can make up for it by dancing, or screaming, or concentrating really hard those good thoughts in your brain, and flinging them towards the stage and/or your immediate section of audience hive (in the hopes of increasing stage directed group energy). For the Entertained at little shows, members of the somewhat intimate to very intimate audience, holding heavy influence on the Entertainer. Things are also much more filled with accountability and the need for action than at Big Shows. Your responsibility is to have a relationship with the Entertainer. Hiss, yell naughty words, or full naughty sentences. Tell them that you love them, if in fact you do. Dance. Oh my God, how much happier relationships would be if everybody danced. Respond, in some way, to the nervous psychobabble or tame speeches that are directed AT YOU by the Entertainer. Make guttural animal noises or throw the wit back. Hell, sitting or standing there and staring at the Entertainer makes a lot of sense too, if that's what you feel. The point is just to be aware of the relationship.

Personally, I am a bit jittery and usually feel compelled to make conversation (however boring or inane....just so that I can let the person know that I am paying some sort of attention) when I am in a relationship with somebody, so I am just naturally compelled to try and dance and make noises at a Rock Show.

But, screw me. Truly. Screw everybody, except the immediate Entity you are engaged in a relationship with (of which, remember, there are sometimes several at once, and many overall, and it is imperative that you pay attention to every and all).

And remember that Rock Shows are relationships that you are involved in when you attend them, and that littler Rock Shows (in comfortably familiar places) are the ones where the intimacy plays a factor, thus making them more dependent on your relationship activity at the time, and that it's ok to scream and dance and say things, and, really, most Entertainers would probably say that they would prefer even demeaning feedback (the confident Entertainer brushing any harsh off as a joke) than none at all. Act a Fool! Act Tribal! Make some Noise!...or don't....it's entirely up to you.

by Wesley Haakenson

Dad's Lebanese Chicken Kabobs

(serves 4)

4 large boneless, skinless chicken thighs, cubed
  (or 2 boneless, skinless chicken breasts)
1 medium red onion, cut into squares/wedges
1 green pepper, cut into squares
1 tablespoon dried mint
1 tablespoon ground cumin
2 teaspoons garlic powder*
2 teaspoons allspice
2 teaspoons pepper
1 tablespoon salt
2 tablespoons olive oil
2 teaspoons lemon juice

 (kabob size)

*Or 4 cloves fresh garlic, minced

Toss your cubed meat and cut-up veggies into a big bowl. In a small bowl mix mint, cumin, garlic powder (or minced garlic), allspice, pepper, salt, olive oil and lemon juice. Whisk with a fork until combined. Pour over the chicken and vegetables and mix until they're coated. Cover and allow to marinate for at least an hour (overnight is ideal).

You can grill this on the barbecue or broil it in your oven, the cook time is the same.

My dad always said that
we'll eat Lebanese food in heaven...

To grill:
If you are using wooden skewers be sure to soak them for 30 minutes before hand, so they don't catch fire on the grill. Skewer meat and vegetables (alternating them looks nice). Cook over direct heat for about 5-6 minutes on each side, depending on how big your chicken chunks are. Cut into the thickest piece to make sure it's cooked through.

...I believe him.

To broil in the oven:
Skewer meat and vegetables. Put the rack in the middle of the oven. Broil meat on high for 5-6 minutes on each side. As above - check thickest piece to be sure it's done.

This is wonderful served with 'Syrian Rice' (page 114) and 'Chopped Greek Salad' (page 74).

I can barely pronounce the actual name of this recipe, much less spell it. Sounds like: "Luh-huh-mish-we"

Chicken with Mushroom & Olive Cream Sauce

(serves 2-4)

1 pound boneless, skinless chicken breasts,
  sliced ½ inch thick
1 tablespoon olive oil
½ medium red onion, sliced
1 (8 ounce) package sliced button mushrooms
¾ cup beef broth
¼ cup heavy cream

½ cup sliced pimento stuffed
  Spanish olives
2 tablespoons chopped fresh thyme
¼ cup beef broth
2 tablespoons flour
½ teaspoon salt
¼ teaspoon pepper

Slice meat and set aside.

Heat olive oil in a medium skillet over medium heat. Add onion, cook and stir for a few minutes. Add mushrooms. Cook and stir until mushrooms start to sweat, about 2 minutes or so. Add ¾ cup of broth, cream, olives and thyme. Mix and bring to a boil.

Add chicken in one even layer, cover and cook for 3-4 minutes. Turn chicken pieces over and cook for another 2-3 minutes. Check thickest piece to see if it's done.

Remove chicken from the skillet and set on a plate. In a small bowl whisk together the other ¼ cup beef broth and flour until smooth. Pour into the skillet with the sauce and whisk until combined. Bring back to a boil, cook and stir for about 2 minutes.

Spoon sauce over chicken. Serve over rice or pasta.

Artwork by Grace Taylor

Main Dishes

Garlic Herb-Butter Chicken

(serves 2)

¼ cup butter
2-4 cloves garlic, minced
1 pound boneless, skinless chicken breasts,
   cut into 1 inch cubes
1 tablespoon chopped fresh parsley

1 tablespoon chopped fresh thyme
1 tablespoon chopped fresh oregano
1 tablespoon chopped fresh cilantro
1 teaspoon salt
¼ teaspoon pepper

In a large skillet, melt butter over medium heat. When butter begins to foam add garlic. Cook and stir for 1 minute. Add chicken and toss. Add parsley, thyme, oregano, cilantro, salt and pepper. Toss until combined. Cook for about 8-10 minutes tossing often. Serve over rice or pasta.

Use any combination of herbs you have on hand for this recipe!

I've heard it's a choice between The Beatles and The Stones and choose The Beatles, then, for the exact same reason I choose them in a battle with Elvis.

From a cultural standpoint you could argue that this far, ex post facto, the work of The Beatles has entered our collective consciousness, and is ultimately a part of every child raised in Western civilization---even if you don't like The Beatles, you're aware of them. Elvis is an archetype, sure, but if we're purely evaluating the music and not marketed notions of what an icon is, it's very difficult to argue the profound impact four young lads from Liverpool imparted.

With The Beatles (ha!), you've all-encompassing statements, things like "All you need is love," "The love you take is equal to the love you make" and "Let it be," all of which today are delivered, believed in, and repeated as mantras, gospel and universal truths.

The Beatles are abstract and attempt to define things which are intangible and ultimately thought of differently by each of us, which is what makes their music so special and personalized. When I think Elvis, I think finite Rock n' Roll with lyrics rooted in what life is, whereas The Beatles lend themselves to examining personal feelings, thoughts, and emotions. The introspection they generate in people who listen to their music is their real value---generations of people believing on some base level that "All you need is love" is much more life-affirming to me than generations saying, "He's a hound dog" and idealizing sock hops and drive-in root beer float palaces.

- Randy Duax - New York, NY - When asked "Elvis or The Beatles?"

Creamy Lemon Rosemary Chicken

(serves 4)

2 tablespoons butter
2 tablespoons olive oil
2-4 tablespoons fresh rosemary, finely
 chopped* (depending on how much you
 like the flavor of rosemary)
2 pounds boneless, skinless chicken
 breasts, sliced ½ inch thick

½ teaspoon salt
½ teaspoon pepper
2 cups chicken broth
3 tablespoons flour
½ teaspoon salt
2 tablespoons lemon juice

Melt butter and olive oil in large skillet over medium heat. Add rosemary. When butter begins to foam, add chicken in one layer. (Unless you have a giant skillet, you'll have to do this in batches.) Season the chicken with salt and pepper and fry for about 4 minutes on each side. As chicken is done, remove it from the skillet and set on a plate. Once all of the chicken is cooked, drain the skillet of its juices and wipe clean. Set the skillet back on the stove.

Keep the heat on the skillet. In a small bowl whisk together the broth and flour until the mixture is smooth without any lumps. (If there are any lumps it'll get even more lumpy as you heat it.) Pour mixture into pan. Add salt and lemon juice, stir and bring to a boil. Cook until sauce reaches your desired thickness. Sometimes this happens right away, sometimes you may need to cook for a minute or so more.

Spoon sauce over chicken. Serve over rice or pasta

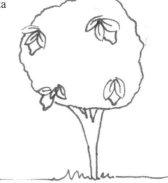

*Remove leaves from stem, then chop 'em up.

Pink Floyd is the reason I am so consumed by music. Before I heard them, I would just listen to whatever was on the radio simply because I didn't know any better. Then a friend introduced me to Pink Floyd and I was, for lack of better words, enlightened. I didn't know music could sound like that or have so much depth. "Wish You Were Here" is the reason I started playing guitar. Whenever I lose the motivation to play, all I need to do is listen to the first 10 seconds of "Wish You Were Here" and I'm compelled to pick up my guitar. That's the beauty of music: it has an intense power over me that I can't live without.

-Mary

Main Dishes

Ginger Chicken with Summer Rice

(serves 4)

1 pound boneless, skinless chicken
  breasts, sliced ½ inch thick
1 teaspoon ground coriander
1 teaspoon ground ginger
½ teaspoon salt
3 tablespoons olive oil
1-2 stalks celery, chopped
¼ medium red onion, diced
2 tablespoons dill pickle relish

2 tablespoons 'Lemon Herb Mayonnaise'
  (page 100)
1 tablespoon canola oil
2 teaspoons cider vinegar
½ teaspoon salt
⅔ cup crumbled Feta cheese
2 cups cooked rice
  (leftover rice works well)*

Add chicken, coriander, ginger and salt into a bowl and toss until chicken is coated. Heat olive oil in a large skillet over medium heat. Add chicken in one layer and fry until done, 4-5 minutes on each side. Remove from heat and allow chicken to cool.

Meanwhile, in a large bowl combine celery, red onion, relish, 'Lemon Herb Mayonnaise', canola oil, vinegar, salt, Feta and rice.

When the chicken has cooled, chop into bite-sized pieces. Add to the rice mixture and stir until combined. Cover and refrigerate for at least 30 minutes before serving (serve cold). This is *delicious* the next day.

*If you are using leftover rice and it's sticky, drizzle some olive oil on it and heat in the microwave for about 30 seconds. Stir to break it up.

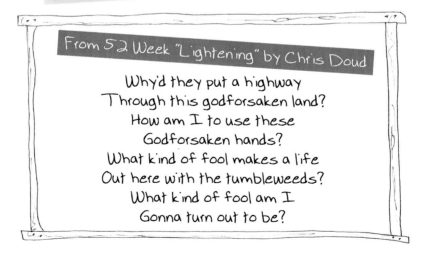

From 52 Week "Lightening" by Chris Doud

Why'd they put a highway
Through this godforsaken land?
How am I to use these
Godforsaken hands?
What kind of fool makes a life
Out here with the tumbleweeds?
What kind of fool am I
Gonna turn out to be?

To read more about the 52-Week Club see pages 87-88

Mom's Chicken & Rice Casserole

(serves 4)

2 cups cooked rice (leftover rice works well)
2 tablespoons olive oil
1 pound boneless, skinless chicken breast tenders*
¼ teaspoon salt
¼ teaspoon pepper
1 (10 ounce) can-cream-of-mushroom soup
½ can milk (use soup can to measure)
½ teaspoon ground sage
½ teaspoon salt
1 cup finely shredded Cheddar cheese
2 cups chopped broccoli

Yes, I use a CAN of cream-of-mushroom soup. If it's good enough for my mom, it's good enough for me!

Preheat oven to 350 degrees.

Cook rice according to package directions and set aside.

Heat olive oil in a large skillet over medium heat. Add chicken tenders and sprinkle with salt and pepper. Sear until lightly browned, about 4-5 minutes. Flip and cook for another 3-4 minutes. Remove from heat and set aside.

While chicken is cooking, in a medium pot set over medium heat add mushroom soup and milk. Whisk until combined and add sage and salt. Bring to a boil, add cheese and stir until melted. Remove from heat.

Spread a little sauce on the bottom of an 8x8 baking dish - just enough to lightly cover it. Spread the rice on top, then the broccoli, chicken and the rest of the sauce. Bake for 30 minutes.

Mom

*My mom used to use drumsticks for this. Just stick the (raw) drumsticks on top of the rice and wedge the broccoli in wherever they fit. Pour sauce on top and bake for 45 minutes to an hour. To see if it's done, cut into a thick piece. When juices run clear, chicken is done.

Chicken Artichoke Casserole

(serves 4-6)

1 tablespoon olive oil
(or oil from artichoke jar)
1 pound boneless, skinless chicken breasts,
chopped into ½ inch cubes
½ teaspoon salt
½ teaspoon pepper
1 cup diced button mushrooms
2 cups chopped fresh baby spinach

2 (6 ounce) jars marinated artichoke hearts,
drained and chopped
½ cup sour cream
1 cup cooked rice (about ½ cup uncooked)
½ teaspoon salt
1 cup shredded Pepper Jack cheese
¼ cup shredded Parmesan cheese

Preheat oven to 350 degrees.

Heat olive oil (or artichoke oil) in a large skillet over medium heat for about one minute. Add chopped chicken and season with salt and pepper. Cook and stir for about 5 minutes. Add the mushrooms, cook and stir for 2 minutes. Add the spinach and toss until spinach is wilted. Remove from heat and set aside.*

In a large bowl mix the artichoke hearts, sour cream, cooked rice, salt and Pepper Jack cheese. Add chicken mixture and stir until combined. Pour and spread evenly into an 8x8 inch baking dish. Sprinkle with Parmesan cheese and bake for 30-45 minutes or until top is brown and bubbly.

*Don't worry if the chicken is a bit undercooked, it will cook the rest of the way in the oven.

I find this to be and unfair question. I always find these questions unfair. Mostly for the reason that I don't want people to know which iconic artists I don't dig. But you asked it, so here goes: I am going to go with The Beatles. Elvis is great but it seems for only a certain mood, whereas The Beatles are impossible to shoehorn into a specific, well, anything. I could rant for you, but just leave with this, The Beatles are the most famous band in history and all of it stems from the fun they obviously had with it all.

- Alexander Ayers - Sacramento, CA - When asked "Elvis or The Beatles?"

Cheesy Chicken Enchiladas

(serves 4-6)

2 tablespoons olive oil
1 pound boneless, skinless chicken breasts, chopped small
1 (4 ounce) can diced mild green chilies
2 cloves garlic, minced
½ cup finely chopped yellow or white onion
1 cup shredded Monterey Jack cheese*
1 cup shredded Cheddar cheese*
1½ cups green enchilada sauce
¼ cup sour cream
4 burrito size flour tortillas

For topping:
½ cup shredded Monterey Jack cheese**
½ cup shredded Cheddar cheese**

*There is no such thing as too much cheese! Pile it on!

Preheat oven to 350 degrees.

Heat olive oil in a large skillet over medium heat. Add chicken, cook and stir for about 5 minutes. Add chilies, garlic and onion. Cook and stir for another 5 minutes. When done, remove from skillet into a bowl and allow to cool to the touch. When cool, add the cheese and mix until combined.

In a small bowl whisk together the enchilada sauce and sour cream.

Pour about ½ cup of the sauce on the bottom of a 8x8 baking dish. Spread it around to cover as much of the bottom as possible. Divide the chicken mixture into 4 portions. Spread each portion evenly in the middle of each tortilla. Roll tightly, tucking ends in, like a burrito. Place enchiladas fold side down in baking dish. Pour the rest of the sauce over the enchiladas. Use a spatula to spread the sauce around so that it completely covers the top. Sprinkle the remaining cheese on top.

Bake enchiladas for 30-35 minutes or until top is brown and bubbly.

**These aren't called 'Cheesy' for nuthin'!

Main Dishes

"Eatith Pilaf, Bb On Your Plate"
by Matt "The Professor" Smith

With music, I can make friends in any town. I have freedom to travel anywhere that I can play, and make the people say: "That fella's a guy to know." Some just dance - and that's sure okay.

If I didn't have music, I'd be playing the spoons right now. My late night walks wouldn't have a certain Slim Harpo swagger, so the street toughs might make a grab for my jewels. I wouldn't strut into the club if I didn't know I was strutting like Jagger. When the jukebox hits it proper, I wouldn't make my Wilson Pickett way to the dance floor. But there would be no jukebox without hits, and what would we even have a floor for? And what would I do, without all my fancy dance kicks, to drive off those un-Slim-Harpo'd street kids. I'd need a harpoon, or a jagged bottle, or a pick axe. You can't walk around cool with all that.

I never use picks or set lists. I once played a show and had a set list. I played a few extra fast-strum rockers that night - none of which were on the list - olive witch gnawed away my unpicked finger tips. My hand was cheesed. There was a good amount of blood that worked up a splatter on my steel guitar. When I noticed, I grabbed my set list: "I knew I brought this for a reason." I used it to towel off the red, then I said: "I got another number goin' out!" People still remember that show.

I rarely use caution. I like garden fresh and Mexican. My combined giddiness caused a knife once to take my knuckle. It was the best salsa we ever had, they all said they still talk about it now.

I was with a woman who behaves in ways that don't make it in to family books - she could, of corset, say worse of me. Nevertheless, we had to eat. It was brunch for her, but dinner for me because I hadn't gone to sleep. Frankly, I was maintaining a slight buzz. On the restaurant porch we sat. I un-shamefully devoured the celery stalk in my Bloody Mary. A disheveled bum was the one who shared the porch. He had scratched together some scratch for a beer, and was sitting there with two arms around it like a bum who'd just scrapped together some scratch for a scotch. I engaged him and was met with craziness about mind control and Vietnam-- all the classics. He asked me to remove my shades, and he said I had the eyes of a mystic. The man was obviously lost in head (out of his head). He gave me his walking stick to reward my mysticism. It's a legitimate walking stick - I tried to refuse, but he insisted. After a few moments, his favor turned in an un-instigated snap, and he wanted to fight me. Now, I've got no qualms about beatin' up an old man with his own stick, particularly if he's tryin' to take my jewels, or tell jokes to my lady friend. My jewels were in the van, so I decided to talk him down. He just wouldn't get sane, though. Then I asked him what kind of music he liked. His eyes jackpotted in joy, we talked of Rock 'n' Roll so cohesively. I've still got the stick. I dropped the lady off.

This Fats Domino record in my hand will be grooved by me tonight. I'll dance along, have a wine, sing aloud. It's the weekend, and the treat is Rock 'n' Roll. These very grooves were served fifty years ago; I don't think they've gone bad. They've spun but haven't turned. In Someteen fifty-nine some youth held the edges, and prepared the needle to set the song he craved. That song's a dud - peas (take none and pass it on). This one moves me every time - pilaf (let it light my soul on fire). How many people have been passed this plate, I wonder. It smells like great grandma's recipe book, and scuffed like my favorite shoes. We listen to songs now as George Jetson eats his supper- an intangerinible file that doesn't smell like it's been handled a hundred times in delight. Digitalia sounds more clear than record, and you don't need wax to make synthetic honey. I don't mind pickin' a few hundred chicken bones outta my gumbo in honor of the chef, a human, a friend.

Family gathers for a meal - there they go; friends gather for a rock show. What's in this? Where's this band from? Roux. New Orleans. At some point you've just gotta dance; at some point you just gotta loosen the belt on your pants. If you can't dance, just say you can, then prove it. That's what I do. Dance like a child who doesn't yet think anyone is looking. Dance like an old man who knows no one ever was. If you can't loosen your belt, I can help.

Am - a sage. CM7 is garlic. F# is sugar, and as far as I know Gm is oregano. I tried it in one key and it didn't work, so I substituted Bb for beef, and rubbed in a little C salt. Every time I played it, I had a better song - that happens best when the bitter's gone. First course, second chorus, third verse. Family and God.

I was a pair of tiny hands putting a whole body in a shuck. The first time I shucked corn: with Great Grandpa Delmer. He sang a lot for a quiet man. That evening was a few sweet Irish/American folk tunes, a healthy osmotic wisdom transfer…And later, corn. It was our only time alone. It is my memory. He died and left me his steel hard hat. He was a carpenter, just like me.

Then his wife passed and left her pot that cooks pilaf, and everything just right. When I get home from work, and put that pot to use I wish they could see me now and hear me sing for my suppers.

All my friends play music, and all of them eat. I don't know if it's a coincidence, but they smile much more than those hipsters that refuse to tap their feet and who gag themselves with spoons. When I croon, the person I want to swoon is that sweet mama who knows her way around the stove. That's far from hip to say, but like anything, once it's in your mouth, your opinion might change.

With my friends, sometimes we trade songs all night and forget to eat, but are sure full. Then again, a lot of evenings have been spent over the grill while dust decorates our guitar case, and we coulda' swore we made music. Those nights that we help each other write, and then get in the kitchen to develop recipes- those are the nights that will always be.

Main Dishes

Sausage & Tomato Rice
(a.k.a. Poor Man's Risotto)
(serves 4-6)

1 cup (uncooked) rice
2 cups chicken broth
1 pound Hot (or Mild) Italian sausage
½ medium onion, sliced and cut into half moons
3 cloves garlic, minced
½ cup heavy cream
1 cup crumbled Queso Fresco cheese
2 cups quartered cherry or grape tomatoes
½ cup chopped flat-leaf (Italian) parsley
1 teaspoon salt

There's nothing fancy about this recipe - it's pretty much a big gooey mess of food - but it's delicious!

Add broth and rice to a large pot. (Use a larger pot than you think you may need. You are going to add the rest of the ingredients to the rice at the end.) Bring to a boil and turn heat to low. Simmer for 15-20 minutes or until water is absorbed.

Meanwhile, cook sausage over medium heat in a large skillet, breaking it up as it cooks. About 5 minutes in, add onions and garlic. Toss and stir until sausage is done, about 4-5 more minutes. Add cream, bring to a boil and turn heat to low. Cook until the cream has reduced by half and remove from heat.

Add the sausage mixture, cheese, tomatoes, parsley and salt to the rice. Stir just until combined, do not over work.

This is the first recipe that ever came to me in a dream. In the dream, I had this dish at a restaurant and wanted to re-create it at home.

I stood outside the restaurant with my brother-in-law and we tried to pick out the ingredients. I asked him which kind of cheese I should use and he said: "Queso Frescooo".

Funny thing is, I'd never heard of Queso Fresco before - but in this dish it was perfect!

"Eureka!"
By Micah Garbarino, Oklahoma City, OK

What's better than finding a $20 bill in the pants you're putting on, or going to the cupboard to discover your kid didn't eat the last Oreo? Putting on an old record and realizing you forgot how good it is. I don't have an iPod (what? that's right, no cell phone either). So, music is not at my fingertips and if I haven't seen the disc for a while, chances are it will stay out of rotation until something in the back of my head says, "Hey, technically-challenged little man. You should really listen to..." Find new music, but keep the old, one is silver, the other is gold, records that is.

Here are 5 albums you must own, no matter what music you typically listen to (in alphabetical order because ranking them would be even harder than deciding on them in the first place...and just in case you're wondering, I'm a folk-rock kind of guy)

IV—Led Zeppelin
Why for cowboys: "Stairway to Heaven" has a better guitar riff than "Free Bird".
Why for the Hip-Hop crowd: The Beastie Boys sampled the heck out of it.
Why for rockers: If you're a rock fan, you don't need a why.

Joshua Tree – U2
Why for cowboys: "Trip Through Your Wire" is one of the best "crossover" songs ever.
Why for the Hip-Hop crowd: "I Still Haven't Found What I'm Looking For" could have been a soul classic.
Why for rockers: The best album from U2. It's laid back but on the edge.

Live at Folsom Prison – Johnny Cash
Why for cowboys: Cash is the king of country. He's at his best here with "Folsom Prison Blues."
Why for the Hip-Hop crowd: "Cocaine Blues," the man in black went to prison before it was cool.
Why for rockers: Cash's back-up band provides driving rhythm that pounds home his direct lyrical style.

London Calling – The Clash
Why for cowboys: This album has a way of poking fun of the elite, it's just a little more funky than twangy.
Why for the Hip-Hop crowd: There is a huge reggae influence here and "Revolution Rock" should be sampled.
Why for rockers: Joe Strummer's and Mick Jones' vocals are perfect for wicked (kind of in a good way) lyrics.

Vampire Weekend – Vampire Weekend
Why for cowboys: You need to broaden your horizons, this is a fun way to do it.
Why for the Hip-Hop crowd: South African flavor that should be in Hip-Hop.
Why for rockers: "A-Punk" is the best single in decades.

Lamb Risotto

(serves 2-4)

1 tablespoon olive oil
½ pound lamb, thinly sliced
½ teaspoon salt
¼ teaspoon pepper
2 cloves garlic, minced
¼ cup pine nuts
4-5 cups chicken broth
2 tablespoons olive oil

½ cup (about ½ medium) finely diced
  red onion
1 cup Arborio rice
½ cup white wine
¼ cup (about 2 ounces) crumbled Feta cheese
¼ teaspoon allspice
2 tablespoons chopped fresh mint

Heat olive oil in a large skillet over medium heat. Add lamb, salt, pepper and garlic. *For rare lamb*: Cook for 2-3 minutes on each side. *For medium*: 4-5 minutes on each side. Use a slotted spoon to remove lamb, set aside. Add about a tablespoon of olive oil to the skillet. Add pine nuts and toss frequently until lightly toasted.

In a medium pot bring broth to a boil. Simmer and maintain over low heat. Set aside ¼ cup for later.

In a medium to large pot heat oil over medium heat. Add onion, cook and stir until soft. Add rice and stir until grains are well coated with oil and translucent, about 3 minutes. Add wine and stir until absorbed.

Add one ladleful of broth and stir. Once the rice absorbs broth, add another ladleful, stirring constantly. Repeat until you have added about 3 cups of broth. Check to see if the rice is done - it should be firm but chewy. If rice is still firm, add another ladleful of broth and check again. When done, remove from heat and add lamb, Feta, allspice, mint and reserved broth. Mix well and serve immediately.

Garnish with crumbled Feta and mint.

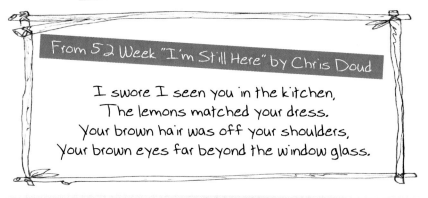

From 52 Week "I'm Still Here" by Chris Doud

I swore I seen you in the kitchen,
The lemons matched your dress.
Your brown hair was off your shoulders,
Your brown eyes far beyond the window glass.

To read more about the 52-Week Club see pages 87-88

Spicy Poblano Chicken Risotto

(serves 6)

2 roasted poblano peppers
2 (7 ounce) cans diced mild green chilies
2 pounds boneless, skinless chicken
  breasts, chopped into ½ inch pieces
½ (10 ounce) can corn
¼ teaspoon salt
¼ teaspoon pepper
8-10 cups chicken broth

2 tablespoons olive oil
½ cup chopped onion
2 cups Arborio rice
1 cup white wine
½ teaspoon salt
½ teaspoon pepper
1 cup shredded Pepper Jack cheese

First, roast the poblano. You can either do this over an open flame or in the oven.

To roast over an open flame: Place poblano directly on grill or over your gas burner. Use tongs to turn it until all sides are black and charred.

To roast in the oven: Preheat oven to 400 degrees. Drizzle pepper with olive oil, sprinkle with salt, pepper and garlic powder. Massage pepper with oil and spices. Roast for 15-20 minutes or until charred all over.

When done roasting, put into a zip top bag and into fridge until cool. Peel and chop.

Heat a large skillet over medium heat. Add the chilies, chicken, corn, salt and pepper. Cook until chicken is done, about 7-10 minutes.

In a medium pot bring broth to a boil. Simmer and maintain over low heat. Set aside ¼ cup for later.

In a medium to large pot heat oil over medium heat. Add onion, cook and stir until soft. Add rice and stir until grains are well coated with oil and translucent, about 3 minutes. Add wine and stir until absorbed.

Add one ladleful of broth and stir. Once the rice absorbs broth, add another ladleful, stirring constantly. Repeat until you have added about 3 cups of broth. Check to see if the rice is done - it should be firm but chewy. If rice is still firm, add another ladleful of broth and check again. When done, add salt, pepper, cheese, chicken/corn mixture, poblanos and reserved broth. Serve hot.

> For an even spicier dish, use one can of mild chilies and one can of hot chilies.
>
> For less spicy, use one poblano and Cheddar instead of Pepper Jack.

Main Dishes

Chicken & Sun-Dried Tomato Risotto

(serves 2-4)

3 tablespoons sun-dried tomato oil
1 pound boneless, skinless chicken breast,
  cut into 1 inch cubes
¼ teaspoon salt
¼ teaspoon pepper
4-5 cups chicken broth
2 tablespoons olive oil

½ medium onion, diced
1 cup Arborio rice
2 cloves garlic, minced
½ cup white wine
¼ cup finely chopped sun-dried tomatoes
½ cup crumbled Feta cheese

Heat the sun-dried tomato oil in large skillet over medium heat. Add chicken, salt and pepper. Cook and stir until chicken is done, about 7-10 minutes.

In a medium pot bring broth to a boil. Simmer and maintain over low heat. Set aside ¼ cup for later.

In a medium to large pot heat oil over medium heat. Add onion, cook and stir until soft. Add rice and stir until grains are well coated with oil and translucent, about 3 minutes. Add wine and stir until absorbed.

Add one ladleful of broth and stir. Once the rice absorbs broth, add another ladleful, stirring constantly. Repeat until you have added about 3 cups of broth. Check to see if the rice is done - it should be firm but chewy. If rice is still firm, add another ladleful of broth and check again. When done, add chicken, sun-dried tomatoes, Feta and reserved broth. Stir until combined and serve hot.

by Shelly Cimoli

Quiche Lorraine

(serves 8)

1 pound bacon
1 (10 ounce) package frozen chopped spinach
1 cup sour cream
4 medium eggs, beaten

2 cups shredded Swiss cheese
½ teaspoon salt
½ teaspoon pepper
2 deep-dish pie crusts

Preheat oven to 350 degrees.

Chop bacon into little pieces and fry until crisp. Set on paper towels to drain. Slowly, a few minutes at a time, defrost the spinach in the microwave. (Or you can do what I never remember to do, and take the spinach out ahead of time and defrost it in the fridge or on the counter.) Squeeze as much water out of the spinach as you can. In a large bowl, mix bacon, spinach, sour cream, eggs, cheese, salt and pepper. Divide mixture evenly between the two pie crusts.

This is one of my favorite dishes that my mom used to make. Actually, it still is. Only now, Dad or I make it. Often we make this on Christmas Eve and eat it for breakfast Christmas morning. This is also excellent served cold.

Bake for 30-45 minutes or until puffed in the middle and a knife inserted in the middle comes out clean. Let cool for 10-15 minutes before serving.

Mexican Quiche

(serves 4)

1 (4.5 ounce) can diced mild green chilies
½ pound ground beef or ground sausage
½ teaspoon salt
½ medium green pepper, chopped
2 (2 ounce) cans sliced black olives, diced
½ cup shredded Cheddar cheese

½ cup shredded Pepper Jack cheese
¾ cup sour cream
3 medium eggs, beaten
½ teaspoon salt
1 deep-dish pie crust

Heat a medium skillet over medium heat. Add chilies. Cook and stir for about 1 minute. Add meat and salt. Cook until almost brown, about 5-6 minutes. Add green peppers and continue cooking until meat is cooked through, another 3-4 minutes. Drain in colander, set aside and allow mixture to cool a bit.

In a large bowl combine the olives, cheese, sour cream, eggs and salt. When the meat mixture has cooled, add to the bowl and mix well. Pour mixture into pie crust.

Bake for 30-45 minutes or until puffed in the middle and a knife inserted in the middle comes out clean. Let cool for 10-15 minutes before serving.

Main Dishes

"Puddles"

The ghost of you speaks to me in dreams.
A chill sweeps over me, and I can't breath.
I hear you whisper "I know you"
And when I awake, my heart breaks a little deeper.
I can still feel your breath on my neck,
I can still hear your voice in my head,
But you're not coming back, cuz he shot you dead.

And when women and wine make men step in puddles,
When lovers serenade each other in foggy old graveyards,
When the wine that I drink at nine in the morning,
Makes me feel like I'm home, that's when I miss you most.

Remember when we sat in that smoky bar,
On a cold Sunday morning in early November?
We smoked cigarettes and drank whiskey all day,
Then we stole that old canoe and floated down the river.
We laid on the shore singing songs to each other
Then we stumbled back to the bar
And you played piano while I sang 'Hey Jude'.

And when women and wine make men step in puddles,
When lovers serenade each other in foggy old graveyards,
When the wine that I drink at nine in the morning,
Makes me feel like I'm home, that's when I miss you most.

Maybe sitting on a barstool instead of a pew
Is the reason he took you away,
Cuz angels can't go into bars that sell whiskey.
And maybe they couldn't see you through the smoke,
So now I'm alone, and you're somewhere near heaven,
Or maybe a little farther south.
But the bar is still smoky, and the pew is still empty,
And whiskey and men still make girls write sad love songs.

And when women and wine make men step in puddles,
When lovers serenade each other in foggy old graveyards,
When the wine that I drink at nine in the morning,
Makes me feel like I'm home, that's when I miss you most.

To read more about the 52-Week Club see pages 87-88

All You Need Is Food

Veggie Herb Quiche

(serves 8)

5 medium eggs, beaten
1 tablespoon chopped fresh thyme
2 tablespoons chopped fresh basil
¾ cup sour cream
1½ cups shredded Fontina cheese
  (or Monterey Jack)
½ teaspoon salt
¼ teaspoon pepper
1 tablespoon olive oil
½ red bell pepper, chopped
½ yellow pepper, chopped
6 spears asparagus, chopped

2 green onions, chopped
¼ teaspoon salt
⅛ teaspoon pepper
2 deep-dish pie crusts

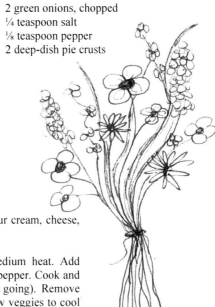

Preheat oven to 350 degrees.

In a large bowl mix eggs, thyme, basil, sour cream, cheese, salt and pepper. Set aside.

Heat olive oil in a large skillet over medium heat. Add peppers, asparagus, green onions, salt and pepper. Cook and stir for 3 minutes (just to get the flavors going). Remove from heat and drain on paper towels. Allow veggies to cool for a few minutes.

When cool, add to egg mixture. Stir until combined and divide evenly into pie crusts.

Bake for 30-45 minutes or until puffed in middle and a knife inserted into the middle comes out clean. Remove from the oven and let it sit for 10-15 minutes before serving.

If you are making this ahead of time, allow to cool completely before covering it with foil and putting it in the refrigerator.

Quiche is the perfect excuse to get rid of those odds and ends that you don't want to go to waste.

You can pretty much use any combination of veggies, herbs and cheeses you having laying around in your fridge.

Main Dishes

Turkey Pot Pie

(serves 4)

1 sheet of puff pastry (from a 17.3 ounce frozen package)
1 tablespoon olive oil
½ pound turkey breast, diced small
¼ teaspoon salt
¼ teaspoon pepper
1 tablespoon butter
1 cup diced potato*
1 large celery stalk, diced*
½ cup diced carrots**
¼ teaspoon salt
¼ teaspoon pepper
1 (10.75 ounce) can cream-of-chicken soup
½ cup frozen peas
1 deep-dish pie crust

Thaw puff pastry according to package directions.

Preheat oven to 350 degrees.

Heat olive oil in a large skillet over medium heat. Add turkey and sprinkle with salt and pepper. Cook and stir for about 10 minutes. Use a slotted spoon to remove the turkey from the skillet into a large bowl. Do not drain the juices!

*Make sure you dice up your vegetables pretty small. Ideally, you want to get some of each ingredient in every bite.

In the same skillet, melt butter. Add potato, cover and cook for 3 minutes. Add celery and carrots. *(If you are using frozen carrots, do not add them now!)* Sprinkle with salt and pepper. Cook and stir for about 3 more minutes. Remove from heat, drain in colander and allow mixture to cool for a few minutes.

To the bowl with the turkey, add the cream-of-chicken soup and peas. *(If you are using frozen carrots, add them here.)* Add the veggie mixture to the bowl and mix well.

Pour into pie crust and use a spatula to spread evenly. If you are using a store-bought crust, run your fingers around the edge of the pie crust to (gently) separate crust from tin. Gently unfold puff pastry and place on top. Tear or cut off each corner to form a circle. Fold and tightly pinch the puff pastry into and under the edges of the lower pie crust. Use a fork to poke tons of holes all over the top of the pastry so it doesn't explode in the oven.

Bake for 1 hour. Remove from oven and allow pie to cool for at least 10 minutes before serving.

**You can use frozen, diced carrots instead. The bags of frozen carrots and peas work perfect.

Green Chili Turkey Taco Melts

(serves 4-6)

1 (32 ounce) container turkey (or chicken) broth
1 pound boneless, skinless turkey breasts
1 teaspoon chili powder
1 teaspoon cumin
½ teaspoon paprika
1 teaspoon dried oregano
¼ teaspoon red pepper flakes

2 (4.5 ounce) cans mild green chilies
¼ cup finely chopped cilantro
1-2 medium vine-ripe tomatoes, diced
½ cup shredded Monterey Jack cheese
½ cup crumbled Queso Fresco cheese
8 small corn tortillas, about 4-5 inches
sour cream
Salsa Verde

Add broth and uncooked turkey meat to a medium sized pot. If the broth doesn't completely cover the meat, add some water until it's covered. Bring to a boil, cover and cook for 15-20 minutes. Check to see if it's done by cutting into the center (or refer to temperature chart at the beginning of this book). Remove from water and allow to cool to the touch. When cool enough to handle, use a couple of forks to shred meat.

While the turkey cooks, add chili powder, cumin, paprika, oregano, red pepper flakes, chilies and cilantro to a bowl. Stir until combined. Once the turkey has been cooked and shredded, add to the bowl and stir until it's coated and everything is evenly combined.

Spray a cookie sheet lightly with cooking spray. Place about ¼ cup of turkey mixture onto one half of each tortilla. Next, sprinkle with diced tomatoes and cheese. Heat under the broiler until the cheese is melted. Spread sour cream and/or salsa onto the other half of the tortilla and fold into a taco. Serve hot.

For me, the draw to the road isn't about not being satisfied in staying in one spot. It's about the idea of doing more good for other people by being out. I believe that what we are doing is important because I know what music has done for me in my life, and what it continues to do for me everyday. So to think about being a part of that in someone's life makes it very easy to make the decision to live with the sacrifices of being on the road so often, and for so long. Not to mention that playing makes it easy for me to release things that would otherwise be difficult to convey or to translate into some other form. Also, if everyone said "No" when we asked to have a place to stay for the night, that may make the decision to be out a little different, but you keep saying that it's okay to sleep on your floor, so...

Home is, as they say, where the heart is, and I think that with us (L.A.H.F.) our heart is with our family. We all have a kinship with each other that is, perhaps, unique to the conventional relationship. We all love our family that is at home tremendously, but with all of us being together - all of the time - it makes it easier for us to bear that burden.

- Dallin Bulkley - Larry & His Flask - Redmond, OR - on "Rambling"

Main Dishes

White Meatloaf

(serves 4)

1 tablespoon olive oil
½ large red bell pepper, diced
½ medium yellow onion, diced
2 cloves garlic, minced
½ cup chopped flat-leaf (Italian)
  parsley, chopped
½ cup panko breadcrumbs
1 teaspoon salt

½ teaspoon pepper
½ cup shredded Gruyere
  (or Parmesan) cheese
2 eggs, beaten
½ pound ground chicken
½ pound ground Mild Italian sausage
½ pound ground turkey
'Tomato Gravy' (page 53)

Preheat oven to 350 degrees.

Heat olive oil in a medium skillet over medium heat. Add red pepper and onion. Sprinkle with about ⅛ teaspoon each of salt and pepper. Cook and stir until soft, about 2-3 minutes. Add garlic, cook and stir for about 1 minute. Remove from heat and set aside to cool for a few minutes.

In a large bowl add parsley, breadcrumbs, salt, pepper, cheese, eggs, meat and pepper/onion mixture. Mix with hands until completely combined. Put the meat on a cookie sheet and use your hands to form it into the shape of a loaf. You can also use a loaf pan, but doing it in a cookie sheet allows more of the grease to come out of the meat. If you use a loaf pan, line the bottom with a few pieces of bread to help soak up the juices.

Rub the loaf with a little bit of the 'Tomato Gravy' (or use ketchup).

Bake for 1 hour and 15 minutes. Serve with the rest of the 'Tomato Gravy'.

Bob Dylan is a mystic. He's an oracle of the vague. His music is roots. His words are vapor. Try to grasp them and they're gone. His music is more intuited than understood and there is no possession of his meanings, only fumbling with ideas. Strung together the words make less sense, but pulled apart, each line supplies an image that conveys an emotion central throughout the rest of the song. The key to appreciating any poet is not to see, but to feel. However confusing his lyrics, there is no denying their power.

- Micah Garbarino - Oklahoma City, OK

Mexican Veggie Rice

(serves 4)

1 cup (uncooked) rice
1 cup water
¾ cup tomato juice
1 (28 ounce) can, whole peeled, stewed
   tomatoes (save juice for rice)
olive oil
salt and pepper
2-3 tablespoons grated Parmesan cheese*
1 tablespoon olive oil
½ cup chopped yellow onion

3 cloves garlic, minced
½ green pepper, chopped
½ red bell pepper, chopped
1 (4.5 ounce) can diced mild green chilies
½ (15 ounce) can black beans,
   drained and rinsed
½ (10 ounce) can corn
½ cup shredded Cheddar cheese
Garnish: cheese, sour cream and
   green onions

Rice: Add rice, water and tomato juice to a medium-large pot. Turn heat to medium and bring to a boil. Reduce heat to a low and simmer (covered) for 15-20 minutes or until all of the liquid is absorbed.

Tomatoes: Preheat oven to 400 degrees. Spray a cookie sheet with cooking spray. Place whole stewed tomatoes on cookie sheet. Drizzle with olive oil and sprinkle with salt, pepper and Parmesan cheese. Roast for 15 minutes.

Veggies: While the rice and tomatoes are cooking, heat oil in a large skillet or pot. Add onion and garlic, cook and stir for about 2 minutes. Add peppers and chilies. Cook for about 5 minutes and add the beans and corn. Remove from heat.

Add the rice to the veggies along with the cheese. Let it cook over low heat for about 5 minutes to melt the cheese.

To serve: Put the rice/veggie mixture on a plate and place 2 or 3 tomatoes on top. Sprinkle with cheese and add a dollop of sour cream and green onions.

This recipe also makes for some delicious leftovers. I like to take the leftovers, add more cheese and sour cream and wrap it in a tortilla.

*Fresh grated Parmesan would be best, but the stuff sold in containers works just as well. It just depends how much of a cheese snob you are. I'm a big fan of cheese, but I'm not opposed to utilizing the money-saving container every once in a while.

Main Dishes

"Nick Drake's Pink Moon"
by Travis Mamone, Easton, MD

It was the summer of 2000 when I first heard it. There was a commercial on TV that had four teens driving at night, on their way to a party. When they get there, however, they look at each other and decide to keep driving into the night. It was supposed to be about how fun it is to drive a Volkswagen, but that's not what I got out of it. What got my attention was the song playing in the background: the gently strummed acoustic guitar, and that voice, so soft and fragile. It was one of the most beautiful sounds I had ever heard in all my seventeen years on earth. Normally, I'd be happy enough blasting my eardrums out with Death Metal, but this was different. This had more emotion and melancholy than anything Korn could ever muster. I had to know who this was.

Later, I found out that voice belonged to Nick Drake and the song was "Pink Moon." I'd heard of the name before, but didn't know anything about him, except that apparently he overdosed on antidepressants when he was just 26. But now that I had put a sound to the name, I quickly bought the album. Drake became the spokesman for my teenage angst and when the darkness of the world overwhelmed me, I put on the album and let him sing me his lullabies. Drake knew that darkness well and he captured it perfectly in his last album, *Pink Moon.*

It's interesting that VW chose "Pink Moon" to sell their cars because the lyrics are actually pretty dark and ominous: "Saw it written and I saw it say/ pink moon is on its way/ and none of you stand so tall/ pink moon's gonna get ye all."

According to medieval culture, a pink moon was considered an omen of coming disaster. Not exactly something you want to convey in a car commercial! Regardless of whatever advertising executives make of it, it's still a beautiful song, and the rest of the album doesn't stray far from the same vibe. Unlike Drake's two previous albums, *Five Leaves Left* and *Bryter Layter*, there is only Drake and his guitar, with a little bit of piano on the title track. The result makes the album more intimate than his other two.

"Place to Be" is another favorite of mine. The haunting lyrics paint a picture of a man who has realized the bright days of his youth are gone and now must find a refuge that can comfort him in his loneliness. In "Parasite" Drake describes himself as a tiny bug on the ground, looking up at the world. Not all the songs are hopeless, though. In "Things Behind the Sun" Drake invites the listener to create something new despite scoffs from "them that stare." Perhaps this is a reference to Drake's disappointment with *Bryter Layter*, which, despite having some great songs, is a bit too overproduced. It's said that he recorded *Pink Moon* without telling anyone at the record label, until he dropped off the master tapes on the receptionist's desk.

Unfortunately, like Drake's life, *Pink Moon* is too short. All the songs are only 2 minutes long (with the exception of "Things Behind the Sun," which is nearly 4 minutes long), which is a shame because many of them can be extended.

For example, the song "Know" is a minute and a half and has only four lines: "Know that I love you/ know I don't care/ know that I see you/ know I'm not there." Engineer John Wood once said 30 minutes was enough for *Pink Moon*, but I disagree. Ever time I listen to it, I play it twice in a row so I can hear Drake longer. It's been eight years since I first heard "Pink Moon." I'm older now and not as angst-ridden as I used to be (thank God). But on days when I feel the world coming down on me, the darkness taunts me, and it seems as though the world will blow itself up shortly—that's when *Pink Moon* comes out. I put the CD in, close my eyes, and let Drake sing me to sleep as he tells me, "Yeah, I've been there, too."

Artwork by Jamin Marshall

Veggie Enchiladas

(serves 4)

1 poblano pepper*
2 tablespoons olive oil
1 medium shallot, finely chopped
2 cloves garlic, minced
1 cup chopped broccoli
1 cup chopped zucchini
½ teaspoon salt
¼ teaspoon pepper
1 (4 ounce) can diced mild green chilies
   (drain juices!)
1 (6 ounce) bag baby spinach, chopped
1 cup shredded Monterey Jack cheese*
1 cup cooked rice
2 cups green enchilada sauce
⅓ cup sour cream
4 burrito size flour tortillas
For topping:
½ cup shredded Cheddar cheese*

Preheat oven to 375 degrees.

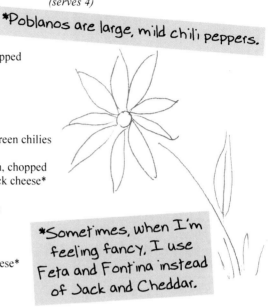

*Poblanos are large, mild chili peppers.

*Sometimes, when I'm feeling fancy, I use Feta and Fontina instead of Jack and Cheddar.

Put the poblano on a cookie sheet, drizzle with olive oil and sprinkle with salt and pepper. Rub oil and spices all over the pepper. Roast in oven for 10 minutes. Flip pepper over and roast for 10 more minutes. Remove and immediately put it into a zip top bag and place in fridge. When cool to the touch, peel and finely chop.

Another option is to blacken the pepper over an open flame (if you have a gas stove or outside grill). To do this, use tongs to lay the pepper directly on the grill, turning it occasionally until the whole pepper is blackened.

Turn oven down to 350 degrees.

Heat olive oil in a large skillet over low-medium heat. Add shallots and garlic. Cook and stir for about 30 seconds. Add broccoli, zucchini, salt and pepper. Cook and stir for about 5 minutes. Add chilies, cook and stir for about 1 minute. Add spinach and cook just until wilted, about 1 minute. Set aside in a colander to allow mixture to cool and drain.

When cool, add poblanos, cheese and rice to the veggie mixture. Stir to combine.

In a small bowl whisk together the enchilada sauce and sour cream.

Spread about ¼ cup of sauce on the bottom of an 8x8 inch baking dish. Divide the veggie mixture into four parts. Put ¼ of the veggie mixture into each tortilla.

(continued)

Fold sides in and roll *tightly* like a burrito. Place in baking dish flap side down. Repeat with the other tortillas and the rest of the mixture. Pour remaining sauce over the enchiladas and sprinkle with Cheddar.

Bake for 30-45 minutes, until brown and bubbly.

All you really need in life is food and shelter. Once you have those locked down, it's all about music. It's almost the same thing, if you think about it. We have soul food and soul music. We have Southern rock and Southern cuisine. Bay Area Thrash, California Pizza Kitchen. Okay, maybe that one doesn't work. But hell man, we have Salsa and salsa! Either way, music is a kind of nourishment on its own. We've all craved a song that's been stuck in our head and when we finally get to our stereos, it can be just as satisfying as sitting down to that enormous pizza you fantasized about all day at work. Music can be cheesy too, right? Can't a song also be bittersweet? "Hey man, play me that tasty lick."

Music and food go together like vans and shag carpets. We can see a musical obsession with food everywhere. George Harrison's second album, the cover is just him sitting down to an enormous table of Indian food. We know that Elvis loved peanut butter and banana sandwiches. Beck even wrote a song called "Satan Gave Me a Taco." If you want to see the greatest example of culinary eroticism by musicians, buy ZZ Top's *Rio Grande Mud* on vinyl. The gate fold is a two panel poster of the most indulgent Mexican meal you have ever seen in your life, with cheese and chilies piled half a foot high. Food is integral to the whole musical process. Who's practice space doesn't have some crumbs by the drum set? Ever gotten cheese puff dust on your guitar? Of course you have.

My favorite musician of all time is a guy from Austin, Texas named Roky Erickson. He's a wonderful singer and along with the rest of the 13th Floor Elevators, he invented Psychedelic Rock. My favorite food has got to be nachos, brought over from Coahuila, Mexico and similarly introduced to the U.S. by way of Texas. Did Roky love nachos as much as me? I don't know. But they go together like bacon and maple syrup, and if I could, I'd have 'em both every day of my life. "Hey man, that drum fill's alright, but could you spice it up?"

- Sean Ford - Trigger Renegade/Professor - Los Angeles, CA

Spinach & Rice Stuffed Zucchini Boats

(serves 4)

4 medium zucchinis
1 tablespoon olive oil
½ teaspoon salt
¼ teaspoon pepper
1 cup finely chopped spinach
1 cup cooked rice*
¼ cup Italian seasoned breadcrumbs
2 tablespoons shredded Parmesan cheese
1 (25 ounce) jar marinara sauce of your choice
2 tablespoons shredded Parmesan cheese

Preheat oven to 350 degrees.

Slice each zucchini lengthwise. Use a spoon or melon-baller to scoop out the middle of the zucchini, leaving about ½ inch on each end. Chop up the stuff that you scooped out, measure out ½ cup and set aside. Discard the rest.

Place zucchinis skin side down in a 9x13 inch baking dish and sprinkle lightly with salt and pepper.

Heat olive oil in a large skillet over low-medium heat. Add the ½ cup of zucchini guts to the oil. Add salt and pepper, cook and stir for 1 minute. Add the chopped spinach and cook until wilted, about 1 minute. Scrape all contents of the skillet into a large bowl.

Add rice, breadcrumbs and 2 tablespoons of Parmesan cheese to the spinach mixture. Mix well until completely combined.

Evenly divide the spinach/rice mixture into each 'zucchini boat'. If you have leftover filling, go back and stuff it in, you'll want to use it all up.

Pour the marinara sauce over the zucchini. Top with shredded Parmesan cheese and place in oven. Bake for 20-30 minutes, depending on how soft you want your zucchini.

*Leftover rice is perfect for this!

Seafood

Spicy Baked Cod – 207

Baked Halibut with Spinach & Tomatoes – 208

Lime & Honey-Glazed Salmon – 209

Ginger Shrimp Risotto – 210

Bethany's Buttery Shrimp – 211

Mahi Mahi Tacos – 212

Ahi Tuna Burgers – 213

Shrimp Cakes – 214

Dreamy Linguini – 215

Three-Cheese Crab Roll-Ups – 216

Creamy Red Pepper Shrimp Pasta – 217

Mahi Mahi Tacos - Page 212

Shrimp Cakes - Page 214

Three-Cheese Crab Roll-Ups - Page 216

Creamy Red Pepper Shrimp Pasta - Page 217

Ahi Tuna Burgers - Page 213

Bethany's Buttery Shrimp - Page 211

Spicy Baked Cod

(serves 4)

1 tablespoon olive oil
2 cups (about 3-4) diced vine-ripe
  tomatoes
¼ cup (about ½ medium) diced shallot
1 clove garlic, minced
½ teaspoon salt
¼ teaspoon pepper
½ teaspoon cumin

½ teaspoon paprika
⅛ teaspoon cayenne
10 fresh basil leaves, chopped (page 18)
2 tablespoons capers
4 (6 ounce) boneless, skinless cod steaks
  or filets
½ cup panko breadcrumbs

Heat oil in a large skillet over medium heat. Add tomatoes, shallots and garlic. Cook and stir for 2 minutes. Add spices, basil and capers. Cook for a few minutes, stirring occasionally, until a thick sauce forms. Remove from heat and allow sauce to cool slightly.

If you are using steaks: Lay fish in a baking dish and cover with the sauce. Top with breadcrumbs and drizzle with olive oil. Bake for 10-15 minutes.

If you are using filets: Spread about ¼ cup or so of the sauce in the middle of each filet. Fold both ends of filet in so that they overlap in the middle. Secure with a toothpick. Place each filet in the baking dish - this may get messy! Pour remaining sauce over the filets, top with breadcrumbs and drizzle with olive oil. Bake for 10-15 minutes.

Love isn't in a house
in an office or a bank vault.

Love is in the wind,
in a smile, on the road.

Love is his laugh,
her eyes, my soul.

Inspired by being blissfully unemployed,
spending weeks on the road with a band,
and coming home to my nephew's laugh.

Baked Halibut
with Spinach & Tomatoes
(serves 4)

2 tablespoons butter
¼ cup (about ½ medium) chopped shallot
2 cloves garlic, minced
2 cups (about 3-4 medium) diced
   and de-seeded tomatoes
4 cups chopped spinach

Preheat oven to 400 degrees.

1 cup chicken broth
¼ cup heavy cream
½ teaspoon salt
¼ teaspoon pepper
1 teaspoon ground coriander
4 (6 ounce) halibut steaks

Melt butter in a large skillet over medium heat. When butter begins to foam, add shallots and garlic. Cook and stir until shallots soften, about 1-2 minutes. Add tomatoes and spinach. Cook and stir until spinach is wilted, about 1 minute. Add broth, cream, salt, pepper and coriander. Mix and bring to a boil. Cook, stirring frequently, until the sauce thickens a bit, about 5 minutes. Remove from heat.

Pour about a quarter of the sauce onto the bottom of an 8x8 inch baking dish and spread it around. Put the halibut on top and pour/spread the rest of the sauce on top of the fish.

Bake in the preheated oven for 20-25 minutes or until fish flakes easily with a fork.

Serve over rice.

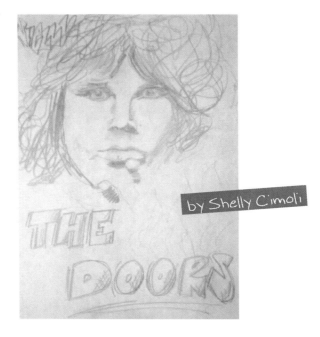

by Shelly Cimoli

Seafood

Lime & Honey-Glazed Salmon
with Warm Black Bean & Corn Salad

(serves 4)

Recipe courtesy of Eddie Nader - Harrison Twp, MI

Salad:
2 tablespoons extra-virgin olive oil
2 large garlic cloves, chopped
½ teaspoon crushed red pepper flakes
1 teaspoon ground cumin
salt and pepper to taste
1 red bell pepper, cored, seeded and chopped
1 (10 ounce) box frozen corn, defrosted
½ cup chicken broth
1 (15 ounce) can black beans,
  rinsed and drained
1 fresh lime (whole)
6 cups baby spinach

Salmon:
2 tablespoons olive oil
1 fresh lime (whole)
3 tablespoons honey
1 teaspoon chili powder
salt and pepper to taste
4 (6 ounce) salmon fillets

Pictured left to right: Eddie, my mom, my dad

Preheat a medium skillet over medium heat with 2 tablespoons of olive oil. Add the garlic, red pepper flakes, cumin, salt and pepper. Cook, stirring occasionally, for 1 minute.

To the cooked garlic add the bell peppers and corn. Cook for 1 minute. Add the chicken broth and continue to cook for another 2 minutes. Add the black beans and cook until the beans are just heated through. Remove the skillet from heat. Add the juice of 1 fresh lime and the spinach. Toss to wilt the spinach and taste to adjust seasoning.

Preheat a medium non-stick skillet over medium-high heat with 2 tablespoons of olive oil. In a shallow dish, combine the juice of 1 fresh lime, honey, chili powder, salt and pepper. Add the salmon fillets to the lime-honey mixture and toss to coat thoroughly. Add the seasoned salmon to the hot skillet and cook about 3-4 minutes on each side.

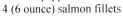

Serve the Lime and Honey-Glazed Salmon on top of the Warm Black Bean and Corn Salad.

Ginger Shrimp Risotto

(serves 4-6 as side dish or 3-4 as main dish)

1 roasted red bell pepper (see page 35)
2 tablespoons olive oil
1 pound shrimp (peeled and de-veined)*
3 tablespoons crushed ginger (from jar)
2 cloves garlic, minced
2 tablespoons olive oil
2 teaspoons lemon juice
1 tablespoon lime juice

½ teaspoon salt
3-4 cups chicken broth
2 tablespoons olive oil
½ cup diced red onion
1 cup Arborio rice
½ cup white wine
1 tablespoon butter
½ teaspoon salt

*You can buy 'em like this.

After red pepper has been roasted and cooled, peel skin off, dice and set aside.

In a large skillet heat oil over medium heat. Add shrimp, ginger and garlic. Cook until shrimp is pink all over, about 3-5 minutes. Remove from heat and put into a bowl. Add the other 2 tablespoons of olive oil, lemon juice, lime juice and salt. Toss until completely combined and set aside.

In a medium pot bring broth to a boil. Simmer and maintain over low heat. Set aside ¼ cup for later.

In a medium to large pot heat oil over medium heat. Add onion, cook and stir until soft. Add rice and stir until grains are well coated with oil and translucent, about 3 minutes. Add wine and stir until absorbed.

Add one ladleful of broth and stir. Once the rice absorbs broth, add another ladleful, stirring constantly. Repeat until you have added about 3 cups of broth. Check to see if the rice is done - it should be firm but chewy. If rice is still firm, add another ladleful of broth and check again. When done stir in butter and salt. Using a slotted spoon, add the shrimp to the rice mixture. Add about 2 tablespoons of the liquid from the shrimp to the risotto and stir to combine.

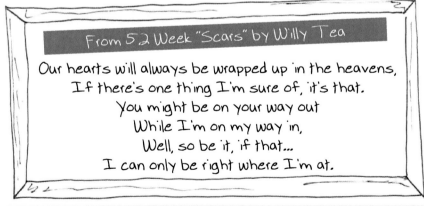

From 52 Week "Scars" by Willy Tea

Our hearts will always be wrapped up in the heavens,
If there's one thing I'm sure of, it's that.
You might be on your way out
While I'm on my way in,
Well, so be it, if that...
I can only be right where I'm at.

To read more about the 52-Week Club see pages 87-88

Seafood

Bethany's Buttery Shrimp
(serves 2-4)

¼ cup butter
2 cloves garlic, minced
1 pound shrimp, peeled and de-veined
½ teaspoon salt
½ teaspoon pepper

1 tablespoon lemon juice
½ teaspoon soy sauce
2 tablespoons chopped flat-leaf
(Italian) parsley

Melt butter over low-medium heat. Add garlic, cook and stir for about 1 minute. Add shrimp, salt, pepper and lemon juice. Cook and stir (or toss) until shrimp is pink all over, about 3-5 minutes. Add soy sauce and toss. Remove from heat and add parsley Toss and serve.

"Home"
by Ian Cook - Larry & His Flask - Redmond, OR

I can see between the slats in that worn out barn.
It's callin' to me across the muddy yard,
A few short steps and I'm in.

There's something in the way the air tastes,
Like fresh cut hay on a warm, summer day.
Like breathin' in pure love.

All your roads lead somewhere,
All mine lead here.

Stop the car, I see a broken tenor guitar.
It's singin' to me, it says: "Please don't leave!"
There's nowhere else I can go.

Watchin' the trees sway in the slow, slow breeze,
I can't help but think: This is my family.
Happiness is here.

All your roads lead somewhere,
All mine lead here.

Ian wrote this song during L.A.H.F's second visit to the Tea Farm. He disappeared into a bedroom for a while, and when he came out, he said, "I wrote a song!" He sat down on the kitchen floor and sang it for us. I think that's when we all knew that they weren't just another band passing through, and we weren't just another stop on their tour. We were family.

Mahi Mahi Tacos

(serves 2-4)

½ teaspoon chili powder
½ teaspoon ground cumin
½ teaspoon salt
¼ teaspoon pepper
1 tablespoon butter
1 clove garlic, minced

1 pound Mahi Mahi* skinned and
  de-boned
2 cups shredded and chopped lettuce
¼ to ½ cup chopped cilantro
5-6 small corn tortillas
'Tomato-Lime Tartar Sauce' (page 51)

In a small bowl mix together the chili powder, cumin, salt and pepper.

In a medium skillet melt the butter over low-medium heat. When the butter begins to foam add the garlic. Cook and stir for about 1 minute.

*A thick piece of Cod or Halibut would also work well.

Rub half of the spice mixture onto one side of the fish. Place the fish, spiced side down, in the heated pan. Rub the rest of the spices onto the top side of the fish. Cook for about 4-5 minutes on each side. When the fish flakes easily, it's done. Usually, I end up breaking up the thicker side with a fork while it's cooking to help it along. Remove from heat and use a fork to flake the fish into pieces. Big pieces or small pieces are both okay, whichever you prefer.

While the fish is cooking, mix the lettuce and cilantro in a bowl and set aside.

To assemble tacos: Spread a little of the tartar sauce onto a tortilla. Add fish and lettuce. Fold into tacos and serve hot!

This goes great with 'Cilantro-Lime Rice'

Make white rice according to package directions. Add 1 tablespoon of lime juice and 1 tablespoon of chopped cilantro for every cup of rice you make.

Well, I do love them both, but to me it's really no contest. The Beatles were creators of high art. Period. Elvis was rad, unforgettable and important to our collective culture, but The Beatles were elevated. Not just as songwriters, but as sound shapers and sonic sculptors, as conceptualists and humorists....of mirroring and magnifying all that makes us humans. To me, they were the equals of almost any artist and forward thinker in human history. But, it's not folly to choose Elvis. He just has a more base appeal. And John Lennon was an Elvis person...

- Aaron Burtch - Grandaddy/The Good Luck Thrift Store Outfit - Turlock, CA
  When asked "Elvis or The Beatles?"

Seafood

Ahi Tuna Burgers

(makes 4 patties)

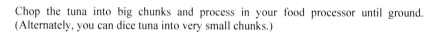

1 ½ pounds Ahi tuna steaks
2 tablespoons mayonnaise
1 tablespoon lemon juice
1 clove garlic, minced
1 tablespoon chopped fresh cilantro
1 tablespoon chopped fresh chives
½ teaspoon salt
¼ teaspoon pepper
1 teaspoon soy sauce
2 teaspoons hot sauce
4 Kaiser rolls or (hamburger buns)
'Lemon Garlic Mayonnaise' (recipe below)
sliced tomatoes
butter lettuce

Chop the tuna into big chunks and process in your food processor until ground. (Alternately, you can dice tuna into very small chunks.)

Add tuna to a medium sized bowl and add mayonnaise, lemon juice, garlic, cilantro, chives, salt, pepper, soy sauce and hot sauce. Mix well.

Form into 4 patties. If you have time, put on a plate, cover with plastic wrap and put in fridge for 1 hour. This allows the flavors to develop a bit.

Take the patties out 10 minutes before you cook and allow them to come back to room temperature.

Fry in vegetable or olive oil for 2-3 minutes on each side.

Serve on Kaiser roll with sliced tomatoes, lettuce and 'Lemon Garlic Mayonnaise'.

Lemon Garlic Mayonnaise:

½ cup mayonnaise
½ tablespoon fresh squeezed lemon juice
1-2 cloves garlic, minced

1 tablespoon chopped fresh oregano
⅛ teaspoon cayenne pepper

Add all ingredients to a small bowl and whisk with a fork until completely combined.

"Food is music you can taste"

Shrimp Cakes

(serves 4)

1 pound shrimp (peeled and de-veined)
¼ cup diced onion
1 medium red bell pepper, diced
½ cup finely chopped flat-leaf
   (Italian) parsley
1 egg, beaten

½ cup panko breadcrumbs
½ cup flour
1 teaspoon salt
½ teaspoon pepper
peanut or canola oil for frying
'Tartar Sauce' (page 51)

Cut tails off shrimp and discard them. Dice shrimp and add to a bowl with onion, bell pepper, parsley, egg, breadcrumbs, flour, salt and pepper. Mix well.

Shape into about six to eight ½ inch thick patties, depending on how big you want them. Heat about ¼ inch of oil in a skillet until hot - about 350 degrees if you have a thermometer. If you don't have a thermometer, you can test the oil by sticking the handle of a wooden spoon into the oil - if the oil around the handle bubbles, it's ready.

Fry for about 3 minutes on each side or until golden brown. Drain on paper towels. Serve with 'Tartar Sauce' over rice or on bread.

To serve over bread (my favorite):
Slice sourdough or French bread of your choice (olive bread is awesome!) about ¾ to 1 inch thick. Toast bread in broiler until it begins to brown, about 30 seconds or so. Remove and spread with tartar sauce, top with shrimp cake and some cheese*. Put under broiler again for a few minutes, just until cheese melts.

*Shredded Fontina is my favorite on this. Goat cheese, Gruyere or Parmesan would also be delicious.

Happy birthday to me!

I know that mixing cheese and seafood is some sort of a food crime, but melted cheese on these shrimp cakes is so good!

(This goes for the next two recipes as well!)

Seafood

Dreamy Linguini

(serves 2-4)

½ pound linguini
1 tablespoon olive oil
2-4 cloves garlic, minced
½ cup heavy cream
2 (6.5 ounce) cans chopped clams
 (save all clam juice!)
½ cup grated Parmesan cheese
½ cup crumbled Ricotta Salata cheese*
2 tablespoons lemon juice
½ teaspoon salt
½ cup chopped flat-leaf (Italian) parsley

*Ricotta Salata can be found in stores that carry a wide variety of 'fancy' cheese and is worth seeking out. If you can't find it, use whole milk Ricotta.

Boil linguini according to package directions. Drain and drizzle with a little olive oil, toss and set aside.

While pasta is boiling, heat oil in a medium skillet over low-medium heat. Add garlic and cook for about 30 seconds. Add cream, clams, clam juice, cheese, lemon juice and salt. Bring to a boil and turn heat to low. Cook until thick and cheese is melted, about 2 minutes. (The Ricotta will still be a bit chunky, but that's ok, this cheese doesn't melt all the way.) Add parsley and pour over linguini. Mix well.

Ricotta Salata is amazing on Pugliese drizzled with olive oil!

This recipe came to me in a dream and has become my super-creamy and cheesy take on Clams & Linguini. I awoke from the dream and immediately wrote the recipe down just as I dreamt it.

Three-Cheese Crab Roll-Ups

(serves 4)

10 lasagna noodles

Sauce:
2 tablespoons olive oil
1 shallot, diced
3 cloves garlic, minced
½ cup white wine
1 (14.5-ounce) can crushed
  (or diced) tomatoes with herbs
½ cup chopped fresh basil
½ teaspoon salt
½ cup heavy cream

Filling:
1 tablespoon olive oil
1 (6 ounce) bag baby spinach
½ cup shredded Parmesan cheese
4 ounces crumbled Feta cheese
½ cup shredded Fontina cheese
2 cups chopped (cooked) crab meat
1 egg, beaten
½ teaspoon salt
½ cup shredded Parmesan cheese

Preheat oven to 350 degrees.

Bring a large pot of water to a boil. Add noodles, about 4 at a time (depending on how much the pot can comfortably hold). Add about a tablespoon of olive oil and stir. Cook the noodles until a tad under-done, about 7-10 minutes (they'll cook more in the oven). Remove and drain on a large piece of foil or on damp kitchen towels until ready to assemble.

To make sauce: Heat olive oil in a medium skillet over medium heat. Add shallots, cook and stir until soft. Add garlic, cook and stir for about 1 minute. Add wine and cook until reduced a bit, about 3-5 minutes. Add tomatoes, basil and salt. Bring to a boil, reduce heat and simmer for about 5 minutes. Add cream and cook an additional 3-4 minutes. Remove from heat.

To make filling: Heat oil in a large pot over low-medium heat. Add spinach and toss constantly until wilted, about 30 seconds to 1 minute. Once spinach starts to cook down it will finish quickly, so don't walk away! Drain in a colander. When spinach is cool enough to handle, squeeze as much liquid out as possible. Add to a bowl with cheese, crab, egg and salt. Mix well.

Spread about ⅓ of the sauce on the bottom of an 8x8 baking dish. Spread some of the filling into the middle of each noodle and roll tightly.* Place rolls flap side down in the baking dish. Pour the rest of the sauce over rolls and sprinkle with ½ cup of Parmesan cheese.

Bake for 20 minutes or until hot, lightly browned and bubbly.

*I find it works best to divide the filling into 10 sections before you start rolling the noodles.

Seafood

Creamy Red Pepper Shrimp Pasta

(serves 4)

½ pound fussili (corkscrew) pasta
2 tablespoons olive oil
2 cloves garlic, minced
½ large red bell pepper, sliced lengthwise
  and cut into 1 inch strips
½ medium shallot, diced
¼ teaspoon salt
¼ teaspoon pepper

1 pound shrimp or prawns, peeled,
  de-veined and tails cut off
¾ cup cream
1 tablespoon lemon juice
¼ teaspoon salt
½ teaspoon pepper
¼ cup chopped flat-leaf (Italian) parsley

Boil pasta according to package directions. Drain and put back into pot. Drizzle with olive oil and toss.

Heat oil in a large skillet over medium heat. Add garlic, red pepper and shallots. Sprinkle with salt and pepper. Cook and stir for about 2 minutes. Add shrimp or prawns. Cook and stir until they are pink all over, about 3-4 minutes. Add cream, lemon juice, salt and pepper. Bring to a boil, reduce heat and simmer until sauce has thickened, about 2-3 minutes. Mix in parsley, pour over pasta and toss until combined.

by Shelly Cimoli

Dessert

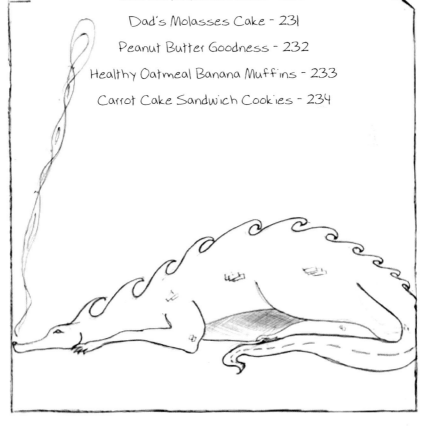

Banana Split Butter Cake - Page 229

Gooies - Page 221

Carrot Cake Sandwich Cookies - Page 234

Chocolate Chip Toffee Bars - Page 228

Chocolate Covered Brownie Bites - Page 227

Dad's Molasses Cake - Page 231

Gooies

(makes approximately 36 one inch squares)

Crust:
¼ cup butter, melted
¾ cup quick oats
2 tablespoons packed brown sugar
2 tablespoons un-sifted flour

Chocolate Layer:
1 cup milk chocolate chips
½ cup sweetened condensed milk
½ teaspoon vanilla

Caramel Layer:
¼ cup water
2 tablespoons light corn syrup
1 cup sugar
½ stick of butter
¼ cup heavy cream
¼ cup sweetened coconut

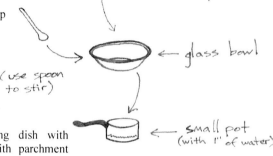

← the good stuff

← glass bowl

(use spoon to stir)

← small pot (with 1" of water)

← heat

Preheat oven to 350 degrees.

Spray an 8x8 inch baking dish with cooking spray and line with parchment paper. Form the paper to the pan and allow paper to flow over the edges. (You're going to be lifting the entire dessert out of the dish when it's complete.) Butter the bottom of the parchment paper and set aside.

In a large mixing bowl combine all ingredients for crust. Press firmly and evenly onto the bottom of the lined baking dish. Bake for 7 minutes. Remove from oven and allow to cool completely - this usually takes 20 to 30 minutes.

When the crust has cooled, start the caramel by placing water, corn syrup and sugar in a large skillet over medium heat. Whisk constantly until it begins to boil. Once boiled, cook, swirling skillet occasionally, until it's a light caramel color, about 10-20 minutes. (Stove temperatures vary - just keep it going until it's the color of caramel!) Add butter and whisk until melted and combined - the mixture will bubble up so be careful. Immediately remove from heat. Add cream and whisk for about a minute or until bubbles are gone and mixture is smooth. Add coconut and mix. Immediately pour over cooled crust. Allow to cool completely in the refrigerator.

Once the caramel layer has cooled, start the chocolate layer. Place a large glass bowl over a small pot filled with about an inch of water* and bring to a boil. Place the chocolate chips, condensed milk and vanilla in the glass bowl. Mix, almost constantly, until everything melts together. Spread evenly over the cooled caramel layer.

*This is called a 'double boiler' - see diagram above

(continued)

For best results, let chocolate cool and put in fridge to sit overnight. At the very least, give it 2 hours to cool and set.

Do not cut or remove from fridge until RIGHT before you are ready to serve! Once these are out of the fridge you've got about 2 hours before the caramel begins to ooze. These are called 'Gooies' for a reason!

To serve: Grab onto the edges of the parchment paper and lift the Gooies out of the baking dish. Cut into 1 inch squares.

Food is important. Very important. Spending months on the road can really let you know just how important it really is. Being in a traveling band and spending so much time away from a stable household, you can't help but learn a lot of things about life and who you are. One of the subtleties of the road is the difference in the food you intake. Cultural differences are a great benefit, but what I am talking about is quality. When you start to have more and more memories of "Ma's home cookin'", you are typically starting to consider the caliber of your menu and comparing the two. It is in this respect that the transformation within yourself of viewing particular pieces as sustenance, versus food and snacks, versus meals and so on.

On tour you are in a position to do more than over indulge in the realm of snacks. I don't know if there is a proper word for 'over indulgence with lack of nutritional value', but perhaps 'tour' can start to become a synonym. It should be clear to the reader that there are forces at work that can not be stopped. So I myself could not say whether or not that it is a personal choice to do these terrible things to yourself. What I can say, however, is that when the opportunity arises to take part in a delicious, hearty, and fulfilling meal, it is one of the joys that you look forward to. The contrast between the two is so great, that you can't help but notice that it is very much the opposite of what you have been in-taking so many times a day.

It is humbling to know that such a basic necessity can be so rich in diversity and that you can put as much love and care into a meal as you so desire. For all the times that people have gone out of their way to give us a wonderful dining experience, all I can do is give my most sincere thanks and hope that I can have the ability to return the favor someday. I hope I have illustrated the point that it means a lot to us for anyone to treat us so well. For the record, this author is near the top, if not at the pinnacle of the list of gratitude. So thanks, Mary! I owe you, Will, Bethany, Rita and Wiley more than one…

- Dallin Bulkley - Larry & His Flask - Redmond, OR

Dessert

Banana Split Pie

(serves 8-10)

2 cups graham cracker crumbs
  (about 12 crackers)
1 stick melted butter
2 sticks of butter, softened
2 cups powdered sugar
2 eggs, slightly beaten

4 bananas, sliced
2 large boxes frozen strawberries, thawed and drained
1 (20 ounce) can crushed pineapple, drained well
1 (8 ounce) container whipped topping
chopped pecans (optional)

Use a food processor to turn graham crackers into crumbs. Pour graham cracker crumbs into the bottom of a 9x13 baking dish. Pour melted butter over crumbs and use a spatula (or your clean hands) to mix well. Spread and pat evenly onto bottom of dish. Set aside.

Place the 2 sticks of softened butter, powdered sugar and eggs in a bowl. Beat with electric mixer for 20 minutes (a must!) and spread over the crust. Layer bananas, strawberries and pineapple (in that order) on top of filling. Spread whipped topping over pineapple. Sprinkle with finely chopped pecans (if desired). Chill at least one hour before serving. Best if chilled overnight.

Lemon Raspberry Trifles
(makes 6 individual trifles)

Lemon curd:
3 eggs
¾ cup sugar
¾ cup lemon juice (fresh is always best!)
1 tablespoon grated lemon zest
½ cup unsalted butter, cubed

Everything else:
1 (12 ounce) package frozen raspberries, thawed
2 tablespoons sugar
½ of a pound cake, cut/torn into cubes*
1 (6 ounce) package fresh raspberries
6 wine glasses**

*You can also use angel food, sponge or any boxed or homemade vanilla cake you prefer.

** ....or margarita..... ....or martini ....or high-ball.... ....or plain ol' water glasses.

To make lemon curd:
In a small bowl whisk together the eggs and sugar. Set aside.

Place a large glass bowl over a small pot filled with about an inch of water. (See diagram on page 221.) Bring to a boil over medium heat. Add lemon juice and lemon zest to the bowl. Stir frequently until hot. (Do not boil!) Pour about ¼ cup into the egg/sugar mixture, whisking constantly. Pour the egg mixture back into the double boiler. Whisk frequently until the mixture is thick like pudding, about 15-20 minutes.

Remove from heat and add butter one cube at a time, stirring until melted. Place plastic wrap directly on the curd (so that it won't form a crust) and place in the fridge to chill.

Puree thawed raspberries in your food processor or blender. Pour through a wire mesh strainer into a bowl to remove seeds, using a spatula to press the puree through. Pour puree back into the food processor or blender, scraping the sides of the bowl. Add sugar and puree until blended. Pour back into bowl and set aside.

To layer trifles:
Place a few cubes of cake into the bottom of each glass. Next, add a few spoonfuls of raspberry puree, followed by fresh berries and a nice sized dollop of the lemon curd. Repeat layers until you reach the top, ending with the lemon curd. Top with a light drizzle of raspberry puree and a fresh raspberry or two.

Dessert

Everyone remembers their first gig. I was 14, four years below the age I was supposed to be at the venue we were at. It was the LA2, a bar in central London, and the year was 1994. On the bill that night were Supergrass and their support were the Bluetones. Special guests, fresh-faced and taking a break from their high-school exams were Ash. All relative unknowns at the time, but within a year all had registered number one records on the British Pop charts. I didn't know it that night, but I was riding the crest of a swelling wave of what the press labeled "Britpop".

To see all three acts back to back on the same small stage, close enough to feel you were up there with them (and, well, we were briefly as we crowd-surfed the moshers), close enough to see the sweat dripping off Gaz's sideburns – all this would become something of a collectors item in the following months.

But what about that night? The noise. The bass drum shaking your ribcage, the electric guitars slicing up the warm air. I was hooked. The whole experience resoundingly kick started my interest in live music.

We met Ash later that evening. The drummer, a chap called Rick, signed my record sleeve. Back then, I thought these bands were immortal. I took great pride in having seen them in a bar, raw and bursting with energy. I caught sight of them before the masses knew who they were. Rick's signature was pinned to my wall for sometime. And yet, it faded and the record sleeve got worn. Nowadays, all 3 bands are in various stages of decay, superseded by the next latest things, consigned to greatest hits packages and limited tours to the old faithfuls. Rick's signature was packed into a box long ago. I'm not even sure where it is now.

But, on one cool night back in the mid-90s, as I sat on the London Underground at midnight, exhausted but exhilarated, with a footprint across my face left by an overzealous crowd-surfer. I wore the smile of someone who felt they were in the middle of something significant.

- Dave Maclure - Natal, Brazil

Artwork by Bethany Taylor

White Chocolate Covered Spice Cake Bites

(makes about 5 dozen 1 ¼ inch bites)

1 (18.25 ounce) box Spice Cake mix
3 eggs, beaten
½ cup vegetable oil
1 (16 ounce) container cream
   cheese frosting

2 (11.5 ounce) bags white chocolate chips
½ cup heavy cream
¼ teaspoon nutmeg
½ teaspoon cinnamon

(You'll need a few very long toothpicks or thin barbecue skewers for this.)

Make the spice cake according to package directions. Allow to cool completely and tear cake into crumbs. Add the frosting and mix until it resembles a thick batter. (I've found it's easiest to just use my hands to do this. It's faster and more thorough - and it's fun to get messy!)

Line a cookie sheet with wax paper. Shape the batter into 1¼ -1½ inch balls and place on wax paper. Put in the freezer for at least an hour or more. Keep the cake balls in the freezer until your chocolate is melted and you are ready to dip.

Now, melt your chocolate. Place a large glass bowl over a small pot filled with about an inch of water. Bring to a boil. (See diagram on page 221.) Add the white chocolate chips to the bowl and stir with a wooden spoon until melted. When chocolate is about ¾ of the way melted, add the cream. Use a whisk to thoroughly mix the cream and chocolate. When completely melted, add the nutmeg and cinnamon.

Line another cookie sheet with wax paper to transfer the dipped balls to. Use your (clean) fingers to pick up a ball. Use a toothpick or skewer to poke it in the flat side it'd been sitting on. Allow the toothpick to only go halfway through the ball (like a lollipop).

Dip the ball in the chocolate and spread the chocolate one of two ways: Either use a spoon to help spread the chocolate around the ball OR use **clean** fingers to spread the chocolate. (Obviously you want to make sure the chocolate isn't super hot if you are using your fingers.) Remove from toothpick and place ball flat side down on lined cookie sheet.

Expect the first few to be not-too-pretty. After doing a bunch you'll get into a rhythm.

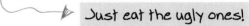 Just eat the ugly ones!

After you've made about a dozen balls and while the chocolate is still soft, sprinkle with cinnamon. Stick covered balls in the fridge until it's time to serve. Once out at room temperature they should hold up just fine for hours without melting - unless it's really hot, of course.

Chocolate Covered Brownie Bites

(makes about 5 dozen 1 ¼ inch bites)

1 (20.03 ounce) box brownie mix
3 eggs, beaten
½ cup vegetable oil
1 (16 ounce) container coconut pecan frosting

2 (11.5 ounce) bags milk chocolate chips
½ cup heavy cream
finely chopped pecans (optional)

Make 'cake-like brownies' according to directions on box. Allow to cool completely and tear cake into crumbs. Add the frosting and mix until it resembles a thick batter. (I've found it's easiest to just use my hands to do this. It's faster and more thorough - and it's fun to get messy.)

Follow dipping directions for 'White Chocolate Covered Spice Cake Bites' on page 226.

While the chocolate is still wet, sprinkle covered balls with chopped pecans.

Music nabbed me early on. I'm lucky to still have a copy somewhere of a song I wrote for my first-grade love interest recorded on a tape recorder that my brother and I used to listen to Star Wars audio cassettes on. Better yet, my mother does. I can remember her trying to convince me I liked "Pop" as I insisted I was a Rocker. I was inundated with 60's and 70's soul most of all. And I loved it. I loved the swagger I felt listening to "Pusherman" and "Superfly" by Curtis Mayfield, as well as the simple innocence of "Kiss and Say Goodbye" by The Manhattans and "Sweet Wanomi" by Bill Withers. There's something about it. At the time, I can remember seeing Billy Idol as such a badass.

I hardly knew his music, but I sure knew his image. Rocker. I was all over the place. I wanted to be a musician so bad. I would sing over the music to songs on the radio with my own adlib lyrics and melody, and it felt good to create. Through high school I mostly forgot about my musical aspirations and got lost in other things. It seemed like a childish pipe-dream to me. Thank God for Saturday nights. My buddy Jansson Stout had been going on and on for a while about this band Petrol from San Francisco and he finally roped me to go to a show in Davis, CA. That band showed me what Rock 'n' Roll was. Michael Shaw: A lead guitarist with seemingly constant puckered lips and a non-homosexual femininity that reeked of fun-loving bigheadedness. Graham Shaw: A true instrument-less front man who somehow compelled onlookers to cram together at the front of the stage, exuding such confidence that even people in the back of the room were shaken by eye contact. Power. It was on from then on. The fear of being the man in front is what makes it so euphoric when you're up there. Doing it. And it is so do-able. Song writing is a completely different animal. Performing is the buzz. Music is the only thing man can truly create. Music is nothing without performance. The two are a beautiful marriage and I'm proud to be a part of it all.

- John Elmasian - Hot Pistol - Sacramento, CA

Chocolate Chip Toffee Bars

(makes about 40 bars)

2 ½ cups all-purpose flour
1 teaspoon baking soda
1 teaspoon salt
2 sticks butter, softened
½ cup granulated sugar
¾ cup packed brown sugar

1 teaspoon vanilla
2 large eggs
1 (11.5 ounce) bag milk chocolate chips
1 (11.5 ounce) bag toffee bits (or 2 cups
  crushed toffee bars)

Preheat the oven to 350 degrees. Lightly grease a 9x13 inch baking dish with cooking spray or butter. In a medium sized bowl mix flour, baking soda and salt. Set aside.

Place the butter, sugar, and brown sugar in the bowl of an electric mixer. Cream until light and fluffy. Scrape down the sides of the bowl with a spatula. Beat in the vanilla and eggs. Gradually add the dry ingredients to the creamed mixture. Continue to mix until a smooth batter forms. Turn off the mixer and fold in the chocolate chips and toffee.

Spread batter into baking dish and bake for 35 minutes. Let cool completely before cutting into squares.

by Shelly Cimoli

Dessert

Banana Split Butter Cake

(makes about 2 dozen 2x2 inch squares)

Cake:
1 (18.25-ounce) box banana cake mix
1 large egg
1 stick butter, melted

Filling:
1 (8 ounce) package cream cheese, softened
2 large eggs
1 teaspoon vanilla extract
1 (16 ounce) box powdered sugar
1 stick butter, melted
1 (1 pound) box frozen strawberries, thawed
¼ cup juice from thawed strawberries

Topping:
1 cup whipped topping*
chocolate syrup
mixed nut toppings
maraschino cherries

Or use whipped cream that comes in the squirt can!

Preheat oven to 350 degrees. Lightly grease a 9x13 baking dish.

Cake: In the bowl of your standing mixer, combine cake mix, egg and butter. Mix well. Pat mixture into the bottom of prepared dish and set aside. Clean the bowl out to use for filling.

Filling: In the bowl of your standing mixer beat the cream cheese until smooth. Add eggs, vanilla and sugar. Beat until creamy. Add butter and mix well. Add thawed and drained strawberries and mix. Pour strawberry mixture onto cake and use a spatula to spread it out evenly.

Bake for 45 minutes. Allow to cool completely in the fridge - this will take at least an hour or so.

When the cake is completely cooled, cut it into 2 inch squares and place on a cookie sheet or tray lined with wax paper. Fill a large zip top bag with the whipped topping. Squeeze the topping into one corner of the bag, cut the corner with scissors and pipe the whipped topping onto each square.* Drizzle squares with chocolate syrup, sprinkle with mixed nuts and top each square with one cherry.

Jacob & Will

Busia's Molasses Cake

2 cups flour
1 cup granulated sugar
1 teaspoon nutmeg or ginger
1 teaspoon cinnamon
1 teaspoon salt
1 stick butter, softened
1 teaspoon baking soda
1 cup buttermilk (or whole milk)
1 egg
2 tablespoons molasses

Preheat oven to 350 degrees.

Add flour, sugar, nutmeg or ginger, cinnamon and salt to a bowl. Mix until combined. Add softened butter and mix until crumbled. Measure out ½ cup and set it aside - this will be used as the topping.

Add baking soda, buttermilk, egg and molasses to the flour mixture and mix just until combined. Do not over mix.

Spread mixture evenly into an un-greased 9x13 inch baking dish. Sprinkle the crumbled topping evenly onto the cake and bake for 20-25 minutes. Test to see if it's done by sticking a toothpick in the middle. If it comes out clean, it's done. Allow to cool for at least 30 minutes before cutting.

From 52 Week "Life Is Beautiful" by Chris Doud

So the boys all whooped it up
Or watched the television,
While the girls watched the turkey cook
And chatted in the kitchen.
And this was way back when gender roles
And stereotypes didn't bother people too much.
We eventually said grace and proceeded
To stuff ourselves good.
Resolutions would make us right again soon.
Or we could try to work it off with a little walk
Around the neighborhood.

To read more about the 52-Week Club see pages 87-88

Dessert

Dad's Molasses Cake

(My dad's version of my mom's mom's cake)

2 cups flour
1 cup granulated sugar
1 teaspoon nutmeg or ginger
1 teaspoon cinnamon
1 teaspoon salt

1 teaspoon baking soda
½ cup butter, softened
1 cup buttermilk (or whole milk)
1 egg
2 tablespoons molasses

Preheat oven to 350 degrees.

Add flour, sugar, nutmeg or ginger, cinnamon, salt and baking soda to a bowl and mix until combined. Add butter, buttermilk, egg and molasses to the flour mixture and mix just until combined. Do not over mix.

Spread evenly into an un-greased 9x13 inch baking dish. Bake for 20-25 minutes. Test to see if it's done by sticking a toothpick in the middle, if it comes out clean it's done. Cool cake completely.

While it bakes make the icing.

When my dad makes his version, Mom always comments: "This isn't my mother's cake!"

Icing:

1 cup powdered sugar
½ stick butter, softened
4 ounces cream cheese, softened
½ teaspoon vanilla

Add all ingredients to your standing mixer (or to a large bowl and use a hand mixer). Mix until combined. Stop once or twice to scrape the sides. When you're done make sure you lick the spatula.

Spread some (or all!) of the icing on the completely cooled cake.

If you want, sprinkle sweetened, shredded coconut or chopped walnuts on top to dress it up a bit.

Mom & Dad in 1975

Peanut Butter Goodness

(serves 6-8)

Recipe courtesy of Marissa Garbarino - Loma Rica, CA

1 (2.1 ounce) box instant chocolate pudding
½ cup of peanut butter (divided in half)
1 (2.1 ounce) box instant vanilla pudding
1 package chocolate sandwich cookies*
1 package peanut butter sandwich cookies**
whipped cream

In a small bowl prepare chocolate pudding as directed. Beat in ¼ cup of the peanut butter.

In another small bowl, prepare vanilla pudding as directed and beat in the rest of the peanut butter.

*You don't need to use the entire package - use as little or as much as you'd like.

This goes for the peanut butter cookies as well.

With desserts like this there are very few rules!

In a deep glass serving bowl, place a layer of peanut butter cookies on the bottom. (Either keep them whole or crumble them and toss them in. I've done it both ways.) When you leave the cookies whole, you're guaranteed cookies as you serve yourself. When they're crumbled it's more of a hit-or-miss, so do as you like.

Pour ½ of the chocolate pudding mixture on top. Put a layer of chocolate sandwich cookies on top of the pudding and spread on ½ of the vanilla mixture. Layer more peanut butter cookies over the vanilla, then more chocolate cookies, followed by more chocolate pudding. Repeat until they're layered up. Top with whipped cream and a few chocolate and peanut butter cookies.

The great thing about this dessert is that you can substitute it with any other cookies or brownies. Add some bananas and change up your flavors of pudding. Try experimenting with candied slivered almonds and adding some almond extract to the pudding.

**The ones that look like this

Dessert

Healthy Oatmeal Banana Muffins

(makes 24 muffins, 120 calories each)

2 cups whole wheat flour
1 teaspoon baking soda
1 teaspoon baking powder
1 teaspoon salt
½ teaspoon nutmeg
¼ teaspoon ginger
½ teaspoon cinnamon
1 cup unsweetened applesauce

1 cup honey
2 large eggs
2 teaspoons vanilla
3 cups oats (not instant)
2 mashed (over-ripe) bananas

Fun additions:
Dried cranberries, raisins
walnuts, blueberries,
etc.

Pre-heat oven to 350 degrees.

Mix flour, baking soda, baking powder, salt and spices in a small bowl and set aside.

In a large bowl mix applesauce, honey, eggs and vanilla. Add flour mixture and stir until just combined. Do not over work. Add oats, mashed bananas and any additional ingredients.

Spray muffin tins with cooking spray. Use an ice cream scooper to scoop mixture into muffin tins.

Bake for 15-20 minutes or until a knife or toothpick inserted in the middle comes out clean.

From 52 Week "Dance Me Around" by Jason Turner

All I wanna do in this broken old town
Is follow my head up into the clouds.
All of the time that I spend with my wife
By the river's edge dancin' all through the night.

Dance me around 'til my feet leave the ground.
Singin' and laughin' under the street light in town.
Pour some kisses, love, here on my mouth
As you dance me around 'til we're fallin' down.

To read more about the 52-Week Club see pages 87-88

Carrot Cake Sandwich Cookies

(makes about 24 sandwich cookies)

Cookies:
1 cup brown sugar (do not pack!)
1 cup granulated sugar
1 cup butter-flavored shortening stick*
2 eggs
2 teaspoons vanilla
2 ¾ cups all-purpose flour
1 ½ teaspoons baking powder
1 teaspoon baking soda
1 teaspoon salt
1 tablespoon cinnamon
1 cup finely grated carrots
1 cup raisins (optional)

Vanilla Spice Filling:
½ cup (room temperature) butter
½ cup (room temperature) cream cheese
1 teaspoon vanilla
¼ teaspoon nutmeg
3 cups powdered sugar

Using shortening instead of butter produces a thicker more 'cake-like' cookie. Don't use margarine or butter substitutes!

Mix sugars and shortening with an electric mixer just until combined and still grainy. (Important not to over mix!) Add eggs and vanilla and mix until combined.

In a separate bowl mix flour, baking powder, baking soda, salt and cinnamon. Add to the sugar mixture a little bit at a time, mixing well after each addition. Add carrots and raisins, stir until combined. (The dough should be really thick and not crumbly.) Cover and place in fridge until chilled, about an hour. (Very important!)

Preheat oven to 350 degrees.

Measure out a heaping tablespoon of dough and place about an inch apart on an un-greased cookie sheet. Bake for 12 minutes. Allow to sit on the cookie sheet for about 5 minutes before removing them to cool on a cooling rack.

Be sure to keep the cookie dough in the fridge in between batches!

To make filling:
Use an electric or standing mixer to cream butter, cream cheese, vanilla and nutmeg until smooth. Add sugar, one cup at a time, beating well after each addition. Once all 3 cups have been added, mix on high for 2-3 minutes or until light and fluffy.

When cookies are ***completely*** cool, spread a generous amount of filling between two cookies.

You will have more than enough filling so don't be stingy with it!

Dessert

Glossary

Behind the Apron

by Emily Webster

Mary Joseph grew up in a family where food was not only important, it was celebrated. Having been raised by inventive, eclectic cooks, it only made sense that Mary would begin cooking meals for people who came into her home. After rave reviews from friends and loved ones, Mary realized that this, above all else, was her passion. Cooking consumed her, she was made for the kitchen, and from there she started on her journey.

Mary's friends and family started hounding her for her recipes. Previously, Mary found joy in throwing things together, experimenting with flavors - in essence, cooking with her heart. When she started writing a family recipe book, the process of seeing her recipes on paper lit a fire in her. In 2006, Mary left her office job and took a job cooking for a family in Sacramento, California, essentially opening up the door for her to write her cookbook while she worked.

Almost simultaneously, a love for music was blossoming in Mary. She would talk for hours with friends about The Beatles, Led Zeppelin, Pink Floyd, Elvis, and other legends and even picked up the guitar and learned some classic songs. Around that time, Mary's sister married Willy Tea, a lyrical, homegrown songwriter, and music got personal. Through her sister and Willy Tea, she met an amazing group of people who lived and breathed music. They wouldn't just talk of other's music, they wrote and played their own night and day. A get together would almost definitely result in playing music and sharing their songs. She soon realized that she was surrounded by some of the best music she had ever heard. Immediately, Mary started singing and writing songs with as much fervor as she cooked. As writing and singing became her greatest form of expression, she realized that she felt an inexplicable bond with other music lovers. If food is the key to one's heart, then music must definitely be the key to the soul.

Food and music! Mary lives for the two, so, sensibly she would create a love letter to both. She rapidly enlisted her talented friends - and eventually many other musicians who crossed her path - to write for her, compiling stories and musings about their musical roots and inspirations, so that their tales and passion could accompany hers on the page.

Mary has found happiness in living her dream. She is currently living at the Tea Farm in Escalon, California, where her love of music and food is even more united. The Tea Farm was built to provide a platform for local singer/songwriters, artists and traveling musicians to share their songs, get some rest and eat a much needed home cooked meal.

It is said that "If more of us valued food and cheer and song above hoarded gold, it would be a merrier world." Mary spends her time with her family and friends happily bringing that merriment to all who pass through her life.